PERL AND CGI

FOR THE WORLD WIDE WEB

VISUAL QUICKSTART GUIDE

by Elizabeth Castro

 Peachpit Press

Perl and CGI for the World Wide Web: Visual QuickStart Guide

by Elizabeth Castro

Peachpit Press

1249 Eighth Street
Berkeley, CA 94710
(510) 524-2178
(510) 524-2221 (fax)

Find us on the World Wide Web at: http://www.peachpit.com
Or contact Liz directly at perl@cookwood.com

Peachpit Press is a division of Addison Wesley Longman

Copyright © 1999 by Elizabeth Castro

Cover design: The Visual Group

ISBN: 0-201-35358-X

0 9 8 7 6 5 4 3 2

Printed in the United States of America

For Andreu and Anna and this new one,
who bring incredible joy to my life.

Special thanks to:

Marjorie Baer, for her encouraging words and helpful editing.

Simon Hayes, for his technical editing and for his help with Perl questions large and small—at all hours of the day and night. You can find his incredibly complete online database and retailing software for bookstores, called Bookware, at http://www.glasscat.com.

Amy Changar, for her astute changes to the formatting and layout, as well as for the production of the book.

Nancy Aldrich-Ruenzel, for her confidence in me.

Larry Wall, for creating Perl and for sharing it with the rest of us.

The denizens of the Perl and CGI newsgroups for their generous sharing of knowledge.

And to Andreu Cabré, who, while I wrote this book, did practically everything else.

Table of Contents

Introduction **13**
What is a program?. *14*
Why Perl? *15*
What about CGI?. *16*
Perl and HTML *17*
Getting Perl. *18*
Internet service providers *19*
Ask your ISP!. *19*
About this book *20*
What this book is not. *21*
The Perl and CGI VQS Guide Web Site *22*

Chapter 1: Perl Building Blocks **23**
Perl data *23*
Operators and functions. *26*
Quotation marks. *28*

Chapter 2: Creating Perl CGI Scripts. **29**
Creating a Perl CGI script *30*
Starting a Perl CGI script. *32*
Writing code in Perl *33*
Creating output for a browser. *34*
Documenting your script *35*
Uploading your script to the server *36*
Changing permissions. *39*
Checking the script's syntax *40*
Running a Perl CGI script. *41*

Chapter 3: Getting Data from Visitors. 43

    Labeling incoming data *44*

    Creating a form *46*

    Creating text boxes *47*

    Creating password boxes. *48*

    Creating larger text areas *49*

    Creating radio buttons *50*

    Creating checkboxes *51*

    Creating menus *52*

    Creating the submit button *53*

    Resetting the form *54*

    Using an image to submit data *55*

    Creating a link to a script *56*

    Using a link to input data to a script. *57*

    Adding default data to a form *58*

Chapter 4: Environment Variables 59

    Using environment variables to parse forms *60*

    Your visitor's browser and platform *62*

    How did your visitor get to your page? *63*

    Viewing all the environment variables *64*

Chapter 5: Getting Data into the Script. 65

    Inputting data from a form or a link *66*

    Inputting data from environment variables *68*

    Inputting scalar data yourself. *69*

    Inputting arrays yourself. *70*

    Inputting hashes yourself *71*

Chapter 6: Working with Scalars 73

    Storing the result of an operation *74*

    Multiplying, dividing, adding, subtracting *75*

    Using more than one operator at a time *76*

    Raising a number to an exponential power *77*

    Getting the remainder of a division *78*

    Connecting strings together. *79*

    Repeating a string *80*

    Operating and assigning in one step *81*

    Incrementing (or decrementing) a variable *82*

Chapter 7: Working with Arrays **83**

Getting a particular item from an array. *84*

Splitting a scalar into an array. *86*

Modifying all the members of an array. *87*

Finding the length of an array *88*

Getting multiple items from an array *89*

Adding items to the beginning of an array *90*

Adding items to the end of an array *91*

Combining two arrays *92*

Removing the first item in an array *93*

Removing the last item in an array. *94*

Replacing an item in an array *95*

Replacing more than one item in an array. *96*

Sorting arrays *98*

Reversing the order of an array's contents *99*

Chapter 8: Conditional Statements **101**

Comparing numbers. *102*

Comparing strings. *103*

Evaluating conditions without comparisons *104*

Testing two or more comparisons at a time. *105*

Creating a basic conditional statement *106*

Adding options for false conditions. *107*

Adding multiple, independent conditions. *108*

Using unless *109*

Repeating a block while a condition is true *110*

Repeating a block while a condition is false *111*

Executing the block at least once *112*

Repeating a block a given number of times. *113*

Repeating a block for each item in an array. *114*

Nesting conditional statements *115*

Chapter 9: Subroutines **117**

Creating a simple subroutine *118*

Using a simple subroutine. *119*

Creating a subroutine that takes input *120*

Calling a subroutine that takes input *121*

Using a subroutine's return value. *122*

Setting the return value manually *123*

Storing subroutines in a separate file *124*

Calling subroutines from an external file *125*

Chapter 10: Working with Hashes **127**
Getting a value by using a key *128*
Getting several values using keys *129*
Getting all of a hash's values *130*
Getting all of a hash's keys *131*
Getting each key and value in a hash *132*
Removing key-value pairs *134*
Checking to see if a key exists *135*

Chapter 11: Analyzing Data **137**
Finding something *138*
Finding and replacing *139*
Seeing and using what was found *140*
Splitting a value into pieces *141*
Constructing search patterns *142*
Tips for constructing search patterns *143*
Matching a single character *144*
Matching a string of characters *145*
Matching a character from a group *146*
Matching a character that's not in the group *147*
Using class shorthands *148*
Limiting the location *149*
Choosing how many to match *151*
Curbing a quantifier's greediness *156*
Matching one element or another *157*
More on using what you already matched *158*

Chapter 12: Remembering What Your Visitors Tell You . . . **161**
About hidden fields *162*
Adding hidden fields to a form *163*
Storing collected data in a hidden field *164*
About cookies *166*
Looking at your browser's cookies *167*
Sending a cookie *168*
Setting a cookie's expiration date *170*
Limiting a cookie to a domain *171*
Limiting a cookie to a part of your server *172*
Limiting cookies to secure connections *173*
Reading and using a cookie *174*
How (and why) your visitors refuse cookies *176*

Table of contents

Chapter 13: Printing and HTML **177**

Formatting output with HTML *178*

Printing several lines at a time *180*

Simplifying paths to images and links. *181*

Creating header and footer subroutines *182*

Outputting a hash as a table. *184*

Outputting an array as a list *185*

Formatting numbers and strings *186*

Formatting numbers as dollars and cents. *187*

Padding numbers *188*

Chapter 14: Files and Directories **189**

Opening a file *190*

Verifying file and directory operations *192*

Writing to an external file. *193*

Getting exclusive access to a file *194*

Reading data from an external file. *195*

Closing a file *196*

Renaming a file. *197*

Removing a file *198*

Checking a file's status *199*

Accessing a directory *200*

Reading the contents of a directory. *201*

Closing a directory *202*

Changing the working directory *203*

Creating a directory *204*

Changing permissions from within a script *205*

Removing a directory *206*

Getting ready to e-mail output *207*

Sending output via e-mail. *208*

Eliminating extra returns *210*

Chapter 15: Debugging **211**

Checking the easy stuff *212*

Creating an error subroutine *214*

Narrowing it down by commenting it out. *215*

Following a variable's progress *216*

Table of contents

Table of contents

Chapter 16: Using Other Folks' Scripts **217**

Using other folks' scripts *218*

Getting other people's scripts *219*

Expanding compressed scripts. *220*

Configuring borrowed scripts *221*

Customizing borrowed scripts. *222*

Appendix A: Parsing Form Input **223**

Creating a subroutine. *223*

Determining which method was used. *224*

Getting name-value pairs from GET. *226*

Getting name-value pairs from POST *227*

Storing name-value pairs in a hash *228*

Using the parsed data *230*

Appendix B: Permissions **231**

Who's the owner? *232*

Default permissions. *233*

Figuring out the new permissions code *234*

Appendix C: Security **235**

Monitoring visitor input *236*

Watching what is sent to the server *237*

Avoiding tainted data. *238*

Appendix D: Unix Essentials **239**

Telnetting to your Unix server. *240*

Executing commands in Unix *242*

Dealing with paths in Unix. *243*

Changing the working directory *246*

Finding out where you are *247*

Listing directory contents *248*

Eliminating files *249*

Creating and eliminating directories *250*

Decompressing tar and zipped files. *251*

Getting help with Unix *252*

Appendix E: Perl and CGI Resources 253

Text editors 254

Telnet programs 255

Other folks' scripts 256

Learning more 257

Index 259

Table of contents

Introduction

So what does it mean to program, anyway? Is it dangerous? And I don't mean that facetiously. Many people have a glorified idea of programming as this complicated thing that only pocket-protector carrying, certified nerds are clever enough to do. And if the rest of us try it we'll probably screw something up, like erase our hard disks or something.

Maybe programmers like this mystique...certainly they don't seem to make it easy to break into the art of programming. Most books that you read about programming start off somewhere in the middle, assuming that you've already done some programming somewhere, and that you're just learning a "new" language, with the basic concepts already under your belt.

This book starts at the very beginning. Even if you've never, ever programmed before, you'll be able to understand this book. At the same time, I won't bore you to tears with a lot of theory or lengthy explanations of esoteric issues. We'll get started right away, but we'll start at the beginning. You don't have to know any Unix commands, you don't have to already know what a variable is, or what arrays are, or any of that incomprehensible programspeak. Let's go.

What about CGI?

If you already have a script written in Perl, what do you need CGI for? CGI is a *protocol* (a way of doing things), not a programming language. In fact, CGI stands for *Common Gateway Interface*. That means that it's the usual way that browsers (like Netscape or Internet Explorer) communicate with servers (the computers that make Web pages available to the Internet). Therefore, any script that sends or receives information from a server needs to follow the standards specified by CGI. When folks talk about *CGI scripts*, they're really talking about scripts written in some programming language (often, but not always, Perl) that follow the CGI protocol.

That means that some Perl scripts are CGI scripts (the ones that follow the CGI protocol) and some are not. It also means that some so-called CGI scripts are Perl scripts (the ones that are written in Perl), but some are not (they are also commonly found written in C, tcl, Visual Basic and AppleScript).

In this book, you'll learn about creating CGI Perl scripts—specifically for getting, processing, and returning information through your Web pages. For information on learning more about non-Web related applications for Perl scripts, consult Appendix E, *Perl and CGI Resources*.

```
                   code.html
<HTML><HEAD><TITLE>Enviro-Web</TITLE></HEAD>
<BODY>

<H2>Figuring your tax deductions</H2>
<FORM METHOD=post ACTION="http://
www.cookwood.com/cgi-bin/lcastro/
taxdeduc.cgi">
Total value of contributions last year? <INPUT
TYPE=text NAME=donation SIZE=10>
 Number of contributions? <INPUT TYPE=text
NAME=times SIZE=5>
<BR>Value of premiums received? <INPUT
TYPE=text NAME=premium SIZE=10>
<HR><INPUT TYPE=submit NAME=submit
VALUE=Submit>
<INPUT TYPE=reset NAME=reset VALUE="Start
over">
</FORM></BODY></HTML>
```

Figure i.3 *Here is the HTML code for a form. When the visitor clicks the submit button, the browser sends the data that the visitor has typed in along with the contents of the NAME attributes to the Perl script referenced in the FORM tag's ACTION attribute.*

```
1    #!/usr/local/bin/perl
2
3    require "subparseform.cgi";
4    &Parse_Form;
5
6    $total = $formdata{'donation'};
7    $times = $formdata{'times'};
8    $premium = $formdata{'premium'};
9
10   $average = $total/$times;
11   $tax_deduction = $total - $premium;
12
13   print "Content-type: text/html\n\n";
14   print "<P>You donated $total dollars last
        year. Thank you.";
15   print "<P>Since you donated $times times,
        that works out to an average of
        $average dollars per donation.";
16   print "<P>Since your premium was worth
        $premium dollars, you can only take a
        tax deduction of $tax_deduction
        dollars.";
```

Figure i.4 *This is the Perl script activated by the HTML page shown in Figure i.3. Lines 13–16 create the Web page that will contain the results of the operations in the earlier part of the script. (For a complete explanation of this particular example, see page 75.)*

Perl and HTML

Because this book focuses on using Perl to enhance your Web pages, you should have at least a rudimentary familiarity with HTML— the language that all Web pages are written in. You don't need to know how to create tables, frames, or styles, or any of HTML's other advanced tags. You don't need to know JavaScript or DHTML. You don't even need to know how to create forms and links—the basic tools for getting data from visitors— since I'll show you how in Chapter 3, *Getting Data from Visitors*. Nevertheless, you *should* know what HTML tags are and how to use them to create a basic Web page.

Perl and HTML work harmoniously together. HTML lets you create links and forms that activate your Perl scripts. And Perl allows you to generate Web pages in which to display a script's results for your visitors.

If you would like to learn or brush up on HTML, you might try my (bestselling!) guide: *HTML 4 for the World Wide Web: Visual QuickStart Guide*, also published by Peachpit Press. For more details, check out *http://www.cookwood.com/* or *http://www.peachpit.com/vqs/html4/*.

Perl and HTML

Getting Perl

Why, you might ask, do you have to *get* Perl when you just want to write something *in* Perl. You don't have to get English to write or understand English, you simply have to know it. However, with Perl scripts, you need something to make them run, and that thing also goes by the name of Perl. Only rarely is it more distinctly called the Perl *interpreter*.

While there are Perl interpreters for many different kinds of computers, this book focuses on using Perl with Unix systems, since most people have their Web pages on Unix servers, and most servers have Perl already installed *(see page 32)*. If your server does not have Perl installed, you'll have to talk to your ISP— or change ISPs *(see page 19)*.

There are several versions of Perl for Unix in use at this writing. While this book assumes you have the current version (5.04), most techniques will work fine with version 4. Although installing Perl on a Unix server is way beyond the scope of this book, you can get up-to-the-minute information about the current versions from *http://www.perl.com/ pace/pub/perldocs/latest.html*.

If you do usually work on a Mac or PC, you can get a Mac or Windows version of the Perl interpreter for testing (see the above-referenced Web page). While some Perl functions work differently in different platforms (most notably, file operations), most of Perl is astonishingly the same from operating system to operating system. Having a local version of Perl can often be useful for testing a bit of a program that just won't work the way you think it should. Make sure you also test the final file on your Unix server.

Figure i.5 *For information about the most current versions of the Perl interpreter, point your browser to http://www.perl.com/pace/pub/perldocs/latest.html*

Getting Perl

Internet service providers

Your connection to the Internet is supplied by your Internet service provider, or ISP. Whether your ISP is a small, independent, local company, or a nationwide concern like AOL, there are several factors that you should keep in mind when choosing where to send your monthly fee.

First, does your ISP allow you to write and execute your own Perl CGI scripts? Since CGI can constitute a security risk, some ISPs either restrict your CGI use to a set of prefabricated scripts or simply don't let you run any at all. Second, what kind of server does your ISP run and does it have Perl installed? This book is specifically for folks using Unix servers with Perl 5.04. Third, what kind of support does your ISP offer? Some ISPs offer round-the-clock technical support and are willing even to offer limited advice on Perl and CGI. Others limit their support to an outdated Web page. Your choice of ISPs is crucial.

Ask your ISP!

Since not everyone uses the same kind of Unix server and because each Unix server is configured differently, in this book, I will sometimes advise you to "Ask your ISP". It's not a cop out. When I tell you to ask your ISP, it's because there's no way to tell from here what the answer will be. I'll usually give you an idea of what to expect, and perhaps something to try if you have a difficult relationship with your ISP, but it's often easiest and fastest to just ask them.

If your ISP is not helpful with such requests, you may prefer to switch ISPs. The kind of information that I advise you to get from them cannot be obtained elsewhere. If they don't help you, they're probably not worth working with.

Internet service providers

About this book

One of the most difficult parts about writing this book was squeezing as much information as possible into each page. Counting the HTML code for the page that activates the Perl script, the way that Web page looks in a browser, the Perl script itself, the explanation for each of the pertinent lines in the Perl script, and the resulting output to the browser (and the HTML code behind it), it is simply impossible to display every step in the life of a Perl script in a column that measures 5 inches long and less than 2.5 inches wide.

Instead, I have focused on what I consider to be the two essential pieces of the puzzle: the Perl script itself—and what each line of code really does—and the way that script plays out in the browser. I have included additional pieces as space permits.

The blocks of Perl code that I display are numbered (in light gray) so that I can explain what each line does without having to repeat each line's contents. *You do not and should not number lines of Perl code in your scripts.*

Primarily due to space restraints, I have not always explained every line of code that is shown, but have focused on the functions being discussed on that page. If you find a line of code that you just don't get, drop me a line *(perl@cookwood.com)* and I'll be happy to translate it into plain English for you.

The Perl script is almost always displayed in its entirety. The particular functions being discussed are highlighted in red, while an explanation of those functions—in "plain English"—is offered in the shaded section below the script. The line numbers are for reference only—do not type them in!

Where space permits, the HTML code is displayed.

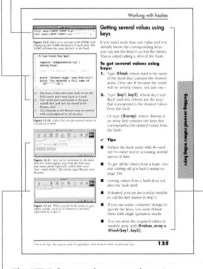

The HTML form used to access the script and the resulting output to the browser after the script is run help you to understand exactly what the script does.

The step-by-step instructions tell you exactly what you need to type to use the Perl element in question. Tips remind you of important points and shortcuts.

Figure i.6 *Because the main focus of the book is on Perl, the script itself is always displayed, together with a description of each of the lines being explained on the page. Where possible, the HTML code, the form as it appears in the browser with the visitor's input, and the output from the script are also displayed. You always have the option of going to the Perl and CGI VQS Guide Web site (see page 22) to see the HTML documents and their source code.*

About this book *(sidebar)*

What this book is not

Perl is an incredibly rich and powerful pro-gramming language that is used in an almost infinite number of ways. You should know that this book is not—nor does it try to be—an exhaustive guide to Perl. Instead, it is a beginner's guide to using Perl for one partic-ular purpose—making Web pages interactive.

This book won't teach you how to use Perl from the command line, how to take advan-tage of Perl's special report-generating functions, nor how to incorporate Perl's advanced features in your scripts. Instead, you'll learn how to use a select group of Perl commands that are useful for making your Web pages interactive. All input is assumed to come from the Web and practically all output will go back to the Web. If you want to use Perl for some non-Web purpose, you'll need a different book *(see page 257)*.

Unix, Macs, and PCs

Perl programs can run on a variety of operat-ing systems, and thus servers, including Mac, Windows NT, and Unix, among many others. Since most people publish their Web pages on Unix servers, this book concentrates on using Perl on those machines.

Of course, that doesn't mean that I expect you to use Unix for everything. In fact, I assume throughout the book that most of you use a Mac or PC to create your scripts—and indeed the rest of your Web page—and then *upload* these files to a Unix server.

Operators and functions

If scalars, arrays, and hashes are the objects on which Perl actions are performed, the actors themselves are called *operators* or *functions*. Simple processes, like addition and multiplication, are represented by symbols and look pretty similar to how you see them in ordinary life. For example, to add 3 and 5 in Perl, you use the addition operator, which is (surprise!) the plus symbol (+), like this: **3 + 5**. To divide the variable $x by the variable $y, you'd use **$x/$y**.

Functions are just operators with names—usually in all lowercase letters—that generally perform slightly more complicated processes. For example, Perl has a function called **print** that sends the specified data to the specified output—which might be the browser or could be an external file.

Some functions operate on scalars, others on arrays or hashes, and still others work differently depending on where you aim them, that is, depending on the *context*. In general, a function's operands are enclosed in parentheses (though experienced Perl programmers often leave these out), and separated by commas if there are more than one.

The operators and functions in Perl that you need for making Web pages interactive are described throughout this book. In addition, they are listed in the index for quick reference.

You can also create your own functions to automate your most common operations. User-defined functions are called *subroutines* and are described in detail in Chapter 9, *Subroutines*.

The plus sign is the symbol for the addition operator.

$sum = 3 + 5;

Figure 1.9 *Operators look like familiar everyday symbols. The addition operator (+) is used to add two numeric values together.*

The shift function

The operand is enclosed in parentheses

shift (@names);

Figure 1.10 *A function's operands are usually enclosed in parentheses. Functions (which are just named operators) generally perform slightly more complicated tasks than operators.*

Result vs. Return value

Functions and operators can affect the value of the data in your script in two ways. Some functions directly change the value of the operands on which they've operated. For example, the **++** operator in the expression **$n++;** *results* in the value of $n being increased by 1.

Other functions leave the variable unchanged and instead have a *return value* that can be analyzed. For example, **print $n;** does not affect the value of $n, it simply sends the contents of $n to output. The return value of any print statement is 1 if it is successful—that is, able to print—and 0 if not. This makes it easy to test if a particular function has been able to run correctly.

Still other functions change the variable *and* have a distinct return value. For example, the **shift** function changes the value of an array by removing its leftmost element and has a return value of the element that was removed. So if @array contains (a, b, c) the result of **shift(@array);** is *(b, c)* while the return value is *a*.

In this book, you'll learn whether a function or operator directly affects the variable, and whether there is a return value that is worth looking at.

Operators and functions

Quotation marks

There are two kinds of straight quotation marks that you'll be using when writing Perl scripts: single and double. You won't need curly quotation marks at all.

Single quotation marks are for enclosing data that you want taken literally, exactly as it appears. Double quotation marks are for enclosing data that may need to be analyzed, or *interpolated*, before processing.

Although you can use the concatenate operator *(see page 79)* to join data together (before, say, printing it), it's much easier and faster to stuff everything into double quotation marks and let Perl interpolate and concatenate the elements on the fly. When Perl interpolates variables within double quotation marks, the *values* of the variables—and not the names of the variables—are printed, which, presumably, is what you want.

To concatenate with double quotes:

1. Type ".

2. Type the constants or variables, or combination of both, that you wish to join together.

3. Type ".

✔ Tip

■ Although this technique is perhaps most useful with printing, you could also assign the result to a scalar variable.

Single quotation marks take their contents literally, exactly as it appears.

print 'You won $5';

Figure 1.11 *The result of this line of code is that the phrase* You won $5 *will be printed. Regardless of whether the $5 was a variable or not, it will not be analyzed.*

Double quotation marks interpolate or analyze the contents of the variables that they contain.

print "You won $prize";

Figure 1.12 *If you use double quotes, any variables contained within will be interpolated before the function does its work. In this case, if the variable* $prize *contains* a new car, *this print statement will output* You won a new car *(and not* You won $prize*).*

Quotation marks

Creating Perl CGI Scripts

Of course, this whole book is about creating Perl CGI scripts. This chapter in particular is about the nuts and bolts of creating the actual files, not the content within them.

You'll learn what software you need to write a Perl CGI script; how and where you should save it; how to upload it to the server, if necessary; how to make it accessible to your audience by adjusting the permissions; how to test its syntax; and finally, and most excitingly, how to run it.

Creating a Perl CGI script

You don't need any special tools to write a Perl CGI script. You can use any word processor, even WordPad or SimpleText, which are included with the basic Windows and Macintosh system software, respectively. Or, you can use the text editors included on the Unix server itself.

Using pico (or some other Unix text editor) on the server means you don't have to worry about the file format or any weird line endings, and you don't have to upload the file to the server, because it's already there. On the other hand, you may be a bit more comfortable with your usual text editor on your Mac or PC. Either way is fine.

To create a new Perl CGI script locally on your Mac or PC:

1. Open a text editor like SimpleText or WordPad.

2. Choose File > New to create a new, blank document **(Figures 2.1 and 2.3)**.

3. Create the script as explained in the rest of this book, starting on page 32.

4. Choose File > Save As.

5. In the dialog box that appears, choose Text Only (or ASCII) for the format **(Figures 2.2 and 2.4)**.

6. If available, choose the option that allows you to save the file with Unix line endings.

7. Choose the directory or folder in which to save the script.

8. Click Save.

Figure 2.1 *In the text editor (this is SimpleText on the Macintosh) choose New to create a new document. Once you've created the script, choose File > Save As to save it.*

Figure 2.2 *Give the file the .cgi extension, choose the Text Only format (the only one available here in SimpleText), choose the desired location, and then click Save.*

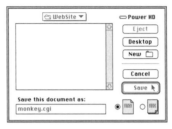

Figure 2.3 *On Windows, choose File > New from Word-Pad (or other text editor). Create the script and then choose File > Save As.*

Figure 2.4 *Give the script the .cgi extension, choose Text Document under Save as type, choose the desired location, and then click Save.*

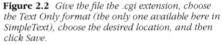

Creating a Perl CGI script

Figure 2.5 *To open the pico text editor on your Unix server, telnet to the server and then type* **pico** *at the command line.*

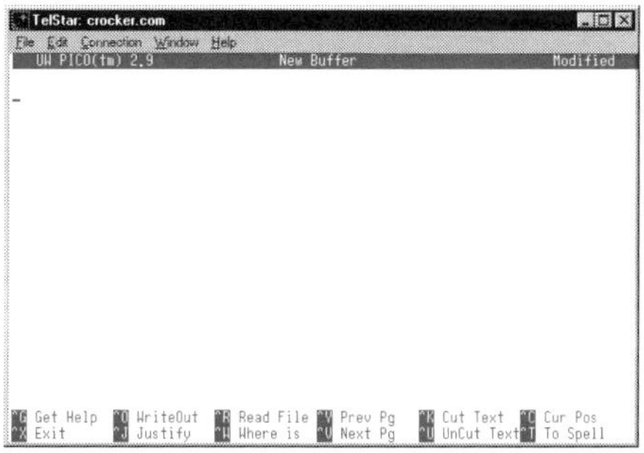

Figure 2.6 *The pico text editor opens in the server (which you access through your Telnet program). Now you start typing your script.*

Figure 2.7 *After you press Control-O, you'll be able to type the desired name for the script at the bottom of the pico window. Make sure to add the path (or press Control-T to go to the directory tree).*

To create a CGI script directly on the Unix server (with pico):

1. Telnet to your Unix server *(see page 240)*.

2. Type **pico**, or whatever program you want to use **(Figure 2.5)**. The text editor opens **(Figure 2.6)**.

3. Create the script as explained in the rest of this book, starting on page 32.

4. Press Control-O (that's the *letter* O) to save your script.

5. At the bottom of the screen, type the file-name for the script, including the path **(Figure 2.7)**.

6. Press Return to save the file. (You'll then have to press Control-X to quit.)

✔ Tips

■ If you create your files locally on your Mac or PC, you should upload them in Text or ASCII format, and not Binary *(see page 36)*.

■ Although you can use SimpleText and WordPad to write your scripts, there are several really robust text editors available. For more details, consult *Text editors* on page 254.

■ Saving your scripts with the .cgi extension makes them easily identifiable to both you and the server. Some servers can execute files with the .cgi extension no matter where they are. Other servers require that you save all your cgi scripts to the cgi-bin directory, and the extension is superfluous. Ask your ISP to be sure *(see page 19)*.

Creating a Perl CGI script

Starting a Perl CGI script

Perl CGI scripts on Unix systems should start with the shebang line—so called because it starts with a *sh*arp (#) and a *bang* (!). The shebang line, which contains the location of the Perl interpreter on your server, enables your scripts to be executed.

To find out where Perl is:

1. Telnet to your Unix server *(see page 240)*.

2. Type **which perl** and then press Enter. The location of the Perl interpreter on your server is revealed.

To start a Perl script:

On the first line of the script, type **#!/usr/local/bin/perl**, where */usr/local/bin/perl* corresponds to the path to the Perl interpreter program on your Unix server that you revealed in the previous step.

✔ Tips

- Another typical shebang line is *#!/usr/bin/perl*. You have to find out where your Perl interpreter is (following the instructions above) to decide which version to use.

- For more information on paths and Unix, consult *Dealing with paths in Unix* on page 243.

- For more information on how to create the actual text document that will contain the script, consult *Creating a Perl CGI script* on page 30.

Figure 2.8 *To find out what version of Perl is on the server, type* **which perl** *at the prompt.*

Figure 2.9 *The server displays the full path to the Perl program. This is the path that you should use in the shebang line.*

```
1   #!/usr/local/bin/perl
```

1: The shebang line consists of the pound symbol (#), the exclamation point (!), and the full path to the Perl program, beginning with a slash.

Figure 2.10 *The shebang line should be the first line in every Perl CGI script that you write.*

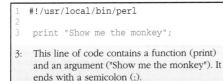

```
1  #!/usr/local/bin/perl
2
3  print "Show me the monkey";
```

3: This line of code contains a function (print) and an argument ("Show me the monkey"). It ends with a semicolon (;).

Figure 2.11 *The semicolon indicates the end of a simple statement in Perl. Only the beginning and ending of blocks escape this rule (see page 106).*

Writing code in Perl

In English, and indeed in many other languages, we end a sentence with a period to contain ideas in understandable chunks. In Perl, you end each "sentence" with a semicolon. Leaving the semicolon out is the cause of innumerable newbie syntax errors.

To write code in Perl:

1. Type the desired code for a particular line.

2. Type **;** (a semicolon).

3. Repeat as necessary. (Seems pretty easy, no?)

✔ Tips

■ The syntax of each particular element of code is described in the corresponding section of this book.

■ The only lines that don't require a semicolon are the first and last lines of a conditional statement *(see page 101)* or the shebang line *(see page 32)*.

■ Nothing should appear after the semicolon except for comments *(see page 35)*. The comments themselves do not need to end with an additional semicolon.

■ There should be no space between the last bit of code and the semicolon.

■ It's considered good style to leave a few empty lines between sections of your script. Due to space restraints, I don't always follow that advice throughout this book. But *you* should.

Writing code in Perl

Creating output for a browser

Perl can be used for many things but since you're using Perl to write CGI scripts for the World Wide Web, you'll want the output from the script to appear in a Web browser, like Netscape Communicator (or Navigator) or Internet Explorer. Although I'll go into more detail about printing later *(see page 177)*, I'll start you off with the basics so you can actually use the examples as you progress through the book.

To create output for a browser:

1. Type **print "Content-type: text/html \n\n";**. There is no space between *html* and the next backslash. Those two backslashes and *n*'s denote newlines and are required. This line tells the browser to expect MIME content of type *text/html*, that is, a Web page. The browser won't be able to display the output at all without this line.

2. On the next line, type **print**.

3. Then type **content**, where *content* is the material that you want to have appear on the Web page. The content can include HTML tags for formatting, strings of text, and variables that contain the processed output from the script (which you'll learn about soon).

4. Type **;** (a semicolon) to complete the print statement.

✔ Tips

- Any strings of text in the content, including HTML tags, must be enclosed in quotation marks. For more details about using quotation marks, see page 28.

- For more information about printing and using HTML in the output, consult Chapter 13, *Printing and HTML.*

```
1   #!/usr/local/bin/perl
2
3   print "Content-type: text/html\n\n";
4   print "Show me the monkey";
```

3: This line prints the all-important MIME content line that browsers require. Without it, browsers don't know what kind of output to expect and they refuse to do anything at all.

4: This is a very simple example of something you might output in the browser.

Figure 2.12 *Your output can range from something as simple as a sentence, as in this example, or as complicated as a full-blown Web page, with formatting, images, and even variables.*

Figure 2.13 *The output appears in the browser. The MIME content line seems invisible, but without it you'd get an Internal Server error because the browser won't know what to do with the output.*

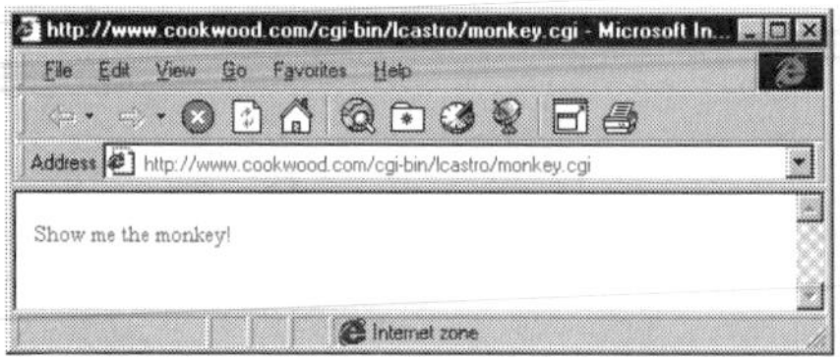

Figure 2.14 *As long as you use standard HTML tags (or none, as in this example), you'll get fairly consistent results across platforms and browsers. This is Internet Explorer 4 for Windows. Figure 2.13 shows Netscape 4 for Macintosh.*

```
1   #!/usr/local/bin/perl
2
3   print "Content-type:text/html\n\n";
4
5   #The next line prints the sentence "Show
    me the monkey"
6   print "Show me the monkey";
```

5: The comment line starts with a # sign and can contain anything you want. It does not need to end with a semicolon.

Figure 2.15 *Comment lines are completely invisible to the user. Use them to remind yourself what you were doing with the code.*

```
1   #!/usr/local/bin/perl
2
3   print "Content-type:text/html\n\n";
4
5   print "Show me the monkey"; #this line
    prints the sentence "Show me the
    monkey"
```

3: Add a comment to a line of code by inserting the # symbol after the semicolon and then following it with the desired information.

Figure 2.16 *Everything after the # sign is considered a comment and is ignored by the interpreter and invisible to the user.*

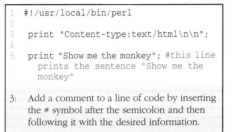

Figure 2.17 *Comments are completely invisible to your visitors. They are strictly for your benefit so you can remember what you were doing, and hopefully, why you were doing it.*

Documenting your script

Although you may live and breathe your script while you're writing it, a few months later you may not recognize your own handwriting, so to speak. It's a good idea to explain what you are doing in your script so that later, when you or someone else come back to update the script, you can figure out why you did something a particular way and not have to invent that same wheel a second or third time.

To add comments on separate lines:

1. At the very beginning of the line, type **#** to begin the comment.

2. Type **comment**, where *comment* explains some part of the following block of code.

3. Repeat steps 1–2 for each line of comments.

You can also add short comments at the end of a line of code.

To add comments on code lines:

1. Type the line of code as described on page 33. Make sure you don't forget the semicolon.

2. After the semicolon, type a space and then **#** to begin the comment.

3. Type **comment**, where *comment* explains some part of the line of code.

✔ Tips

■ Each individual line of comments must start with its own pound sign (#).

■ Comment lines do not need to end with a semicolon (or *anything* in particular, for that matter).

Documenting your script

Uploading your script to the server

If you create the script on a Mac or PC (which is perfectly fine), you'll then have to upload it to the Unix server with an FTP program like Fetch (for Mac) or WS_FTP (for Windows). If you create the script directly on the server *(see page 31)*, you can skip this section.

To change your preferences for uploading CGI scripts from a Mac (with Fetch):

1. Launch Fetch, or other FTP program.

2. Choose Customize > Preferences **(Figure 2.18)**.

3. In the Preferences dialog box that appears, click Upload, the third tab. The Upload preferences appear **(Figure 2.19)**.

4. Choose Text in the menu next to Default text format.

5. Deselect the Add .txt suffix in text files option.

To upload your script to the server from a Mac (with Fetch):

1. Launch Fetch, or other FTP program.

2. If the New Connection window isn't already open, choose File > New Connection **(Figure 2.20)**.

3. In the New Connection window, type the server name (or IP address) in the Host box **(Figure 2.21)**.

4. Type your user name and password in the User ID and Password boxes.

5. Click OK. Fetch opens the connection with the server.

Figure 2.18 *In Fetch (on the Mac), choose Customize > Preferences.*

Figure 2.19 *Click the Upload tab at the top of the Preferences dialog box to see the Upload preferences. Then choose Text for the Default text format and make sure to deselect the Add .txt suffix to text files option.*

Figure 2.20 *In Fetch (on the Mac), choose File > New Connection to open a connection to your site for uploading files.*

Figure 2.21 *In the New Connection dialog box, type the name or IP address in the Host box, your user ID in the User ID box, and your password in the Password box. If you like, you can type the desired destination directory in the Directory box. Then click OK.*

Uploading your script to the server

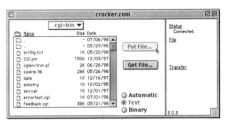

Figure 2.22 *Navigate to the directory into which you wish to upload your CGI scripts. On many servers, CGI scripts must be located in the cgi-bin directory in order to work properly. Ask your ISP to be sure. Then click Put File (or drag the file from the desktop).*

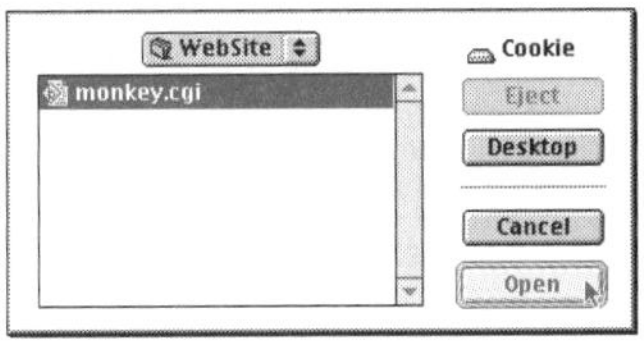

Figure 2.23 *After clicking Put File, choose the desired file from the dialog box that appears and click Open.*

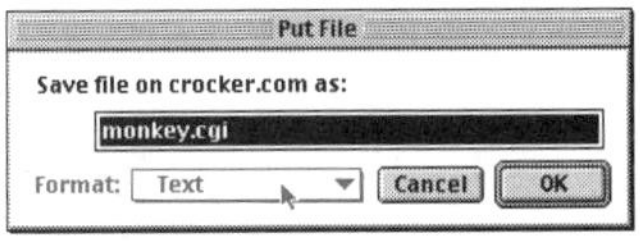

Figure 2.24 *In the Put File dialog box, confirm that the name of the script is correct and that the format is Text.*

6. If necessary, navigate to the directory on the server into which you wish to upload the script **(Figure 2.22)**.

7. Make sure Text is selected (below the Get File button).

8. Click Put File and choose the file you wish to upload from the dialog box that appears **(Figure 2.23)**.

Or, drag the desired script from your desktop to the Fetch window.

9. In the Put File dialog box that appears, confirm the name of the script you're uploading and make sure the Format is set to Text **(Figure 2.24)**.

✔ Tips

- Some ISPs require that you upload your CGI scripts to the cgi-bin directory. Others let you run CGI scripts from wherever you like, as long as they have the .cgi extension. To be sure, ask your ISP *(see page 19)*.

- Information about uploading files from Windows machines is on the next page (page 38).

- You can find Fetch's home page at *http://www.dartmouth.edu/pages/softdev/fetch.html.*

Uploading your script to the server

To upload files from Windows (with WS_FTP Pro):

1. Launch WS_FTP Pro, or other FTP transfer program.

2. Click Connect at the bottom of the main WS_FTP window. The Session Properties dialog box appears.

3. Enter your server's name or IP address in the Host Name/Address box **(Figure 2.25)**.

4. Type your user ID and password in the corresponding boxes.

5. Click OK to return to the main WS_FTP window.

6. On the left side of the window, navigate to the directory on your hard disk that contains the file you wish to upload and select the desired script **(Figure 2.26)**.

7. On the right side of the window, navigate to the directory on the server to which you wish to upload the script.

8. Click the ASCII option below the left list.

9. Click the Upload button (the right pointing arrow) between the panes. The file will be uploaded.

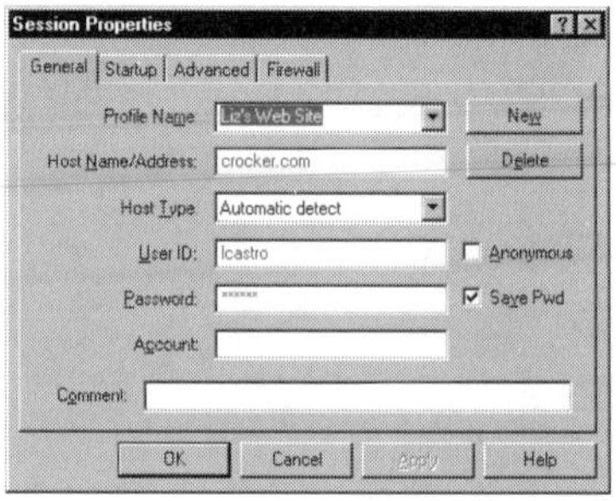

✔ Tips

- Some ISPs require that you upload your CGI scripts to the cgi-bin directory. Others let you run CGI scripts from wherever you like, as long as they have the .cgi extension. To be sure, ask your ISP *(see page 19)*.

- For details on uploading files from a Macintosh, see page 36.

- You can find WS_FTP's home page at *http://www.ipswitch.com/products/ws_ftp/*.

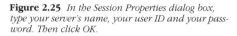

Figure 2.25 *In the Session Properties dialog box, type your server's name, your user ID and your password. Then click OK.*

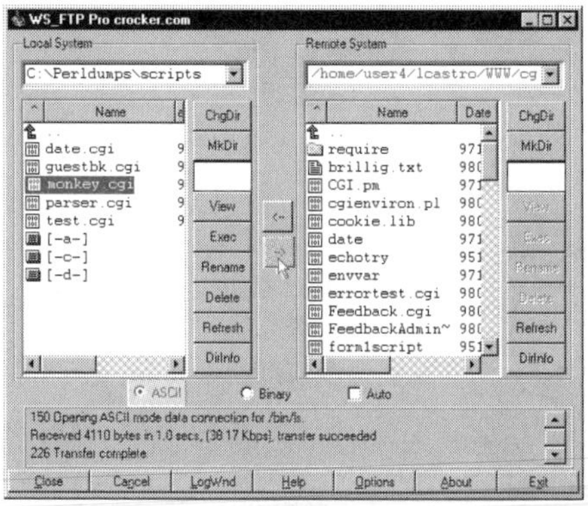

Figure 2.26 *In the left pane (your hard disk), choose the script you want to upload. On the right side (your server), choose the directory into which you wish to place the uploaded script. Click the ASCII option below the left list. Then click the Upload button between the frames.*

Uploading your script to the server

Figure 2.27 *Normally, the chmod function gives no feedback whatsoever. Still, as long as you're sure you typed the right permissions code, no news is probably good news.*

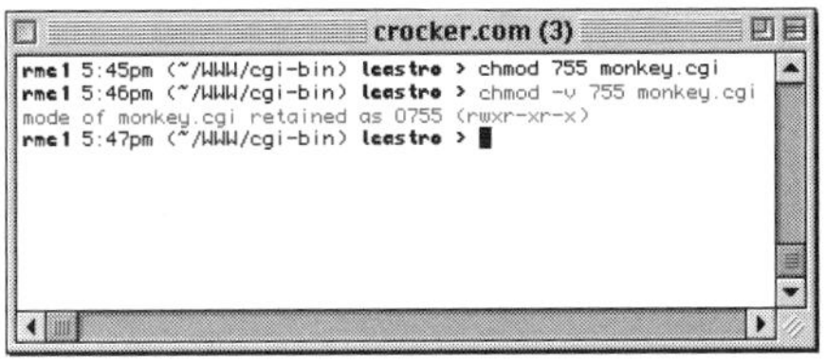

Figure 2.28 *If you use the -v flag with chmod, you'll get a message telling what permissions a file or directory has, and if they've changed or not.*

Changing permissions

When you first upload a file to the Unix server, it is generally set so that only the owner can read and write to it, and everyone else can just read it. In order for others (and thus any browser) to be able to execute it, you have to change the permissions.

To change a file or directory's permissions:

1. Telnet to the Unix server *(see page 240)*, and, if necessary, navigate to the directory that contains the file or directory whose permissions you want to change *(see page 246)*.

2. Type **chmod**.

3. If desired, type **-v** so that you'll get a message confirming the permissions.

4. Type **oge**, where *o* is the number that indicates the *o*wner's permissions, *g* is the number that indicates the *g*roup's permissions, and *e* is the number that indicates *e*veryone else's permissions.

5. Type **scriptname**, where *scriptname* is the full name of the script whose permissions you want to change.

6. Press Enter. The permissions are set. Unless you use **-v** there is no confirmation.

✔ Tips

- Use 755 for files, like CGI scripts, that need to be executed. Use 644 for non-executables, including log files, configuration files, preferences files, external subroutines, libraries, and others.

- For more information about permissions, consult Appendix B, *Permissions*.

Changing permissions

Checking the script's syntax

The one thing about communicating with a computer is that you have to be very precise. Leave off a semicolon, and the computer gets very testy. Misspell a variable name and it may decide to hang up on you altogether. Perl has a handy command for finding typos and other minor syntax errors.

To test a Perl script:

1. Telnet to your Unix server *(see page 240)*.

2. Navigate to the directory that contains the script in question.

3. Type **perl -c scriptname**, where *script-name* is the full name of the script whose syntax you want to check. The Perl interpreter will advise you of any syntax problems in the script, but it won't run the script.

```
1   #!/usr/local/bin/perl
2
3   print "Content-type: text/html\n\n";
4   print "Show me the monkey';
```

4: I've created an error by using a single quote to end the print statement that I had started with a double quote.

Figure 2.29 *Syntax errors are often hard to spot, even when they're highlighted with a second color. (The error is at the end of line 4.)*

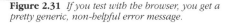

Figure 2.30 *Using the -c flag is a quick and easy way to find syntax errors in your script.*

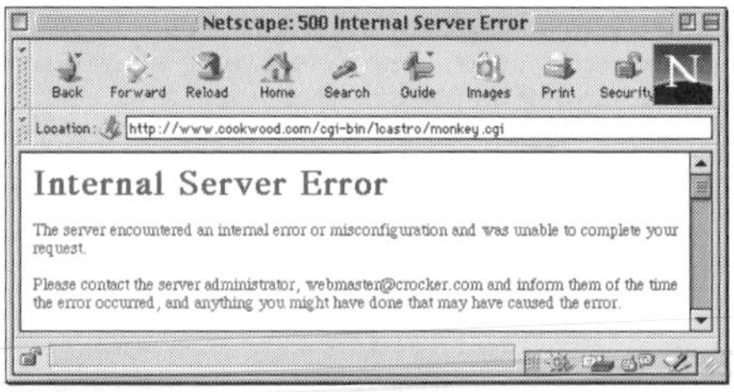

Internal Server Error

The server encountered an internal error or misconfiguration and was unable to complete your request.

Please contact the server administrator, webmaster@crocker.com and inform them of the time the error occurred, and anything you might have done that may have caused the error.

Figure 2.31 *If you test with the browser, you get a pretty generic, non-helpful error message.*

Figure 2.32 *Launch the browser that you want to run the script in.*

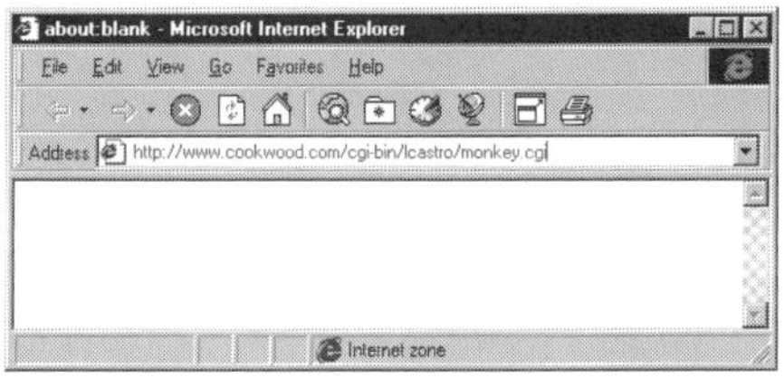

Figure 2.33 *Type the script's URL—not the path within the server—in the Address box in IE and in the Location box in Netscape.*

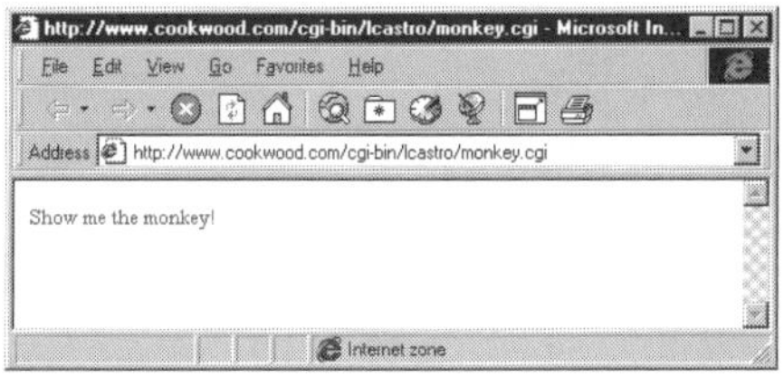

Figure 2.34 *When you press Enter, the browser sends the request to the server, the server processes the script and sends the output to the browser, and the browser displays the output.*

Running a Perl CGI script

Once you've written your script, uploaded it, changed its permissions, and checked its syntax, you're ready to try it out. You can either point your browser directly at the CGI script that you want to run or you can set up a form that activates the script when you press its submit button.

To run a Perl CGI script with no input:

1. Launch your browser **(Figure 2.32)**.

2. Type the URL of the script in the browser **(Figure 2.33)**.

3. Press Enter. The browser sends your request to the server, and then the server runs the script and sends the output, if any, back to the browser **(Figure 2.34)**.

✔ Tips

- It doesn't matter what browser you use.

- Actually, you can input data to the script when you type its URL in the browser. For more details, consult *Using a link to input data to a script* on page 57 and then instead of creating the link, just type the URL in the browser.

- You can also use a link to activate a script. For more details, see page 56.

- For details on running a script with a form, see Chapter 3, *Getting Data from Visitors*.

- How, oh, how do you find out what the URL is? You'd think (or I did) that the URL would be the same as the server name plus the path to the script. Unfortunately, that's not always true. It all depends on how your ISP has set up the server. You have to ask your ISP *(see page 19)* what the URL is for your cgi-bin directory, and then construct the full URL by tacking on the script name.

Getting Data from Visitors

By far, the easiest and most common way to get input from your visitors is with a form on your Web page. Creating a form is pure HTML; no Perl scripting is required. Perl becomes a factor when you want to look at and process the data.

In this chapter, you'll learn how to create all of the different elements of a form, with special emphasis on making the data easy to collect and process. If you are already familiar with HTML and form creation, you can skip this chapter—although you might want to skim through it to catch the scripting-focused tricks that I've added.

Another way to get input from visitors is by creating a link to a script. You'll learn how to do that at the end of this chapter.

Labeling incoming data

Perhaps the most crucial part of collecting data from your visitors is making sure the information is properly labeled so you know what you've received. For example, if you receive a piece of data that contains "Maplewood", is that the visitor's preference of materials for the bed they're ordering or is it the name of the town where they want the bed shipped? If the data from a radio button simply says "Yes", what exactly is the visitor agreeing to?

As the designer of the HTML form, you decide on the labels that will accompany incoming data on its journey to your CGI script. In your HTML document, you set the NAME attribute for each form element so that it clearly and distinctly identifies the data that that particular element collects.

Creating the data itself

There are basically two kinds of form elements: those that allow free-form input (text boxes, password boxes, and larger text areas), and those that the visitor can select but not type in (radio buttons, checkboxes, and menus). For the former, the value is set to the free-form input. For the latter, you, the form designer, will set the VALUE attribute to create the actual data that is sent to the server when the visitor uses one of these fields.

The visitor never sees the VALUE attribute (unless they look at your source code) but when they check a button or checkbox, or select an option in a menu, the corresponding VALUE attribute identifies the visitor's choices to you and to your CGI script. If you don't set the VALUE attribute for radio buttons, checkboxes, or menus, the default value is a vague, pretty useless "on".

```
code.html
<FORM ACTION="http://www.cookwood.com/cgi-
bin/lcastro/namevalue.cgi" METHOD=POST>

Name: <INPUT TYPE="text" NAME="name">
Address: <INPUT TYPE="text" NAME="address"
SIZE=30>

<P>City: <INPUT TYPE="text" NAME="city">
State: <INPUT TYPE="text" NAME="state" SIZE=2
MAXLENGTH=2>
Zipcode: <INPUT TYPE="text" NAME="zip" SIZE=5
MAXLENGTH=5>
<HR>

<B>Type of wood:</B>
<SELECT NAME="woodtype">
<OPTION VALUE="Mahogany">Mahogany
<OPTION VALUE="Maplewood">Maplewood
<OPTION VALUE="Pine">Pine
<OPTION VALUE="Cherry">Cherry
</SELECT>

<B>Size:</B>
<INPUT TYPE="radio" NAME="size" VALUE="K">
King <INPUT TYPE="radio" NAME="size"
VALUE="Q">Queen <INPUT TYPE="radio"
NAME="size" VALUE="T">Twin <INPUT
TYPE="radio" NAME="size" VALUE="S">Single

<P><B>Extras:</B>
<INPUT TYPE="checkbox" NAME="extras"
VALUE="foot">Footboard
<INPUT TYPE="checkbox" NAME="extras"
VALUE="drawers">Drawers (for underneath)
<INPUT TYPE="checkbox" NAME="extras"
VALUE="casters">Casters
<INPUT TYPE="checkbox" NAME="extras"
VALUE="nosqueak">Squeak proofing

<HR>Would you like us to call you before
shipping your bed? <INPUT TYPE="radio"
NAME="call_first" VALUE="Yes"> Yes
<INPUT TYPE="radio" NAME="call_first"
VALUE="No"> No
<P>Would you like us to share your name,
address, and bedding preferences with every
mailing list on the continent?
<INPUT TYPE="radio" NAME="mail_list"
VALUE="Yes"> Yes
<INPUT TYPE="radio" NAME="mail_list"
VALUE="No"> No

<HR>
<INPUT TYPE="submit" VALUE="Order Bed">
<INPUT TYPE="reset" VALUE="Start Over">
```

Figure 3.1 *Here is the HTML code for a typical Web form. Don't worry too much about all the details. Instead, concentrate on the NAME and VALUE attributes. Notice, for example, how free-form elements have no VALUE attribute set, while radio buttons, checkboxes, and the menu have both NAME and VALUE attributes.*

Figure 3.2 *Here is the form on the Web page after the visitor has entered the data. Note that only the highlighted elements are sent to the server. Everything else, including for example, the radio button labels, are just descriptions so that the visitor knows what to do.*

Figure 3.3 *This is the information that arrives at the server and that is processed by the CGI script. Notice that it is the NAME attribute—and not the label that appears in the Web form—that gets sent. Also notice how important it is that the NAME attribute clearly describe the information in the corresponding VALUE—in particular with the identical Maplewood values, but also with non-obvious values like Q.*

HTML labels vs. the NAME attribute

Only the contents of the NAME and VALUE attributes (and the text entered by the visitor in free-form fields) are sent to the script. Don't confuse either of these with the plain-text labels that you use to identify the different fields on your Web page **(Figure 3.2)**. While the plain-text labels are essential for helping your visitor know where they should type each piece of information, the script doesn't care if they exist at all.

Creating a form

A form has three important parts: the FORM tag, which includes the URL of the CGI script that will process the form; the form elements, like fields and menus; and the submit button which sends the data to the CGI script on the server.

To create a form:

1. Type **<FORM**.

2. Type **ACTION="script.url">** where *script.url* is the location on the server of the CGI script that will run when the form is submitted.

3. Type **METHOD=POST**.

4. Create the form's contents, as described on pages 47–54.

5. Type **</FORM>** to complete the form.

✔ Tips

■ In order for your visitor to send you the data on the form, you'll need either a submit button (if your form contains fields, buttons, and other elements that your visitors will fill in) or an active image. For details about submit buttons, consult *Creating the submit button* on page 53. For information on active images, consult *Using an image to submit data* on page 55.

■ You can also use the GET method to process information gathered with a form. However, since the GET method limits the amount of data that you can collect at one time, I recommend using POST.

■ Even if you use the POST method, you can still append data to the URL in step 3 which will be processed via GET. For more details, see page 57.

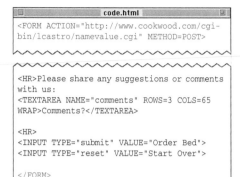

```
┌──────────── code.html ────────────┐
<FORM ACTION="http://www.cookwood.com/cgi-
bin/lcastro/namevalue.cgi" METHOD=POST>
~~~~~~~~~~~~~~~~~~~~~~~~~~~~~~~~~~~~~~~~

<HR>Please share any suggestions or comments
with us:
<TEXTAREA NAME="comments" ROWS=3 COLS=65
WRAP>Comments?</TEXTAREA>

<HR>
<INPUT TYPE="submit" VALUE="Order Bed">
<INPUT TYPE="reset" VALUE="Start Over">

</FORM>
```

Figure 3.4 *Every form has three parts: the FORM tag, the actual form elements where the visitor enters information, and the SUBMIT tag which creates the button that sends the collected information to the server (or an active image).*

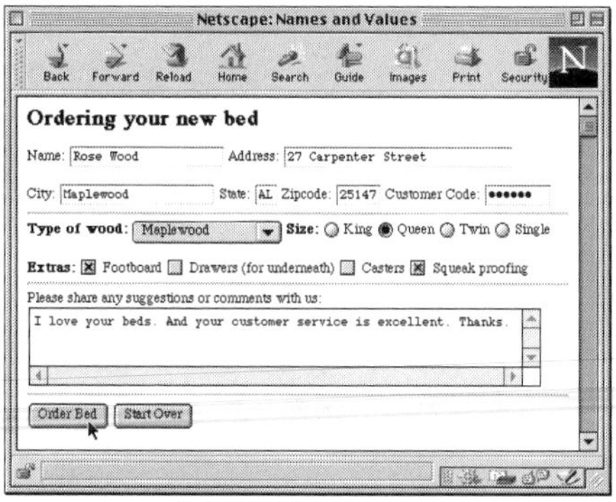

Figure 3.5 *A form gives you a great way to get information and feedback from your visitors.*

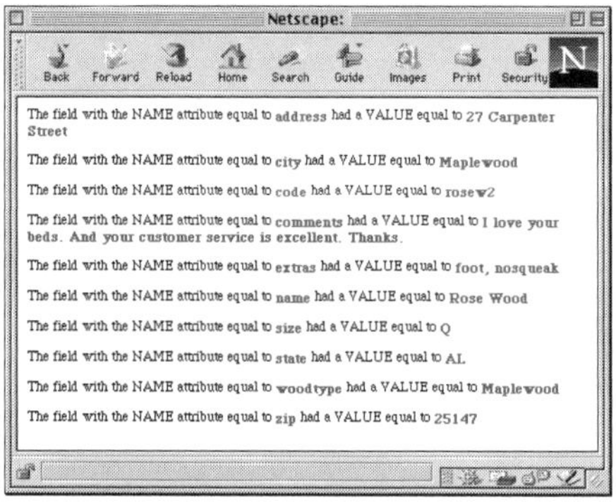

Figure 3.6 *Here is an example of one of many ways to compile the incoming data.*

Creating a form

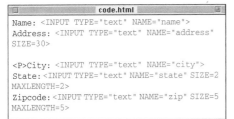

```
code.html
Name: <INPUT TYPE="text" NAME="name">
Address: <INPUT TYPE="text" NAME="address"
SIZE=30>

<P>City: <INPUT TYPE="text" NAME="city">
State: <INPUT TYPE="text" NAME="state" SIZE=2
MAXLENGTH=2>
Zipcode:<INPUT TYPE="text" NAME="zip" SIZE=5
MAXLENGTH=5>
```

Figure 3.7 *While it's essential to set the NAME attribute for each text box, you only have to set the VALUE attribute when you want to add default values for a text box.*

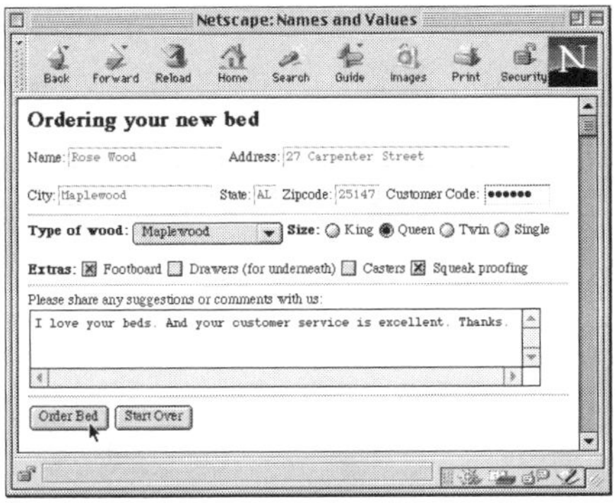

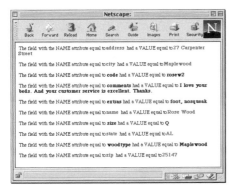

Figure 3.8 *Text boxes can be different sizes to accommodate different types of fields.*

Figure 3.9 *It's important to give descriptive names to your text boxes (with the NAME attribute) so that you know what information you're receiving.*

Creating text boxes

Text boxes can contain one line of free-form text—that is, anything that the visitor wants to type—and are typically used for names, addresses, and the like.

To create a text box:

1. If desired, type the label that will identify the text box to your visitor (for example, **Name:**).

2. Type **<INPUT TYPE="text"**.

3. Type **NAME="name"**, where *name* is the text that will identify the input data to the server (and your script).

4. If desired, type **VALUE="value"**, where *value* is the data that will initially be shown in the field and that will be sent to the server if the visitor doesn't type something else.

5. If desired, define the size of the box on your form by typing **SIZE=n**, replacing *n* with the desired width of the box, measured in characters.

6. If desired, type **MAXLENGTH=n**, where n is the maximum number of characters that can be entered in the box.

7. Finish the text box by typing a final **>**.

✔ Tips

■ Even if your visitor skips the field (and you haven't set the default text with the VALUE attribute), the NAME attribute is still sent to the server (with an undefined, empty VALUE).

■ The default SIZE is 20. However, visitors can type up to the limit imposed by the MAXLENGTH attribute. Still, for larger, multi-line entries, it's better to use text areas *(see page 49)*.

Creating text boxes

Creating password boxes

A password box is similar to a text box, but when the visitor types in it, the letters are hidden by bullets or asterisks.

To create password boxes:

1. If desired, type the label that will identify the password box to your visitor (for example, **Enter password:**).

2. Type **<INPUT TYPE="password"**.

3. Type **NAME="name"**, where *name* is the text that will identify the input data to the server (and your script).

4. If desired, define the size of the box on your form by typing **SIZE=n**, replacing *n* with the desired width of the box, measured in characters.

5. If desired, type **MAXLENGTH=n**, where n is the maximum number of characters that can be entered in the box.

6. Finish the text box by typing a final **>**.

✔ Tips

■ Even if nothing is entered in the password box, the NAME is still sent to the server (with an undefined VALUE).

■ You could set default text for VALUE (as in step 4 on page 47), but that kind of defeats the purpose of a password.

■ The only protection the password box offers is from folks peering over your visitor's shoulder as she types in her password. Since the data is not encrypted when the information is sent to the server, moderately experienced crackers can discover the password without much trouble.

```
                    code.html
Customer Code: <INPUT TYPE="password"
NAME="code" SIZE=8>
```

Figure 3.10 *The NAME attribute identifies the password when you compile the data with your form-parsing script.*

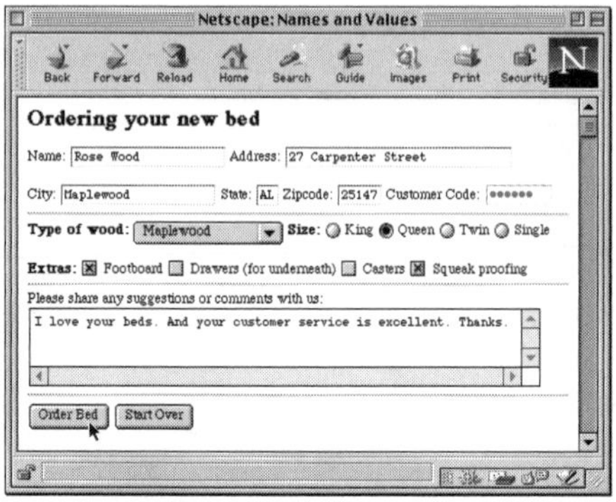

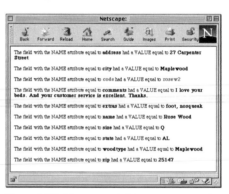

Figure 3.11 *When the visitor enters a password in a form, the password is hidden with bullets.*

Figure 3.12 *The password data appears as regular text after processing by a form-parsing script. Password boxes are not high-security! (See last tip.)*

```
▓▓▓▓▓▓▓▓▓    code.html    ▓▓▓▓▓▓▓▓▓
<HR>Please share any suggestions or comments
with us:
 <TEXTAREA NAME="comments" ROWS=3 COLS=65
WRAP>Comments?</TEXTAREA>
```

Figure 3.13 *The VALUE attribute is not used with the TEXTAREA tag. Default values are set by adding text between the opening and closing tags (as in "Comments?" here).*

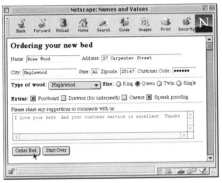

Figure 3.14 *The visitor can override the default text simply by typing over it.*

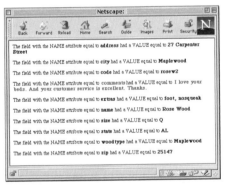

Figure 3.15 *Text areas are great for getting longer comments and suggestions from visitors. They are typically used in guestbooks and bulletin boards.*

Creating larger text areas

In some cases, you want to give the visitor more room to write. Unlike text boxes *(see page 47)*, text areas may be as large as your page, and will expand as needed if the person enters more text than can fit in the display area. They're perfect for eliciting questions and comments.

To create larger text areas:

1. If desired, type the explanatory text that will identify the text area.

2. Type **<TEXTAREA**.

3. Type **NAME="name"**, where *name* is the text that will identify the input data to the server (and your script).

4. If desired, type **ROWS=n**, where *n* is the height of the text area in rows. The default value is 4.

5. If desired, type **COLS=n**, where *n* is the width of the text area in characters. The default value is 40.

6. If desired, type **WRAP** so that when the visitor types, the lines are automatically wrapped within the margins.

7. Type **>**.

8. Type the default text, if any, for the text area. You may not add any HTML coding here.

9. Type **</TEXTAREA>** to complete the text area.

✔ Tips

■ There is no use for the VALUE attribute with text areas.

■ Visitors can enter up to 32,700 characters in a text area. Scroll bars will appear when necessary.

Creating larger text areas

Creating radio buttons

Remember those old-time car radios with big black plastic buttons? Push one to listen to WFCR; push another for WRNX. You can never push two buttons at once. Radio buttons on forms work the same way (except you can't listen to the radio).

To create a radio button:

1. If desired, type the introductory text for your radio buttons. You might use something like **Select one of the following**.

2. Type **<INPUT TYPE="radio"**.

3. Type **NAME="radioset"**, where *radioset* both identifies the data sent to the script and also links the radio buttons together, ensuring that only one per set can be checked.

4. Type **VALUE="data"**, where *data* is the text that will be sent to the server if the radio button is checked, either by you (in step 5) or by the visitor.

5. If desired, type **CHECKED** to make the radio button active by default when the page is opened. (You can only do this to one radio button in the set.)

6. Type the final **>**.

7. Type the text that identifies the radio button to the visitor. This is often the same as VALUE, but doesn't have to be.

8. Repeat steps 2-7 for each radio button in the set.

✔ Tip

■ If you don't set the VALUE attribute, the word "on" is sent to the script. It's not particularly useful since you can't tell which button in the set was pressed.

```
code.html
<B>Size:</B>
<INPUT TYPE="radio" NAME="size"
VALUE="K">King
<INPUT TYPE="radio" NAME="size"
VALUE="Q">Queen
<INPUT TYPE="radio" NAME="size"
VALUE="T">Twin
<INPUT TYPE="radio" NAME="size"
VALUE="S">Single
```

Figure 3.16 *The NAME attribute serves a dual purpose for radio buttons: it links the radio buttons in a given set and it identifies the values when they are sent to the script. The VALUE attribute is crucial since the visitor has no way of typing a value.*

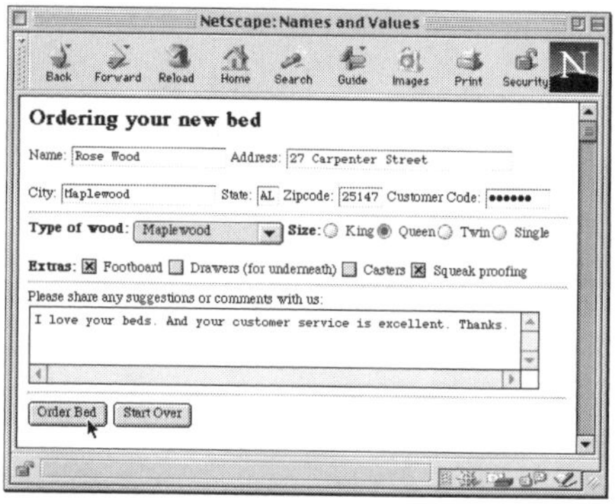

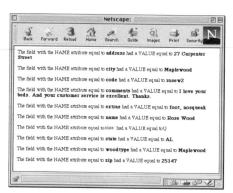

Figure 3.17 *The radio buttons themselves are created with the HTML tags. The labels (King, Queen, etc.) are created with plain text alongside the HTML tags.*

Figure 3.18 *Note that it is the VALUE (Q) and not the label (Queen) that gets sent to the script.*

```
code.html
<P><B>Extras:</B>
<INPUT TYPE="checkbox" NAME="extras"
VALUE="foot">Footboard
<INPUT TYPE="checkbox" NAME="extras"
VALUE="drawers">Drawers (for underneath)
<INPUT TYPE="checkbox" NAME="extras"
VALUE="casters">Casters
<INPUT TYPE="checkbox" NAME="extras"
VALUE="nosqueak">Squeak proofing
```

Figure 3.19 *Notice how the label text (not high-lighted) does not need to match the VALUE attribute. That's because the label text identifies the checkboxes to the visitor in the browser while the VALUE identifies the data to the script.*

Figure 3.20 *The visitor can check as many boxes as necessary. Each corresponding value will be sent to the script, together with the checkbox set's name.*

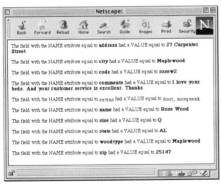

Figure 3.21 *Since the visitor has chosen two check-boxes, both values (but not their labels, of course) are sent to the script. This particular script separates multiple values with a comma.*

Creating checkboxes

While radio buttons can accept only one answer per set, a visitor can check as many checkboxes in a set as they like. Like radio buttons, checkboxes are linked by the value of the NAME attribute.

To create checkboxes:

1. If desired, type the introductory text (something like **Select one or more of the following**) for your checkboxes.

2. Type **<INPUT TYPE="checkbox"**. (Notice there is no space in the word *checkbox*.)

3. Type **NAME="boxset"**, where *boxset* both identifies the data sent to the script and also links the checkboxes together.

4. Type **VALUE="value"** to define a value for each checkbox. The value will be sent to the server if the checkbox is checked (either by the visitor, or by you as described in step 5).

5. Type **CHECKED** to make the checkbox checked by default when the page is opened. You (or the visitor) may check as many checkboxes as desired.

6. Type **>** to complete the checkbox.

7. Type the text that identifies the checkbox to the user. This is often the same as the VALUE, but doesn't have to be.

8. Repeat steps 2-7 for each checkbox in the set.

✔ Tip

■ If you don't set the VALUE attribute, the word "on" is sent to the script. It's not particularly useful since you can't tell which box in the set was checked.

Creating menus

Menus are perfect for offering your visitors a choice from a given set of options.

To create menus:

1. Type the introductory text, if desired.

2. Type **<SELECT**.

3. Type **NAME="name"**, where *name* will identify the data collected from the menu when it is sent to the server.

4. Type **SIZE=n**, where *n* represents the height (in lines) of the menu.

5. If desired, type **MULTIPLE** to allow your visitor to select more than one menu option (with Ctrl or Command).

6. Type **>**.

7. Type **<OPTION**.

8. Type **SELECTED** if you want the option to be selected by default.

9. Type **VALUE="value"**, where *value* specifies the data that will be sent to the server if the option is selected.

10. Type **>**.

11. Type the option name as you wish it to appear in the menu.

12. Repeat steps 7-11 for each option.

13. Type **</SELECT>**.

✔ Tips

■ If you add the SIZE attribute in step 4, the menu appears more like a list, and there is no automatically selected option (unless you use SELECTED).

■ If SIZE is bigger than the number of options, visitors can deselect all values by clicking in the empty space.

```
code.html
<B>Type of wood:</B>
<SELECT NAME="woodtype">
<OPTION VALUE="Mahogany">Mahogany
<OPTION VALUE="Maplewood">Maplewood
<OPTION VALUE="Pine">Pine
<OPTION VALUE="Cherry">Cherry
</SELECT>
```

Figure 3.22 *Menus are made up of two HTML tags: SELECT and OPTION. You set the common NAME attribute in the SELECT tag and the individual VALUE attribute in each of the OPTION tags.*

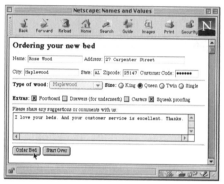

Figure 3.23 *There's no way for a visitor to select nothing in a menu unless you set the SIZE attribute. The default selection is either the first option in the menu or the one you've set as SELECTED in step 8.*

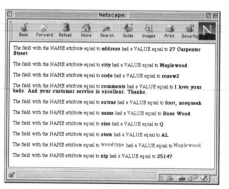

Figure 3.24 *Notice that the NAME attribute (woodtype) and not the label (Type of wood:) is what gets sent to the script.*

```
<INPUT TYPE="submit" VALUE="Order Bed">
```

Figure 3.25 *If you leave out the NAME attribute, the name-value pair for the submit button will not be passed to the script. Since you usually don't need this information, that's a good thing.*

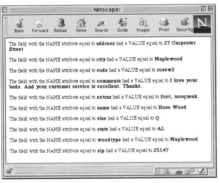

Figure 3.26 *The most important function of the submit button is to activate the script that will collect the data from the other fields. You can personalize the button's contents with the VALUE attribute. (The phrase* Order Bed *is clearer for your visitors than the default* Submit Query*).*

Figure 3.27 *If there is no NAME attribute specified for the submit button, not even the submit button's VALUE attribute will be gathered by the script. But, hey, what do you need it for anyway?*

Creating the submit button

All the information that your visitors enter won't be any good to you unless they send it to the server. You should always create a submit button for your forms so that the visitor can deliver the information to you. (If you use images as active elements in a FORM area, see page 55.)

To create a submit button:

1. Type **<INPUT TYPE="submit"**.

2. If desired, type **VALUE="submit message"** where *submit message* is the text that will appear in the button. The default submit message is *Submit Query*.

3. Type the final **>**.

✔ Tips

- The name-value pair for the submit button is only sent to the script if you set the NAME attribute. Therefore, if you omit the NAME attribute, you won't have to deal with the extra, usually superfluous submit data.

- On the other hand, you can create multiple submit buttons (with both the NAME and VALUE attributes) and then write your CGI script to react according to which submit button the visitor presses. Of course, it would be much easier just to use a set of radio buttons for the same purpose.

- Although the standard HTML 4 specifications allow for fancier button creation (including fonts and images), most browsers don't recognize the code yet. You can get more details in my HTML book: *HTML 4 for the World Wide Web: Visual QuickStart Guide*, also published by Peachpit Press.

Creating the submit button

Resetting the form

If humans could fill out forms perfectly on the first try, there would be no erasers on pencils and no backspace key on your computer keyboard. You can give your visitors a reset button so that they can start over with a fresh form (including all the default values you've set).

To create a reset button:

1. Type **<INPUT TYPE="reset"**.

2. If desired, type **VALUE="reset message"** where *reset message* is the text that appears in the button. The default reset message is *Reset*.

3. Type **>**.

✔ Tip

■ The name-value pair for the reset button is only sent to the script if you set the NAME attribute. Therefore, if you omit the NAME attribute, you won't have to deal with the completely superfluous reset data—which is usually something like "reset, Reset".

```
code.html
<INPUT TYPE="reset" VALUE="Start Over">
```

Figure 3.28 *You can use any text you wish for the reset button.*

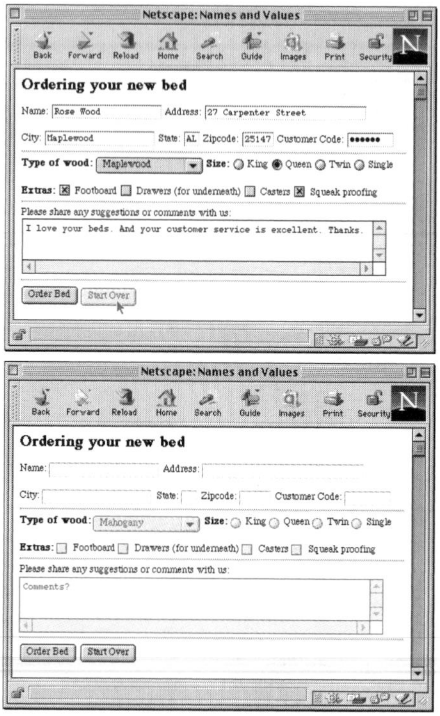

Figure 3.29 *If your visitor clicks the reset button, all the fields are set to their default values.*

```
                    code.html
<FORM ACTION="http://www.cookwood.com/cgi-
bin/lcastro/zonemap.cgi" METHOD=POST>

<BR><INPUT TYPE="radio" NAME="infotype"
VALUE="time">Local time
<INPUT TYPE="radio" NAME="infotype"
VALUE="weather">Local weather
<INPUT TYPE="radio" NAME="infotype"
VALUE="directions">Directions
<INPUT TYPE="radio" NAME="infotype"
VALUE="statistics">City statistics

<P><INPUT TYPE="image" SRC="zonemap.gif"
NAME="coord">
</FORM>
```

Figure 3.30 *If you use an active image, you don't need a submit button.*

Figure 3.31 *You can have both regular form elements (like the radio buttons) and an image map in the same form. When the visitor clicks the map, all of the data is sent to the script.*

Figure 3.32 *The browser appends a period and an x to the NAME attribute (coord) and uses this name (coord.x) to identify the x coordinate of the location where the visitor clicked. The same happens with the y coordinate. Notice that the information from the radio button is also collected.*

Using an image to submit data

You may use an image—called an active image—as a combination input element and submit button. In addition to submitting the data from the other fields in the form, a click on the image sends the current mouse coordinates to the server in two name-value pairs. The names are generated by adding .x and .y to the value of the NAME attribute. The values correspond to the actual horizontal and vertical locations (where 0,0 is the top left corner) of the cursor.

To use an image to submit data:

1. Create a GIF or JPEG image.

2. Type **<INPUT TYPE="image"**.

3. Type **SRC="image_url"** where *image_url* is the location of the image on the server.

4. Type **NAME="name"**. When the visitor clicks on the image, the x and y coordinates of the mouse will be appended to the name defined here and sent to the server.

5. Type the final **>** to finish the active image definition for the form.

✔ Tips

- Setting the VALUE attribute has no effect. The values are set to the mouse coordinates automatically.

- *All* the form data is sent when the visitor clicks the active image. Therefore, it's a good idea to explain how to use the active image and to place the image at the end of the form so that the visitor completes the other form elements before clicking the image and sending the data.

Using an image to submit data

Creating a link to a script

Some simple—but still useful—scripts require no input at all. For example, you might create a CGI script that outputs the exact time (according to the server). In that case, the visitor doesn't have to input any data, they simply have to ask what time it is. Although you could conceivably create a form with a solitary submit button and no fields, an easier way would be to create a *link* that activates the script.

To create a link to a script:

1. In the HTML document, type **<A HREF="script.cgi">**, where *script.cgi* is the name of the script that you want to have activated when the visitor clicks the link.

2. Type the label for the link. This is what the visitor will see (usually underlined) on the Web page.

3. Type **</A>**.

✔ Tip

■ For more information on the gettime.cgi script used in this example, check the Web site *(see page 22).* I didn't show it here because I want you to focus on how to activate a script with a link, not on how the script works.

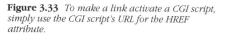

Figure 3.33 *To make a link activate a CGI script, simply use the CGI script's URL for the HREF attribute.*

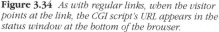

Figure 3.34 *As with regular links, when the visitor points at the link, the CGI script's URL appears in the status window at the bottom of the browser.*

Figure 3.35 *When the visitor clicks the link, the script is activated, and in this case, displays the correct local time. Notice also that the URL of the script appears in the Location bar.*

```
┌─────────── code.html ───────────┐
<HTML><HEAD>
<TITLE>Time Page</TITLE>
</HEAD>
<BODY>

<H1>What time is it?</H1>

<P>In <A HREF="http://www.cookwood.com/
cgi-bin/lcastro/getlocaltime.cgi?zone=EST&
place=Hartford">Hartford, Connecticut</A>?

<P>In <A HREF="http://www.cookwood.com/
cgi-bin/lcastro/getlocaltime.cgi?zone=CT&
place=Dallas">Dallas, Texas</A>?

<P>In <A HREF="http://www.cookwood.com/
cgi-bin/lcastro/getlocaltime.cgi?zone=MT
&place=Denver">Denver, Colorado?</A>

<P>In <A HREF="http://www.cookwood.com/
cgi-bin/lcastro/getlocaltime.cgi?zone=PT
&place=Eureka">Eureka, California?

</BODY></HTML>
```

Figure 3.36 *Each link has two name-value pairs appended to the URL. When the visitor clicks a link, the browser sends the corresponding pair of values to be processed by the script. Note that there are no spaces in any of the URLs.*

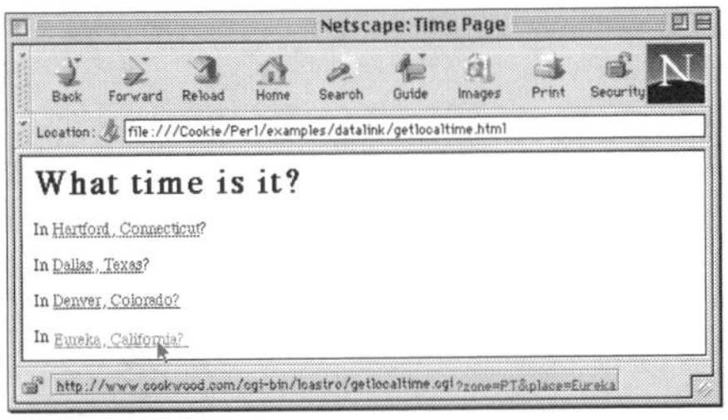

Figure 3.37 *Now when a visitor points at a link, not only does the link's URL show up in the status bar at the bottom of the browser, but the data that will be sent to the script also appears.*

Figure 3.38 *When the visitor clicks the link, the data is sent to the script to be processed and the browser displays the result. Notice also that the input appears at the end of the script's URL in the Location bar.*

Using a link to input data to a script

You can also create links that contain certain pre-input data so that when the visitor clicks the link, that data is sent to the server and processed by the script.

To use a link to input data to a script:

1. Type **<A HREF="script.cgi**, where *script.cgi* is the CGI script that will process the data when the visitor clicks the link.

2. Type **?key=value**, where *key* is the name of the data you're sending and *value* is the actual data itself. There is no space between the script name and the question mark.

3. If desired, type **&key2=value2**, where *key2* is the name of the second piece of data and *value2* is the actual second piece of data. There is no space between the first value (from step 2) and the ampersand (&).

4. Repeat step 3 as desired.

5. Type **">**.

6. Type the label text for the link.

7. Type **</A>**.

✔ Tips

■ If you were sending data from a form, the key would correspond to the contents of the NAME attribute while the value would correspond to the contents of the VALUE attribute.

■ For details on the script used in this example, check the Web site *(see page 22)*. For now, I want you to focus on how to send data to the script, not how the script works.

Adding default data to a form

In the same way you can append data to a URL in a link, you can add that data to the URL in the ACTION attribute of your FORM tag. Each time a visitor clicks the submit button, both the appended information from the URL and the information the visitor has entered in the form will be sent to the server.

To add default data to a form:

1. In your Web page, type **<FORM ACTION="http://script.cgi**, where *script.cgi* is the URL for the script that will process the form and the extra data.

2. Type **?key=value**, where *key* is the name of the data you're sending and *value* is the actual data itself. There is no space between the script name and the question mark.

3. If desired, type **&key2=value2**, where *key2* is the name of the second piece of data and *value2* is the actual second piece of data. There is no space between the first value (from step 2) and the ampersand (&).

4. Repeat step 3 as desired.

5. Type **"**.

6. Type **METHOD=POST**.

7. Type **>** to complete the form tag.

8. Create the form elements as usual. For more details, see pages 47–54.

9. Type **</FORM>** to finish the form.

10. Create additional Web pages that access the same script but with different appended data, as necessary.

```
<FORM ACTION="http://www.cookwood.com/cgi-
bin/lcastro/cityinfo.cgi?city=Eureka"
METHOD=POST>
```

Figure 3.39 *You can add default data to the URL for the ACTION attribute in the FORM tag. This data is sent to the script together with the contents of the fields when the visitor clicks submit.*

Figure 3.40 *When the visitor clicks the submit button on the Eureka page, the city name "Eureka" is input automatically, and the script knows which local time to output.*

```
<FORM ACTION="http://www.cookwood.com/cgi-
bin/lcastro/cityinfo.cgi?city=Hartford"
METHOD=POST>
```

Figure 3.41 *On the Hartford Web page, the only difference in the FORM tag is that Hartford is appended to the script's URL.*

Figure 3.42 *When the visitor clicks the submit button on the Hartford page, the city name "Hartford" is input automatically, and the script again knows which local time to output.*

Environment Variables

One of the keystones of CGI is a collection of data called *environment variables* that are set each time the browser sends information to the server. Perhaps the most important of these variables, from a Perl CGI perspective, describe which method was used to send the data to the server (GET or POST), how much data was sent (for POST), and even what the data was (for GET). Other environment variables show what IP address a visitor has, what browser they're using, and what server you're using, among others.

The available environment variables may change according to what server you have and what information is sent from the browser. If, for example, you set up your form with the GET method, certain environment variables are set. If the form uses the POST method, other variables are set.

The environment variables are stored in the special %ENV hash which is set each time a script is run. Don't worry yet about what a hash is or how to get to the information stored in these variables. The important thing is to simply be aware that this information is available. You'll learn how to process this data on page 68.

Using environment variables to parse forms

Perhaps the most crucial environment variables are those that contain information about the data that is being passed to the server. There are three key environment variables that hold this information.

POST or GET?

What happens to the data when a visitor presses the submit button on a form or clicks a link to a CGI script? The simple answer is that the data goes to the server. However, to get a hold of that data in order to process it with your script, you'll need to know *how* it was sent.

The data from a form can be sent in one of two ways: POST or GET. (I generally recommend using POST *(see page 46)*, since this method allows for unlimited quantities of input data.) Data appended to a link *(see page 57)* is always sent with GET. If you append data to a URL in the FORM tag *(see page 58)*, that data is sent via GET while the rest of the data from the form is sent via POST.

While you can rely on the knowledge you already have about what method is being used—that is, if you created a form that uses the POST method, you know it uses the POST method!—you can also use the REQUEST_METHOD environment variable to determine the method that was used. For example, if you have a general form-parsing subroutine (like the one included in this book—see page 66) that can be used to parse information coming via GET, POST, or both, the contents of the REQUEST_METHOD environment variable can tell you exactly which method was used.

```
1   #!/usr/local/bin/perl
2
3   print "Content-type: text/html\n\n";
4   print "<P>The Request Method was:
        $ENV{'REQUEST_METHOD'}";
5   print "<P>The data from GET was:
        $ENV{'QUERY_STRING'}";
6   print "<P>The data from POST had
        $ENV{'CONTENT_LENGTH'}bytes. You can
        find it in standard input.";
```

3: The all important MIME content line.
4: To access the value in the %ENV hash that corresponds to the REQUEST_METHOD key, you use $ENV{'REQUEST_METHOD'}.
5: This line prints out the value that corresponds to the QUERY_STRING key, if any, in the %ENV hash.
6: This lines prints the length of the posted data, if any, in bytes, which is stored in the %ENV hash with the CONTENT_LENGTH key.

Figure 4.1 *For more information on accessing individual values in a hash, see Chapter 10, Working with Hashes. This script is used for each of the three examples on these two facing pages.*

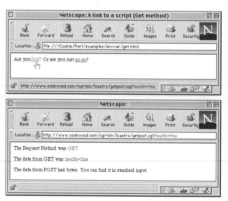

Figure 4.2 *When a visitor clicks a link, the data is sent to the server with the GET method. Therefore, the REQUEST_METHOD is set to GET, the QUERY_STRING contains the sent data, and the CONTENT_LENGTH is undefined (notice that it is completely absent from the third line in the bottom illustration).*

```
<FORM ACTION="http://www.cookwood.com/cgi-bin/lcastro/getpost.cgi" METHOD=POST>

How are you? <INPUT TYPE=text NAME=health>
<INPUT TYPE=submit VALUE="Send data">
</FORM>
```

Figure 4.3 *I recommend that you always use the POST method for forms.*

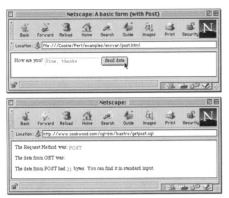

Figure 4.4 *When a visitor submits the data from a form that uses post (see Figure 4.3 on page 60), the REQUEST_METHOD is set to POST and the CONTENT_LENGTH is set to the number of bytes in the incoming data (21). The data itself is stored in the server's standard input area. Notice that the QUERY_DATA variable is empty.*

```
                    code.html
<FORM ACTION="http://www.cookwood.com/cgi-
bin/lcastro/getpost.cgi?form=health"
METHOD=POST>
How are you? <INPUT TYPE=text NAME=health>
<INPUT TYPE=submit VALUE="Send data">
</FORM>
```

Figure 4.5 *You can append default data to the ACTION attribute's URL in the FORM tag. The method for the data from the form is still POST.*

Figure 4.6 *The visitor can't see the appended data (top). However, all three environmental variables are now set: the method is still POST, and the CONTENT_LENGTH contains the number of bytes in the posted data. Meanwhile, the QUERY_STRING variable contains the appended data.*

Information sent via the GET method is stored in the QUERY_STRING variable **(Figure 4.2)**. So, once you know the GET method was used, you can access the QUERY_STRING variable to see (and process) the input data.

Information sent via POST **(Figure 4.3)** is not saved in an environment variable—and is therefore not restricted as far as length goes. Instead, it is sent to a place called *Standard Input*, which is a sort of holding area on the server for incoming data. So, once you know that POST has been used, you then know where to find the posted data. To access data in the standard input area, you'll need to know how much data you're looking for. The exact length of posted data, in bytes, is stored in the third essential form-parsing variable, called CONTENT_LENGTH **(Figure 4.4)**.

Finally, appended data to the form's ACTION URL is sent via GET while the data from the form elements themselves are sent as usual by POST **(Figures 4.5 and 4.6)**.

Note: Since QUERY_STRING is only used with the GET method, it will be empty or undefined when you use the POST method. Likewise, the CONTENT_LENGTH variable (and indeed standard input) is empty when you use the GET method. If you use POST and GET at the same time *(see page 58)*, the REQUEST_METHOD will be set to POST (assuming that's the method you set in the FORM tag), the CONTENT_LENGTH variable will contain the length of the (posted) data coming from the form, and the QUERY_STRING will contain the data appended to the URL in the ACTION attribute in the FORM tag.

Using environment variables to parse forms

Your visitor's browser and platform

There are also environment variables that you can use to "spy" on your visitors. For example, it's relatively easy to find out which browser and platform your visitor is using.

The HTTP_USER_AGENT environment variable contains the name and version of the visitor's browser. Notice that both Netscape and Internet Explorer identify themselves as "Mozilla", which is actually a code name for Netscape. Explorer then continues on to inform you that it is "compatible", presumably with Mozilla, and that it is really MSIE, which one can assume stands for *Microsoft Internet Explorer*.

The value of HTTP_USER_AGENT also reveals the visitor's computer platform, although each browser uses a different syntax to convey this information. Still, you should be able to match either Win or 95, or Mac, to determine your visitor's platform. You could conceivably tailor your output for each browser, ensuring that HTML tags or JavaScript compatible with one browser are not used by the other.

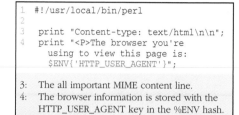

```
1   #!/usr/local/bin/perl
2
3   print "Content-type: text/html\n\n";
4   print "<P>The browser you're
    using to view this page is:
    $ENV{'HTTP_USER_AGENT'}";
```

3: The all important MIME content line.
4: The browser information is stored with the HTTP_USER_AGENT key in the %ENV hash.

Figure 4.7 *For more information on accessing individual values in a hash, see Chapter 10, Working with Hashes.*

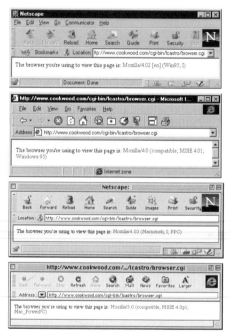

Figure 4.8 *From top to bottom, I've accessed the script shown in Figure 4.7 with Netscape Communicator for Windows, Internet Explorer 4 for Windows, Netscape Communicator 4 for Macintosh, and Internet Explorer 4 for Macintosh.*

```
1    #!/usr/local/bin/perl
2
3    print "Content-type: text/html\n\n";
4    print "<P>Before coming to this
         page, you were looking at
         $ENV{'HTTP_REFERER'}";
```

3: The all important MIME content line.
4: The URL of the page that your visitor was looking at before they jumped to the page that accesses this CGI script is stored with the HTTP_REFERER key in the %ENV hash.

Figure 4.9 *For more information on accessing individual values in a hash, see Chapter 10, Working with Hashes.*

Figure 4.10 *Imagine that a visitor is checking out Yahoo's home page.*

Figure 4.11 *Then they type in the name of a script, or of a page that contains a form or a link to a script.*

Figure 4.12 *The URL stored in the HTTP_REFERER variable will reveal the visitor's earlier trip to Yahoo.*

How did your visitor get to your page?

One of the most intriguing bits of data stored in the environment variables is the URL of the page your visitor was looking at before they ran your CGI script. In many cases, this URL corresponds to a page that has a link to your page. By keeping track of these URLs, you can see where your traffic is coming from. It can be an extremely valuable marketing tool.

The URL of the page the visitor was visiting before running your script is stored in the HTTP_REFERER environment variable. However, *referer* is a bit of a misnomer. Imagine what happens if your visitor was visiting, say, the Artichoke Home Page and then finds your URL in a magazine and types it in the Location bar? You may think that the Artichoke Home Page contains a link—or any kind of relationship—to your page, when in fact, it simply was the page that the visitor happened to be looking at before typing in your URL.

You should also keep in mind that if the visitor executes your script by pressing a link or a submit button on one of your pages, the HTTP_REFERER variable will contain the URL of that particular page. You can use this as a security precaution to make sure that the script is always run from one of your pages *(see page 236)*.

So, while the HTTP_REFERER environment variable can be interesting, it's not always pertinent. Keep that in mind as you analyze your data.

Viewing all the environment variables

If you would like to see all the environment variables available to you, you can create a little script to do just that. Remember, however, that the results depend on how the script is called (with POST or GET), and on what server you use.

To view the environment variables:

1. Create, upload and change the permissions of the script shown in Figure 4.13. For more details, consult Chapter 2, *Creating Perl CGI Scripts* and Chapter 16, *Using Other Folks' Scripts*.

2. Open your browser.

3. Type the URL of the script you created in step 1. The environment variables available on your server will appear.

✔ Tip

■ You can also create a simple form that calls the script (by using the script's URL in the ACTION attribute—see page 46) in order to see the environment variables that are set if you use the POST method.

```
1   #!/usr/local/bin/perl
2
3
4   print "Content-type: text/html\n\n";
5   print "<HTML><HEAD><TITLE>Environment
      Variables</TITLE></HEAD><BODY>";
6
7   foreach $env_var (keys %ENV) {
8       print "<BR><FONT COLOR=red>
        $env_var</FONT> is set to <FONT
        COLOR=blue>$ENV{$env_var}</FONT>";
9   }
10
11  print "</BODY></HTML>";
```

7: This foreach loop goes through each of the elements in the special ENV hash, where the environment variables are stored, and prints each one's name (in red) and value (in blue).

Figure 4.13 *This simple script prints out all of the available environment variables to your browser.*

Figure 4.14 *The environment variables that are currently set will be displayed in the browser.*

Getting Data into the Script

In Chapter 3, *Getting Data from Visitors*, and Chapter 4, *Environment Variables*, I talked about how to get data from your visitor to the server. In this chapter, you'll learn how to pass that data from the server to your Perl script. Once you've entered the data into the Perl script, you can start to process the data and generate the desired output.

Inputting data from a form or a link

When a visitor to your Web site clicks on a link to a CGI script or presses the submit button on a form, the name-value pairs *(see page 44)* from the link or the form are sent to the server in one big, long stream. For that data to be at all useful, you have to separate, or parse, the stream into intelligible chunks. CGI scripts for parsing forms are probably the most commonly used scripts on the Web, and while one can be used alone, a parsing script most often serves as the backbone of another script that processes those individual chunks of data. Because they are so essential to working with Web data, I'll introduce you to one version of the form-parsing script here. However, I won't explain it in detail until Appendix A, *Parsing Form Input.*

To input data from a form or a link:

1. Download the script shown in Figure 5.1 from the Web site *(see page 22)*. You can type it in from scratch as long as you type it exactly as it appears here.

2. Create a form *(see page 43)*, using the URL of the script in step 1 for the ACTION attribute in your FORM tag.

   Or create a link to the CGI script with the necessary data appended to the end *(see page 57)*.

3. Wait for a visitor to click a link to a CGI script or press the submit button in a form (or test it yourself). At that point, the data is sent to the server and the script parses the incoming information—and in this example, also prints it out for your review.

```
1   #!/usr/local/bin/perl
2
3   if ($ENV{'REQUEST_METHOD'} eq 'GET')
    {
4     @pairs = split(/&/,
      $ENV{'QUERY_STRING'});
5   } elsif ($ENV{'REQUEST_METHOD'} eq
    'POST') {
6     read (STDIN, $buffer,
      $ENV{'CONTENT_LENGTH'});
7     @pairs = split(/&/, $buffer);
8   } else {
9     print "Content-type: text/
      html\n\n";
10    print "<P>Use Post or Get";
11  }
12
13  foreach $pair (@pairs) {
14    ($key, $value) = split (/=/, $pair);
15    $key =~ tr/+/ /;
16    $key =~ s/%([a-fA-F0-9][a-fA-F0-9])/
      pack("C", hex($1))/eg;
17    $value =~ tr/+/ /;
18    $value =~ s/%([a-fA-F0-9][a-fA-F
      0-9])/pack("C", hex($1))/eg;
19
20    $value =~s/<!--(.|\n)*-->//g;
21
22    if ($formdata{$key}) {
23      $formdata{$key} .= ", $value";
24    } else {
25      $formdata{$key} = $value;
26    }
27  }
28
29  print "Content-type: text/html\n\n";
30  foreach $key (sort keys(%formdata)) {
31    print "<P>The field named <B>$key</B>
      contained <B>$formdata{$key}</B>";
32  }
```

3: Lines 3–27 actually parse the form data and make it ready for processing. For complete details, see Appendix A, *Parsing Form Input.*

29: Lines 29–32 are not part of the form-parsing sequence. These lines simply print out each piece of data garnered from the form or link, together with its name. You'll most likely want to use more complicated processing, but this at least shows you what the form-parsing sequence has produced.

Figure 5.1 *Here is one rendition of the all-important script that parses form data. The highlighted portion is the essential part. The rest of it is for displaying the results in a simple way.*

Figure 5.2 *Create a form (or a link to a CGI script). The form can have any number of fields in it. Then wait for a visitor to view the form, enter the information, and press Submit (or test it yourself).*

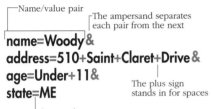

Figure 5.3 *When the data gets to the server, it looks like this—one long stream of names and values separated with equals signs, and an ampersand delimiting each pair. Spaces are substituted with plus signs. Note that I've added line returns here so that you can see where one pair starts and the next ends. There are no returns or newlines in the actual data stream.*

Figure 5.4 *In this example, our script parses the data and then prints it out in a meaningful way. Often you'll want to do a lot more with the data than just print it out. (That's what the rest of the book is for!)*

✔ Tips

■ This script works equally well with posted data as it does with "gotten" data. In other words, you can use it to parse data from a link, and from a form that uses the GET method, as well as with forms that use the POST method.

■ This form-parsing script places the name-value pairs gathered from the HTML form or link in a hash called *%formdata*. Each NAME attribute from the HTML form corresponds to a *key* in the %formdata hash. Each VALUE attribute (or the data typed manually by the visitor in text boxes, password boxes, or larger text areas) corresponds to a *value* in the %formdata hash. For more information on name-value pairs in the HTML code, consult *Labeling incoming data* on page 44. For more information on working with hashes, see Chapter 10, *Working with Hashes*.

■ Don't worry too much yet about how the form-parsing script works. Right now, it's more important to be able to use it. I'll explain the script in full detail in Appendix A, *Parsing Form Input*.

■ In most of the examples in the rest of this book, I call the form-parsing script from a subroutine—which is just an easy way to access one frequently used script from another. Hopefully, this will help keep the examples clean so that you can concentrate on the particular Perl function that's being discussed. Nevertheless, the form-parsing sequence will always work just as it's described here. For more details on subroutines, consult Chapter 9, *Subroutines*.

Inputting data from a form or a link

Inputting data from environment variables

As I discussed in Chapter 4, *Environment Variables*, each time a visitor clicks a link to a CGI script or presses the submit button on a form, Perl stores a wealth of information in a collection of variables called *environment variables*. Armed with the data that the environment variables contain, you'll be able to tell what page the visitor was looking at before they came to your page, what browser they're using, and much more. You can assign the value of an environment variable to one of your own variables for later processing.

To input data from environment variables:

1. Type **$scalar**, where *scalar* is the name of your variable that will hold the information from the environment variable.

2. Type **=** (the equals sign).

3. Type **$ENV{'env_var'}**, where *env_var* is the name (or key) of the desired environment variable.

4. Type **;** to end the line.

✔ Tips

■ The particular environment variables available to you depend on the server you use. You can see a list of typical environment variables on page 59.

■ The %ENV hash functions like any other hash. For more information on working with hashes, see Chapter 10, *Working with Hashes*.

■ You can get more than one value at a time from the %ENV hash. For more details, see page 129.

```
1   #!/usr/local/bin/perl
2
3   $browser = $ENV{'HTTP_USER_AGENT'};
4   $from = $ENV{'HTTP_REFERER'};
5
6   print "Content-type: text/html\n\n";
7   print "<P>You're browsing this page with
        $browser";
8   print "<P>And before this page, you were
        looking at $from";
```

3: This line stores the value related to the HTTP_USER_AGENT key (which tells what browser the visitor is using) in the $browser variable.

4: This line stores the value related to the HTTP_REFERER key (which tells what page the visitor is coming from) in the $from variable.

6: The all important MIME content line.

7: We'll print a simple statement with the contents of the $browser variable.

8: And another simple print statement with the $from variable.

Figure 5.5 *You can use environment variables for simple operations like telling your visitors what you know about them, or you can create more complicated scripts that, for example, count the number of times your site has been visited, from where, and from which browser.*

Figure 5.6 *While printing this information may wow your visitors, keeping track of it may serve to be a valuable marketing tool. Knowing where your visitors are coming from can help you generate even more traffic; knowing what browsers your visitors use can help you tailor output to their needs.*

```
1   #!/usr/local/bin/perl
2
3   $rate = 55;
4   $distance = 400;
5   $driver = "Marion";
6   $destination = "42 Indy Place";
7
8   $name = $driver;
9
10  print "Content-type: text/html\n\n";
11  print "The rate is $rate, the distance
        is $distance, the driver is $driver,
        the destination is $destination.
        And the driver's name really is
        $name";
```

3:   The scalar variable $rate is set to the number 55.

4:   The scalar variable $distance is set to 400.

5:   The scalar variable $driver is set to the string "Marion".

6:   The scalar variable $destination is set to the string "42 Indy Place".

8:   The scalar variable $name is set to the current value of $driver, which is "Marion" (line 5).

Figure 5.7 *Notice that you set scalar variables to individual pieces of data. A "piece of data" can be a number (as for $rate and $distance), a string (as for $driver and $destination), or another scalar variable (as with $name). Strings can contain any number of letters, digits, symbols, or a combination of both.*

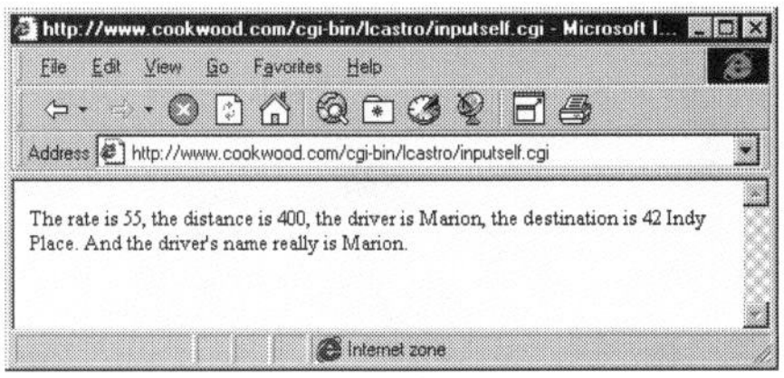

Figure 5.8 *The value of each variable is printed. Once you know a little more Perl, you'll be able to combine this static data with incoming information from your visitors.*

Inputting scalar data yourself

Some data is the same all the time—you'll want to add this kind of data to the script manually. You store individual pieces of data in a scalar variable *(see page 25)*. Later you can refer to the variable by name to perform calculations on the data it contains.

To input scalar data yourself:

1. At the beginning of the line, type **$name**, where *name* is the label of the scalar variable.

2. Type **=** (the equals sign).

3. Type **value**, where *value* is the number or string that you want to store. If the value is a string, you'll have to enclose it in single or double quotes.

4. Type **;** to complete the line.

✔ Tips

■ Storing data in a variable is also called *assigning a value to* the variable.

■ You're probably more used to seeing the equals sign in a non-active sort of way, as in *5 = 2 + 3*. In Perl, think of the equals sign as something more like *gets* or *is assigned the value of.*

■ Strings (but not numbers) should be enclosed in quotation marks. For more details, consult *Quotation marks* on page 28.

■ Make sure you use just one equals sign. There are ways to combine the equals sign with other symbols for different effects *(see pages 82 and 102).*

Inputting arrays yourself

You can also manually input lists of constant data—like the names of the days of the week—when necessary.

To input items in an array:

1. At the beginning of the line, type **@name**, where *@name* is the label for the array.

2. Type **=** (the equals sign).

3. Type **(element1,** where *element1* is the first item in the array.

4. If desired, type **nextelement,** where *nextelement* is the next item in the array.

5. Repeat step 4 as desired, remembering to separate each element with a comma.

6. Type **)** to complete the listing.

7. Type **;** to finish the line.

✔ Tips

■ You should enclose string elements in quotation marks *(see page 28)*. Make sure you put the separating commas *outside* the quotes! An equivalent but faster technique is to precede the parentheses with **qw**. Then you don't need to use quotation marks (or commas) at all. For example, **("one", "two")** is the same as **qw(one two)**.

■ You can use numbers, strings, scalar variables, or even arrays as elements to be assigned to the new array. And you may use a combination of each.

■ You can replace some or all of the existing values or add additional values to an array. For more details, see Chapter 7, *Working with Arrays*.

```
1  #!/usr/local/bin/perl
2
3  @days = ("Monday", "Tuesday",
     "Wednesday", "Thursday", "Friday",
     "Saturday", "Sunday");
4
5  print "Content-type: text/html\n\n";
6  print "These are the days of the
     week:";
7  print "<P>";
8  print "@days";
```

3: The array @days now contains the names of each of the days of the week.
5: The all important MIME content line.
6: This simple print statement creates a label for the rest of our output.
7: The <P> is the HTML tag that creates a new paragraph. A simple newline (\n) would be ignored by the browser.
8: By enclosing the array in double quotes, its elements are printed one after the other with a space in between.

Figure 5.9 *Once you've input an array (line 3), you can manipulate it or combine it with visitor input. Here we stick to just printing it out.*

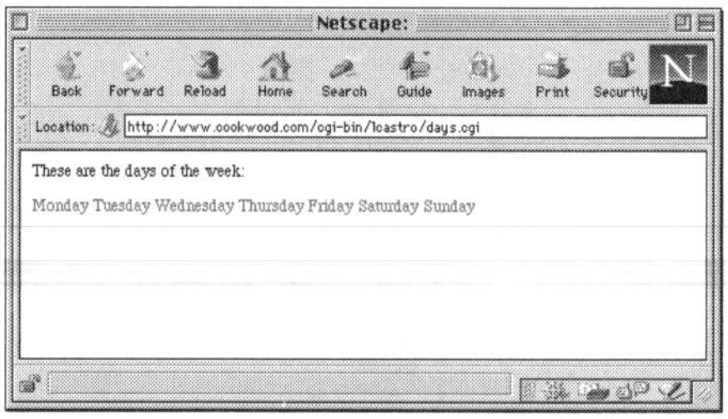

Figure 5.10 *Notice that the members of the array are printed in precisely the same order as they were input.*

Inputting arrays yourself

```
1  #!/usr/local/bin/perl
2
3  %chores = ("Monday", "vacuum",
     "Wednesday", "mop", "Friday", "wash
     windows");
4
5  print "Content-type: text/html\n\n";
6  foreach $day (keys (%chores)) {
7    print "<P>On $day, we have to
       $chores{$day}\n";
8  }
```

3: The %chores hash now contains three pairs of linked values, "Monday" and "vacuum", "Wednesday" and "mop", and "Friday" and "wash windows".

5: The all important MIME content line.

6: There is no simple way to print all the members of a hash, so to show you how we've input the values, I'll give you a sneak preview of the *foreach* block which does just that *(see page 114)*.

7: The print statement prints an HTML paragraph tag followed by a key in the hash and its corresponding data.

8: The foreach block ends with a curly bracket.

Figure 5.11 *It doesn't matter what order you enter the paired data in since you normally reference one half of the pair with the other half.*

Figure 5.12 *Each pair in the hash has a key (in this example, the days) and a value (in this case, the chores).*

Inputting hashes yourself

The only difference between inputting the values to an array and inputting values to a hash is that with a hash, you have to be careful about the order of the elements: elements must be assigned in pairs with the first element in the pair being the *key*, or identifier, and the second element being the *value*, or actual data.

To assign values to a hash:

1. At the beginning of the line, type **%hash**, where *hash* is the name of the hash.

2. Type **=** (the equals sign).

3. Type **(** to begin the hash.

4. Type **key, value** where *key* is the label for the first element and *value* is the corresponding data.

5. For each set of values, type a comma and then repeat step 4.

6. Type **)** to complete the hash.

7. Type **;** to complete the line.

✔ Tips

■ You can use **qw** with hashes as well *(see page 70)*.

■ Although you may add the pairs of keys and values in a particular order, Perl does not maintain the pairs in order. You should access the values in a hash using the keys *(see page 128)* and not rely on the order you used to define the hash.

■ If you have an array that is in the format: (key, value, key, value,...), you can convert it into a hash by using **%hash = @array**.

■ For more details on adding, modifying, or eliminating pairs from a hash, see Chapter 10, *Working with Hashes*.

Inputting hashes yourself

Working with Scalars

As I discussed in Chapter 1, *Perl Building Blocks (see page 25)*, a scalar is any *individual piece of data*, whether it be a number or a string, a constant or a variable. Scalar variables always start with a dollar sign ($)—the *s* shape is supposed to remind you of the word *scalar*.

Note: Each of the example scripts on the pages that follow works in tandem with a form, created with HTML. Unfortunately, there just isn't always enough room to show you the scripts, the HTML code for the form (which reveals the names of the fields), the input that our example visitor types into the fields on the form, *and* the result of the script, given that input. Since the aim of this book is to teach you Perl and CGI, I'll focus on the script code and the result of the script. Where there's room, I'll show you the form and the input and the HTML code behind it. If you're interested, you can find all the forms and Perl scripts online *(see page 22)*.

Storing the result of an operation

In Chapter 5, *Getting Data into the Script*, you learned how to input a simple initial value to a scalar variable *(see page 69)*. You can also assign the result of an *expression* to a scalar variable—which lets you store the outcome of the operation for future use.

To store the result of an operation:

1. Type **$scalar**, where *scalar* is the name of the variable that will contain the result of the expression.

2. Type = (the equals sign).

3. Type the expression. See pages 75–82 for more information on common number and string operators.

✔ Tips

■ You can update the value of a variable by using it on both sides of the assignment. For example, **$age = $age + 1** adds 1 to the $age variable and then saves the result back in the $age variable itself. This is where it's very important to remember that the equals sign doesn't exactly mean *equals*, it means *gets* or *is assigned the value of* (**Figure 6.2**).

■ The most common mathematical and string operators are discussed on pages 75–82.

```
1   #!/usr/bin/perl
2
3   $sales_Jan = 5467;
4   $sales_Feb = 234;
5   $sales_Mar = 8875;
6   $sum_1Q = $sales_Jan + $sales_Feb +
       $sales_Mar;
7   $avg_1Q = $sum_1Q / 3;
```

3: The variable $sales_Jan is assigned an initial value of 5467.
4: The variable $sales_Feb is assigned an initial value of 234.
5: The variable $sales_Mar is assigned an initial value of 8875.
6: The right-hand expression evaluates the sum of the three variables, which have values of 5467, 234, and 8875. The result (14576) is assigned to the variable $sum_1Q.
7: First $sum_IQ, which has a value of 14576 (line 10), is divided by 3, with a result of approximately 4858.67. Then the result is assigned to the variable $avg_1Q.

Figure 6.1 *You can assign the result of a complicated (or simple) expression to a variable and then use that variable (with its new value) in a later operation.*

```
1   #!/usr/bin/perl
2
3   $counter = 1;
4   $counter = $counter + 1;
5   $counter = $counter + 5;
```

3: We assign the numeric constant 1 to the variable $counter. Giving a variable an initial value is called *initializing* the variable.
4: The right-hand expression adds 1 to the value of the variable $counter, which we know is 1 (line 3) giving a result of 2. This new value is then assigned to $counter.
5: The right hand expression adds 5 to the value of the variable $counter, which this time is 2 (line 4), giving a result of 7. Again, the result is assigned to $counter for future operations.

Figure 6.2 *If you assign the result back to the same variable as in this example, the variable will then contain the new value.*

```
1   #!/usr/local/bin/perl
2
3   require "subparseform.lib";
4   &Parse_Form;
5
6   $total = $formdata{'donation'};
7   $times = $formdata{'times'};
8   $premium = $formdata{'premium'};
9
10  $average = $total/$times;
11  $tax_deduction = $total - $premium;
12
13  print "Content-type: text/html\n\n";
14  print "<P>You donated $total dollars last
    year. Thank you.";
15  print "<P>Since you donated $times times,
    that works out to an average of
    $average dollars per donation.";
16  print "<P>Since your premium was worth
    $premium dollars, you can only take a
    tax deduction of $tax_deduction
    dollars.";
```

10: To get the average donation, we divide the total yearly deductions ($total) by the number of contributions ($times). The result is saved in $average.

11: Next, we subtract the premium value ($premium) from the total donations ($total) and store the result in $tax_deduction.

15: This lines prints the result of the division.

16: The result of the subtraction is printed here.

Figure 6.3 *Arithmetic operations are particularly useful for Web stores or other sites where you have to calculate numeric data.*

Figure 6.4 *The visitor enters the necessary data and submits the form.*

Figure 6.5 *Saving the results of the mathematical operations in another variable makes it easy to incorporate them into print statements (or other operations) later.*

Multiplying, dividing, adding, subtracting

Perl lets you perform basic mathematical operations on scalars with the same symbols you've been using since second grade: + for addition, - for subtraction, * for multiplication and / for division. These symbols are called *mathematical operators*. The scalars that you operate on are called *operands*.

To multiply, divide, add, or subtract:

1. Type the first operand. It can be a numerical constant like **12**, a scalar variable like **$distance**, or an entire expression in itself, like **$age + 1**.

2. Type the mathematical operator: *****, **/**, **+**, or **-**.

3. Type the second operand.

✔ Tips

■ You can store the result of a mathematical operation in a variable. For example, in **$result = $first * $second**, the product of the values of $first and $second is stored in $result.

■ If you use more than one mathematical operator in a given expression, you may need to use parentheses to control the order in which operations are carried out *(see page 76)*.

■ If you use a mathematical operator on a string, Perl converts the string to a number (stripping it of any non-numeric symbols, or changing it to zero if there are no numbers at all) and then uses the result in the calculation. The results are probably not what you might expect.

Chapter 6

Using more than one operator at a time

What happens if you use more than one operator in a single expression? Imagine, for example, the expression 2 * 3 + 5. Is the result 11 or 16? For Perl, and indeed most mathematicians, the answer is 11 because the multiplication operator takes *precedence* over the addition operator. Multiplication's precedence over addition means you multiply 2 * 3 and *then* add 5.

You can override precedence rules by using parentheses. The expression inside the parentheses is always evaluated before the expressions and operators outside the parentheses. For example, the result of 2 * (3 + 5) is 16 because the parentheses have precedence over multiplication, and thus the numbers within the parentheses are added before the sum is multiplied by 2.

When two operators have equal precedence, Perl then looks at the *associativity* of the operators. Left associativity means the two operands to the left are executed first. Right associativity means the two right operands are executed first. If you check the precedence table on the Web site *(see page 22)*, you'll see that multiplication and division have equal precedence and left associativity. Since left associativity means that with operators of equal precedence the left two operands are executed first, an expression like 12 / 2 * 3 is equivalent, but perhaps more clearly represented by, (12 / 2) * 3, with a result of 18 (and not a result of 2, which is 12 divided by the product of 2 and 3).

What are the basic precedence rules? Exponentiation takes precedence over division, multiplication, taking the remainder of division, and repeating (all of which have equal precedence), which in turn take precedence over addition, subtraction, and concatenation (which have equal precedence).

```perl
1   #!/usr/bin/perl
2
3   $div = 40 / 5 + 3;
4   $parens = 40 / (5 + 3);
5   $subadd = 9 - 3 + 5;
6   $parens_subadd = 9 - (3 + 5);
7
8   print "Content-type: text/html\n\n";
9   print "div is $div, parens is $parens,
    subadd is $subadd and parens_subadd is
    $parens_subadd";
```

3: In the right-hand expression, there are two operations, division and addition. Division has precedence, and so we first divide 40 by 5 (getting 8) and then add 3, with a final result of 11, saved in the $div variable.

4: The operators and numbers are the same as in line 3, but here we've added parentheses so that the addition is carried out first. Thus, we first add 5 and 3 and then divide 40 by the result (8), with a final result of 5.

5: In this expression there are two operators of equal precedence. Since they have left associativity, we operate on the two left operands (9 and 3) first. Thus, we subtract 3 from 9, getting 6 and then add 5 for a final result of 11.

6: Again, the numbers and operators are the same as in line 5, with parentheses added to give precedence to the second half of the expression. Thus, we add 3 and 5 and subtract the result (8) from 9, with a final result of 1.

Figure 6.6 *The rules of precedence determine which operations are carried out first in expressions with multiple operators.*

Figure 6.7 *The expected results.*

```
 1   #!/usr/local/bin/perl
 2
 3   require "subparseform.lib";
 4   &Parse_Form;
 5
 6   $number = $formdata{'number'};
 7   $power = $formdata{'power'};
 8
 9   $result = $number ** $power;
10
11   print "Content-type: text/html\n\n";
12   print "<P>You entered $number with an
        exponent of $power";
13   print "<P>$number raised to the $power
        power is $result.";
```

9: In the right-hand expression, we raise the value of $number to the value of $power. The result is stored in $result.

13: This simple print statement reminds the visitor what they typed in and prints out the result of raising their number to the desired power.

Figure 6.8 *This script spends a bit of time getting the values from the visitor, a millisecond raising the number to a power, and then a bunch more time outputting the data. It's not atypical.*

Figure 6.9 *The visitor can enter any number they wish in the form boxes. When they click the Do it (submit) button, the numbers are sent to the server and the script is processed.*

Figure 6.10 *It's a good idea to remind your visitor what information they requested.*

Raising a number to an exponential power

Multiplying a number by itself a given number of times is known as raising the number to an exponential power. For example, 3 raised to the fourth power (3^4) is equivalent to 3 * 3 * 3 * 3, or 81. Perl uses two asterisks ** as the operator for exponential power.

To raise a number to an exponential power:

1. Type the scalar that you want to raise to an exponential power. You can use a scalar constant, a scalar variable, or even an expression.

2. Type ** (two asterisks).

3. Type the power to which you wish to raise the scalar or expression in step 1.

✔ Tips

■ Don't put a space between the two asterisks.

■ You can assign the result to a scalar variable. For example, if you use **$result = $number ** 5**, with $number equal to 3, $result will be set to 243 (that is, 3^5).

■ The exponential power operator takes precedence over the simple mathematical operators discussed on page 75. That means that if you use an expression like 2 ** 7 + 1, the answer is 129 (1 added to 2^7) and not 256 (2 to the sum of 7+1). You can override precedence with parentheses. For more details on precedence, consult *Using more than one operator at a time* on page 76.

Getting the remainder of a division

When you divide 13 by 3, the answer is 4 with a *remainder* of 1. Perl has a built-in function to give you the remainder of a division operation. The operator is called *modulus*.

To get the remainder of a division:

1. Type the first number or scalar variable (the dividend).

2. Type % (the percent sign).

3. Type the number (or scalar variable) that you wish to divide into the number in step 1.

✔ Tips

■ You can assign the result (that is, the remainder itself) to a scalar variable. For example, if you use **$result = $number % 5**, with $number equal to 14, $result will be set to 4.

■ Perl eliminates the decimal part of a number before taking the modulus. Thus, 34.7 % 5 is calculated as 34 % 5 and results in a remainder, or modulus, of 4.

```
1   #!/usr/local/bin/perl
2
3   require "subparseform.lib";
4   &Parse_Form;
5
6   $dividend = $formdata{'dividend'};
7   $divisor = $formdata{'divisor'};
8
9   $result = $dividend % $divisor;
10
11  print "Content-type: text/html\n\n";
12  print "<P>You entered $dividend for
        the dividend and $divisor for the
        divisor";
13  print "<P>The remainder of $dividend
        divided by $divisor is $result";
```

9:   In the right-hand expression, we want the remainder of $dividend when divided by $divisor. The remainder is stored in $result.

12: This simple print statement reminds the visitor what they typed and gives the remainder of the division.

Figure 6.11 *The* dividend *is the number that you divide the* divisor *into.*

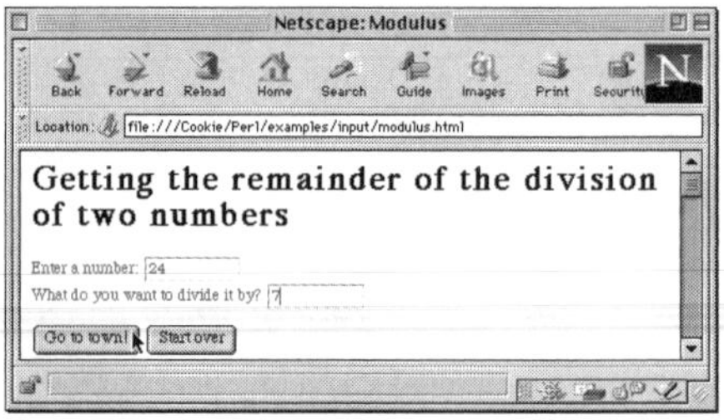

Figure 6.12 *The visitor can enter any numbers they wish in the form boxes. When they click the Go to town! (submit) button, the numbers are sent to the server and the script is processed.*

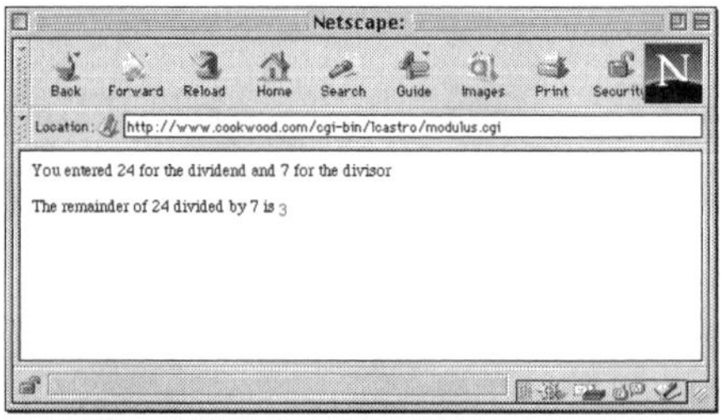

Figure 6.13 *The script processes the incoming information and then outputs the results.*

Getting the remainder of a division

```
1   #!/usr/local/bin/perl
2
3   require "subparseform.lib";
4   &Parse_Form;
5
6   $first = $formdata{'first_name'};
7   $married = $formdata{'fiance_last'};
8
9   $fullname = $first . " " . $married;
10
11  print "Content-type: text/html\n\n";
12  print "Congratulations! Your married
       name would be $fullname.";
```

9:   This lines joins the woman's first name
     ($first) with a space (" "), and then with her
     fiancé's last name ($married).

Figure 6.14 *The period, or concatenation operator,
is for connecting strings together.*

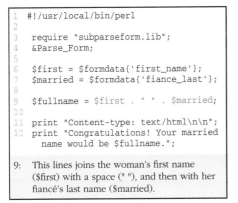

Figure 6.15 *The visitor enters both her and her
fiance's names in the appropriate fields. When she
clicks Marry Me (the submit button), the information
is sent to the server and the script.*

Figure 6.16 *The script takes the woman's first name
and concatenates it with a space and the fiancé's
last name and then prints out the result. Just one
more reason to keep one's own name...*

Connecting strings together

Although it might seem logical to use the
addition symbol (+) to connect strings
together, Perl has a separate operator for connecting or *concatenating* strings: the period.

To connect strings together:

1. Type the first string, in single or double
   quotation marks *(see page 28)*.

2. Type **.** (a period).

3. Type the string that you wish to connect
   to the end of the first string.

4. Repeat steps 2 and 3 as desired.

✔ Tips

■ You can use variables and expressions in
  both steps 1 and 3, as needed.

■ You can also assign the result to a variable. For example, **$string = "Barry
  Gold" . "water"** would result in $string
  containing the value "Barry Goldwater".
  Notice that the concatenation operator
  connects the two strings without adding
  extra spaces.

■ Make sure you use the period (.) for adding strings and the plus sign (+) for
  adding numbers. For example, **2 + 3**
  would result in *5*, but **2 . 3** results in *23*.
  In a similar way, **"water" + "melon"**
  results in *0*, while **"water" . "melon"**
  results in *"watermelon"*. Finally, an
  expression like **"3x" + "4y"** results in *7*
  but **"3x" . "4y"** results in *"3x4y"*. For
  more information on getting the sum of
  two numbers, see page 75. For more
  details on strings versus numbers, consult
  page 23.

■ Double quotation marks are an easy way
  to concatenate strings *(see page 28)*.

Repeating a string

Perl has an operator for repeating a string a given number of times. It's not a particularly common function in CGI scripts, but maybe you'll find a use for it.

To repeat a string:

1. Type the string (in the form of a constant or variable) that you want to repeat.

2. Type **x** (a lower case letter x).

3. Type **n** where *n* is the number of times you want the string to be repeated.

✔ Tips

■ You can use a mathematical expression for step 3. Something like **$repeats * 4** is perfectly legal.

■ You can assign the resulting value (the repeated string) to a variable in order to save it for a later calculation.

■ Don't confuse the repeat operator (x) with the multiplication operator (*) for numbers. For example, because Perl expects the operands next to the repeat operator (x) to be strings, 2 x 3 results in 222 while 2 * 3 (where Perl expects the operands to be numbers) results in the perhaps more expected 6. For more information on numbers and strings, consult *Numbers and strings* on page 23. For more information on multiplying numbers, consult *Multiplying, dividing, adding, subtracting* on page 75.

```
1   #!/usr/local/bin/perl
2
3   require "subparseform.lib";
4   &Parse_Form;
5
6   $base = $formdata{'base'};
7   $school = $formdata{'school'};
8   $cheer = $base x 2 . $school;
9
10  $number = $formdata{'number'};
11  $repeat = $formdata{'repeat'};
12  $repeat_number = 3 x 5;
13
14  print "Content-type: text/html\n\n";
15  print "<FONT SIZE=+2>The cheer is
        <B>$cheer</B>.";
16  print "<P>And the number, $number,
        repeated $repeat times is
        <B>$repeat_number<B></FONT>";;
```

8: The right-hand expression repeats the value of the $base variable twice, concatenates that with $school and stores the result in $cheer. Notice that the repeat operator has precedence over the concatenate operator.

12: If you use the repeat operator on a number, Perl converts the number into a string and then completes the operation.

Figure 6.17 *The repeat operator repeats a string as many times as you can stand.*

Figure 6.18 *You can't see it, but I've entered a space after Hurrah in the first field.*

The cheer is Hurrah Hurrah Pennsylvan-i-a.

And the number, 3, repeated 5 times is 33333

Figure 6.19 *Is this the most contrived example you've ever seen, or what? If you find a good use for the repeat operator in your CGI scripts, I'd like to hear about it.*

```
1   #!/usr/local/bin/perl
2
3   require "subparseform.lib";
4   &Parse_Form;
5
6   $counter = $formdata{'counter'};
7
8   $counter +=1;
9
10  print "Content-type: text/html\n\n";
11  print "<FONT SIZE=+2>If you add one to
        your number, the result is
        <B>$counter</B>";
12
13  $counter +=5;
14  print "<P>If you add 5 to that, the
        result is <B>$counter</B></FONT>";
```

6: The initial value for $counter is specified by
    the visitor.

8: The binary operator adds 1 to the value of
    $counter and then stores the result back into
    $counter.

13: This line adds 5 to the current value of
    $counter (which is now 1 plus whatever the
    visitor had entered), and then stores the
    result back into $counter.

Figure 6.20 *Notice that the print statements in both lines 11 and 14 use the $counter variable, since it always contains the latest value.*

Figure 6.21 *The visitor enters the initial value for the $counter variable.*

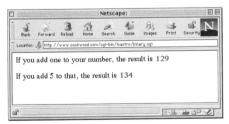

Figure 6.22 *Binary operators save you time and typing.*

Operating and assigning in one step

Updating the value of a variable by assigning it the result of an operation on itself is quite common. For that reason, Perl offers a special operator to save you typing called *the binary assignment operator.* It takes the form of the regular operator followed by the equals sign, which makes sense if you think of it as both operating and assigning a value to the variable.

To update a variable with the binary assignment operator:

1. Type **$scalar**, where *scalar* is the name of the variable that both holds the current value and that will hold the result of the operation.

2. Type the operator (*, **/**, **+**, **-**, **%**, ******, **.**, etc.)

3. Type **=** (the equals sign).

4. Type the second operand.

✔ **Tips**

■ Using a binary assignment operator is equivalent to carrying out the operation and the assignment individually. In other words, **$age = $age + 1** is equivalent to **$age +=1**. The second variation is simply faster to type.

■ The binary assignment shortcut works for both numbers and strings. In fact, the operators work just as they usually do; this is just a shortcut so you don't have to write out the variable name twice.

Operating and assigning in one step

Incrementing (or decrementing) a variable

Perl has a shorthand for the common operation of adding 1 to a variable (or subtracting 1 from it). You can use the operator either before or after the variable. In both cases, the variable itself is modified. If the operator precedes the variable, the return value *(see page 27)* of the operation is the incremented value while if the operator goes after the variable the return value is the value before it was incremented.

To increment/decrement a variable (and the result):

1. Type **++** (for adding 1) or **--** (for subtracting 1).

2. Type the variable.

To increment/decrement a variable (but not the result):

1. Type the variable.

2. Type **++** (for adding 1) or **--** (for subtracting 1).

✔ Tips

■ Whether you put the autoincrement operator before or after the variable largely depends on whether you're assigning the result to another variable. If you are, you just have to decide if you want the second variable to use the incremented value (use ++ before) or the value before it was incremented (use ++ after).

■ The autoincrement operator (but not autodecrement) works on strings as long as they contain only numbers and letters.

```perl
1  #!/usr/bin/perl
2
3  $counter = 13;
4  ++$counter;
5  $watch = ++$counter;
6
7  $counter = 13;
8  $counter++;
9  $watch = $counter++;
```

4: The autoincrement operator adds 1 to the value of $counter, which was 13 (line 3). The result (14) is then assigned back to $counter.
5: The autoincrement operator adds 1 to the value of $counter (14) and then assigns the result (15) back to $counter. *Then*, it assigns the result of the operation (15) to $watch. Note that $counter is equal to $watch.
7: We reassign the initial value of 13 to $counter so that we can compare the two operators on an even footing.
8: The autoincrement operator adds 1 to the value of $counter, which is 13 (line 7). The result (14) is then assigned back to $counter. There is no difference here from line 4.
9: The value of $counter (14) is assigned to $watch, and *then* the autoincrement operator does its thing, adding 1 to the current value of $counter (14) and then assigning the result (15) back to $counter. Now $counter and $watch have different values (15 and 14 respectively). Compare these results with the results from line 5.

Figure 6.23 *If you're not assigning the result of the entire expression to another variable, the placement of the autoincrement operators doesn't matter (lines 4 and 8). It's when you assign the result to a new variable ($watch), as in lines 5 and 9, that the order becomes important.*

Working with Arrays

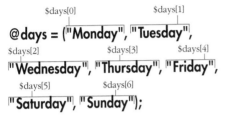

@days = ("Monday", "Tuesday",
"Wednesday", "Thursday", "Friday",
"Saturday", "Sunday");

Figure 7.1
Each element in an array is automatically numbered, starting from 0. You can use the number—together with the array name and some square brackets—to identify, use, and modify individual elements of the array as if they were independent

While a scalar is an individual piece of data, an array is a *collection* of pieces of data. While scalar variables begin with a dollar sign ($), array variables begin with an at sign (@). The idea is that the *a* in *at* will remind you of the *a* in *array*.

The elements in an array are automatically numbered for easy reference **(Figure 7.1)**. For better or worse, the numbering starts with 0 and not 1. That means that the fifth element is numbered 4—stay alert!

You've already learned how to enter a list of items into an array variable *(see page 70)*. In this chapter you'll learn how to create arrays in other ways and to manipulate them once they're set up.

Note: Each of the example scripts on the pages that follow works in tandem with a form, created with HTML. Unfortunately, there just isn't enough room to show you the scripts, the HTML code for the form (which reveals the names of the fields), the input that our example visitor types into the fields on the form *and* the result of the script, given that input. Since the aim of this book is to teach you Perl and CGI, I'll show you the script code and the result of the script. You'll usually be able to reconstruct what the HTML code and form looked like. And you can find the HTML—as well as Perl scripts—online *(see page 22)*.

Getting a particular item from an array

The elements in an array are automatically numbered, starting with 0 (not 1!). You use the numbers, often called an *array index*, to grab and use a particular item in the array.

To get a particular item from an array:

1. Type **$array_name**, where *array_name* is the name of the array that contains the desired element.

2. Type **[n]**, where *n* is the number of the desired item in the array (the leftmost item is 0, the next item is 1, and so on). There is no space between the array name and the left bracket.

✔ Tips

■ Note that when you access an individual member of an array, you use a dollar sign ($) and not an at sign (@). It makes sense when you think of scalars ($) as individual pieces of data and arrays (@) as lists of pieces of data.

■ Use a negative value for *n* to get items starting from the end of the list. (The last item is numbered -1, the second to last item is -2, and so on.)

■ To store an item from an array in a scalar variable, use **$scalar = $array[n]**.

■ You can use a scalar variable for *n*, as in **$array[$index];**. You can also use expressions, as in **$array[$index-1];**

■ To get more than one item at a time from an array, consult *Getting multiple items from an array* on page 89.

```
1   #!/usr/local/bin/perl
2
3   @days = qw(Sunday Monday Tuesday
        Wednesday Thursday Friday
        Saturday);
4
5   print "Content-type: text/html\n\n";
6   print "The first day of the week is
        $days[0]";
7
8   print "<P>The third day of the week is
        $days[2]";
```

3: This line assigns the list of days of the week to the array @days. For more details on qw, consult *Inputting arrays yourself* on page 70.

6: The expression $days[0] references the first item in the list, that is, *Sunday*. Notice that the first item is numbered 0, the second item is numbered 1, and so on.

8: In this line, we get the third element of the array with $days[2] and print an explanatory statement around it.

Figure 7.2 *Notice that when you access an individual member of the array, you use the dollar sign ($), not the at sign (@).*

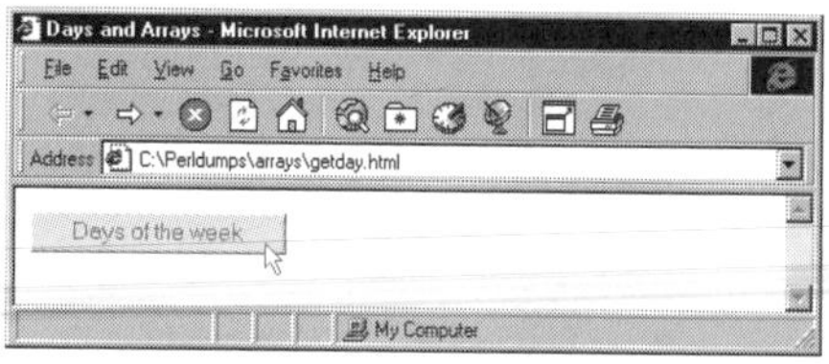

Figure 7.3 *This particular script doesn't require any input from the visitor, the submit button (with the descriptive title) simply sets it in motion.*

Figure 7.4 *It's true, this example is pretty boring since it always will give the same results. For a more interesting example of accessing individual elements of an array, check out the next page!*

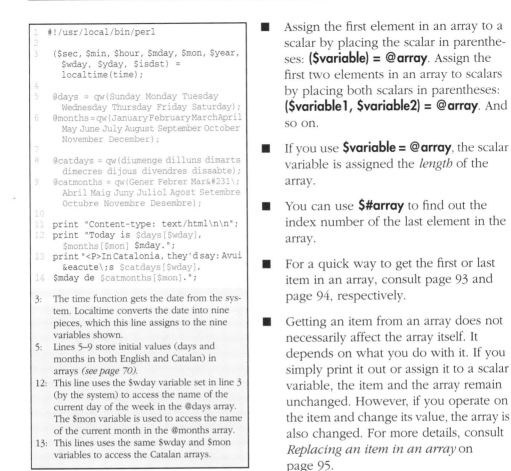

```
1   #!/usr/local/bin/perl
2
3   ($sec, $min, $hour, $mday, $mon, $year,
    $wday, $yday, $isdst) =
    localtime(time);
4
5   @days = qw(Sunday Monday Tuesday
    Wednesday Thursday Friday Saturday);
6   @months = qw(January February March April
    May June July August September October
    November December);
7
8   @catdays = qw(diumenge dilluns dimarts
    dimecres dijous divendres dissabte);
9   @catmonths = qw(Gener Febrer Mar&#231\;
    Abril Maig Juny Juliol Agost Setembre
    Octubre Novembre Desembre);
10
11  print "Content-type: text/html\n\n";
12  print "Today is $days[$wday],
    $months[$mon] $mday.";
13  print "<P>In Catalonia, they'd say: Avui
    &eacute\;s $catdays[$wday],
14  $mday de $catmonths[$mon].";
```

3: The time function gets the date from the system. Localtime converts the date into nine pieces, which this line assigns to the nine variables shown.

5: Lines 5–9 store initial values (days and months in both English and Catalan) in arrays *(see page 70)*.

12: This line uses the $wday variable set in line 3 (by the system) to access the name of the current day of the week in the @days array. The $mon variable is used to access the name of the current month in the @months array.

13: This lines uses the same $wday and $mon variables to access the Catalan arrays.

Figure 7.5 *The $wday and $mon variables have values from 0–6 and 0–11, respectively. They work perfectly with the array element numbering system but may confuse you if you have trouble thinking of say, 2, as March (and not February).*

Figure 7.6 *It doesn't matter what's in the array (be it English or Catalan days and months, or a list of groceries or whatever), you can easily access each element that it contains.*

- Assign the first element in an array to a scalar by placing the scalar in parentheses: **($variable) = @array**. Assign the first two elements in an array to scalars by placing both scalars in parentheses: **($variable1, $variable2) = @array**. And so on.

- If you use **$variable = @array**, the scalar variable is assigned the *length* of the array.

- You can use **$#array** to find out the index number of the last element in the array.

- For a quick way to get the first or last item in an array, consult page 93 and page 94, respectively.

- Getting an item from an array does not necessarily affect the array itself. It depends on what you do with it. If you simply print it out or assign it to a scalar variable, the item and the array remain unchanged. However, if you operate on the item and change its value, the array is also changed. For more details, consult *Replacing an item in an array* on page 95.

Getting a particular item from an array

Splitting a scalar into an array

When a visitor checks more than one check-box or option in a menu, the form-parsing subroutine included in this book (and indeed most others) creates one scalar variable with several "answers" separated with commas. You use the split function to convert that scalar into an array.

To split a scalar into an array:

1. Type **@array**, where *array* is the name of the array that will contain the items in the scalar variable.

2. Type **=** (the equals sign).

3. Type **split (/,/, $scalar)**, where *scalar* is the name of the variable that contains the comma-delimited items.

4. Type **;** to end the line.

✔ Tips

■ This will only work if the scalar variable contains a bunch of items separated by commas, which would be the case if you wish to process a menu or set of check-boxes from a form.

■ For more information on the split function, consult *Splitting a value into pieces* on page 141.

```
1   #!/usr/local/bin/perl
2   require "subparseform.lib";
3   &Parse_Form;
4
5   $class = $formdata{'class'};
6   @classes = split(/,/, $class);
7
8   print "Content-type: text/html\n\n";
9   print "<H1>You chose:</H1><UL>";
10
11  foreach $item (@classes) {
12          print "<LI>$item";
13  }
14  print "</UL>";
```

5: As usual, this line copies the data from the form-parsing subroutine *(see page 66)* into a scalar variable.

6: The split function uses the comma (the first argument in the function) to decide where to divide the contents of the scalar variable $class into sections *(see page 141)*.

11: We can now access individual items of the array using the foreach loop *(see page 114)*.

Figure 7.7 *The form-parsing subroutine merely puts both choices in a single scalar. The split function lets you divide them into individual elements of an array for separate processing.*

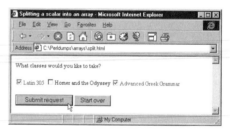

Figure 7.8 *This technique is only important if you have checkboxes or a menu in your form where your visitors can select more than one option.*

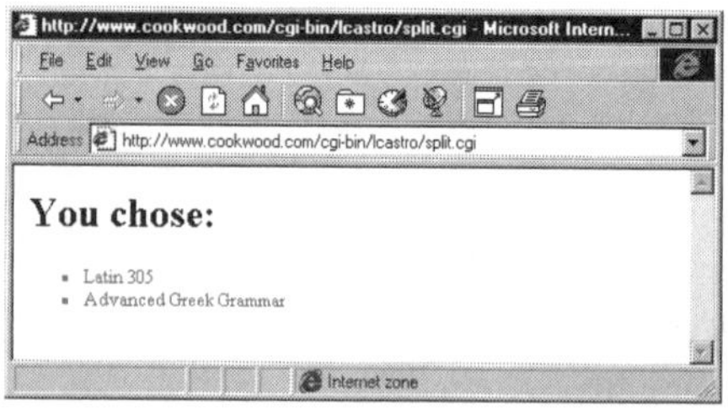

Figure 7.9 *Creating an array from a scalar makes it possible to treat each individual item separately. In this example, I've given them extra HTML formatting (the tags <H1>, <UL>, <LI>, etc.) to help them stand out. You wouldn't be able to create an HTML list out of a single scalar variable. For more details on outputting arrays as HTML lists, see page 185.*

```
1   #!/usr/local/bin/perl
2
3   require "subparseform.lib";
4   &Parse_Form;
5
6   @numbers = split(/,/,
       $formdata{'number'});
7   print "Content-type: text/html\n\n";
8   print "The numbers you entered were:";
9   foreach $number (@numbers) {
10    print "<LI>$number";
11  }
12  foreach $number(@numbers) {
13    $number = sqrt($number);
14  }
15
16  print "<P>The square roots of those
       numbers are: ";
17  foreach $number(@numbers) {
18    print "<LI>$number";
19  }
```

6:   In this line, we combine lines 5 and 6 from Figure 7.7.

8:   Lines 8–11 simply print each of the numbers the visitor entered. I've included it so that *you* can see what the original array contains.

13: Each time the $number variable is altered, the @numbers array is also permanently changed. At the end of this loop, the @numbers array no longer contains the original numbers, but rather the square roots of those numbers.

16: Lines 16–19 print out the new contents of the array. I've created a separate foreach loop so that the one under discussion (lines 12–14) is as simple and clear as possible. Nevertheless, the two foreach loops could be easily combined by putting line 18 after line 13.

Figure 7.10 *When you operate on a member of an array, the array itself is permanently altered.*

Figure 7.11 *The original array is printed out in the top part of the page. After modifying each element in the array, the new array contains completely different elements.*

Modifying all the members of an array

It seems strange but if you operate on each member of an array, say in a **foreach** loop, the array is permanently changed. You can take advantage of this fact to modify the whole array at once.

To modify all the members of an array:

1. Type **foreach**.

2. Type **$item**, where *item* is the name of the variable that will act as a stand-in for each member of the array.

3. Type **(@array)**, where *array* is the name of the array that you wish to change.

4. Type **{**.

5. On the next line, create an expression that changes the value of the $item variable. Remember to end the line with a semicolon.

6. On the next line, type **}**.

✔ Tips

- Beware of functions that seem to change a variable but don't. For example, the *result* of **sqrt ($item)** is the square root of $item, but the *value* of $item remains unchanged. On the other hand, **$item++** results in 1 plus the value of $item, *and* the variable $item will now contain the new value. This is why line 13 in the example in Figure 7.10 stores the value of the sqrt function back into $number. For more details, see page 27.

- To replace one element of an array, see page 95. To replace several, but not all, of the elements, see page 96.

Finding the length of an array

Once you or your visitor have entered an array, it's often useful to know how many elements the array contains. There are three ways to get the *length* of an array.

To store the length of an array in a scalar variable:

1. Type **$scalar**, where scalar is the name of the variable that will contain the length of the array.

2. Type **=** (the equals sign).

3. Type **@array**, where *array* is the name of the array whose length you want.

To get the length of an array another way:

1. Type **scalar**. (That's *not* a variable. You really have to type the word "scalar".)

2. Type **(@array)**, where array is the name of the array whose length you're interested in. The result of this expression is the length of the array.

An array name prefaced with **$#** returns the index number of the last item in the array *(see last tip on page 85)*. You can add 1 to this to get the number of elements in the array.

To use the index number to get the length of an array:

Type **$#array + 1**. The result of the expression is the number of elements (or length) of the array.

✔ Tip

- If you assign the array to another array (e.g., **@array = @otherarray**), instead of the length, you'll get a copy of the original array.

```
1   #!/usr/local/bin/perl
2
3   require "subparseform.lib";
4   &Parse_Form;
5
6   $class = $formdata{'class'};
7   @classes = split(/,/, $class);
8   $amount = @classes;
9
10  print "Content-type: text/html\n\n";
11
12  print "<H2>You chose $amount classes.
       They are:</H2><UL>";
13
14  foreach $item (@classes) {
15     print "<LI>$item";
16  }
17
18  print "</UL>";
```

8: This line stores the length of the @classes array in the $amount variable.

12: This print statement uses the $amount variable to display how many classes the visitor has chosen (that is, how many elements are in the @classes array).

Figure 7.12 *The easiest way to get the length of an array is to assign the array to a scalar variable.*

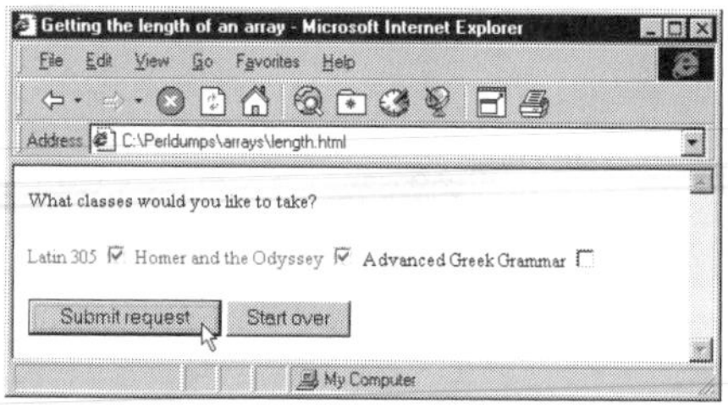

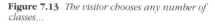

Figure 7.13 *The visitor chooses any number of classes...*

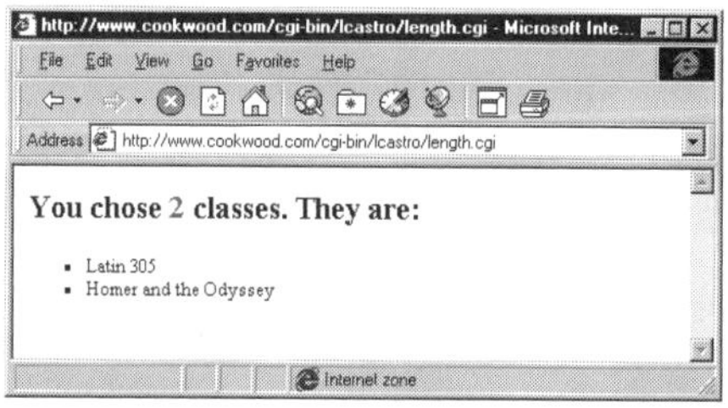

You chose 2 classes. They are:

- Latin 305
- Homer and the Odyssey

Figure 7.14 *...and by counting the elements in the newly created array, you can determine how many classes they chose.*

```
1   #!/usr/local/bin/perl
2
3   require "subparseform.lib";
4   &Parse_Form;
5
6   @days = qw(Sunday Monday Tuesday
      Wednesday Thursday Friday
      Saturday);
7
8   @choice = split(/,/,
      $formdata{'choice'});
9
10  print "Content-type: text/html\n\n";
11
12  print "You chose @days[@choice]";
```

6:   The @days array is set to the English days of the week.

8:   The @choice array contains the choices the visitor has entered in the form.

12: Since the fields' values are numbers, they can be easily used here to access the @days array.

Figure 7.15 *If you wanted to format this example in the same way I did the one Figure 7.9 on page 86, you could assign @days[@choice] to a third array and then use foreach to format and print out each item individually.*

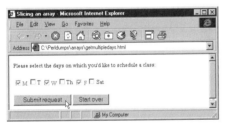

Figure 7.16 *The value of these checkboxes is not their name but rather their number. Monday is 1, Tuesday is 2, and so on.*

Figure 7.17 *In this example, the script grabs the elements numbered 1, 3, and 5 (corresponding to the values of the boxes checked) in the @days array and prints them out.*

Getting multiple items from an array

You can extract more than one item at a time from an array. This is called taking a *slice*. You can assign the slice to an array or use it in some other expression.

To get multiple items from an array:

1. Type **@array**, where *array* is the name of the array that contains the desired items.

2. Type **[n**, where *n* is the number of the desired item in the array (the leftmost item is 0, the next item is 1, etc.)

3. Type **, m**, where *m* is the number of the next desired item in the array.

4. If desired, repeat step 3 as many times as necessary, remembering to separate each array index with a comma.

5. Type **]**.

✔ Tips

■   If you want to assign the resulting items to another array, use **@resulting_items = @array[n, m]**;. It wouldn't make sense to assign more than one item to a scalar variable; you have to assign a slice to another array.

■   As shown in the example, it's perfectly fine to use an array for *n* and *m*, as in **@array[@otherarray]**. You can also use scalar variables, as in **@array[$index_n, $index_m]**; or expressions, as in **@array[$index_n, $index_n + 1]**;.

■   For details on changing multiple elements in an array, consult *Replacing more than one item in an array* on page 96.

Adding items to the beginning of an array

Once you've defined an array, you may need to add items to it. Perl has a special function for adding items to the beginning of an array.

To add one or more items to the beginning of an array:

1. Type **unshift(@array,**, where @array is the array to which you want to add items.

2. Type **newelement,**, where *newelement* is a scalar constant, a scalar variable, or an array whose elements you wish to add to the beginning of the array mentioned in step 1.

3. If desired, type **nextnewelement,**, where *nextnewelement* is an additional scalar or array that you wish to add to the array in step 1.

4. Type **)**.

5. Type **;** to finish the line. The array now contains the new elements followed by its original contents.

✔ Tips

■ As always, separate each item in the array with a comma. String constants should be delimited with quotes.

■ You can also add items to the beginning of an array using assignment: **@array = (newelement, @array)**. Again, the new-element can be a scalar constant, variable or an array.

■ It doesn't make much sense to add a hash to an array because the order of the pairs in a hash is arbitrary, and thus there is no way to control the order of the resulting items.

```
1   #!/usr/local/bin/perl
2
3   require "subparseform.lib";
4   &Parse_Form;
5
6   @classes = ("Latin 305", "Advanced Greek
       Grammar");
7   $newclass = $formdata{'newclass'};
8
9   unshift(@classes, $newclass);
10
11  print "Content-type: text/html\n\n";
12
13  print "<H2>You added $newclass. Your
       complete list is now:</H2><UL>";
14
15  foreach $item (@classes) {
16      print "<LI>$item";
17  }
18  print "</UL>";
```

6: For simplicity, I've manually created the array here *(see page 69)*. It would usually come from visitor input.

7: The $newclass variable gets data from the visitor through the form-parsing subroutine.

9: The unshift function adds the value of $new-class to the beginning of the @classes array.

Figure 7.18 *You don't need to assign the result of the unshift function to another array. The array specified in the first argument is itself permanently modified.*

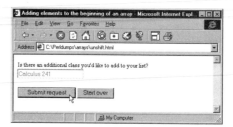

Figure 7.19 *The visitor adds the new class which will be stored in the $newclass variable.*

Figure 7.20 *If you use unshift to add the an element to an array, the new element appears at the beginning of the array (cf. Figure 7.23).*

```
1   #!/usr/local/bin/perl
2
3   require "subparseform.lib";
4   &Parse_Form;
5
6   @classes = ("Latin 305", "Advanced
       Greek Grammar");
7   $newclass = $formdata{'newclass'};
8
9   push(@classes, $newclass);
10
11  print "Content-type: text/html\n\n";
12
13  print "<H2>You added $newclass. Your
       complete list is now:</H2><UL>";
14
15  foreach $item (@classes) {
16      print "<LI>$item";
17  }
18  print "</UL>";
```

6: For simplicity, I've manually created the array
    here *(see page 70)*. It would usually come
    from visitor input.

7: The $newclass variable gets data from the
    visitor through the form-parsing subroutine.

9: The push function adds the value of $new-
    class to the end of the @classes array.

Figure 7.21 *You don't need to assign the result of
the push function to another array. The array specified in the first argument is itself permanently
modified.*

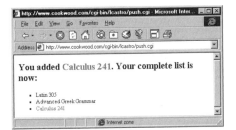

Figure 7.22 *Again, the visitor types the name of the
new class and submits the data.*

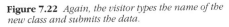

Figure 7.23 *The push function adds the new value
to the end of the array (cf. Figure 7.20).*

Adding items to the end of an array

You can also add items to the end of an existing array.

To add one or more items to the end of an array:

1. Type **push(@array**, where *@array* is the
    name of the array to which you want to
    add items.

2. Type **newelement,**, where *newelement* is
    a scalar constant, a scalar variable, or an
    array whose elements you wish to add to
    the end of the array mentioned in step 1.

3. If desired, type **nextnewelement,**, where
    nextnewelement is an additional scalar or
    array that you wish to add to the array in
    step 1.

4. Type **)**.

5. Type **;** to finish the line. The array now
    contains its original contents followed by
    the new elements.

✔ Tips

■ As always, separate each item in the array
   with a comma. String constants must be
   delimited with quotes. Or, use qw *(see
   page 70)*.

■ You can also add items to the end of an
   array using assignment: **@array =
   (@array, newelement)**. Again, the *newelement* can be a scalar constant, variable
   or an array.

■ It doesn't make much sense to add a hash
   to an array because the order of the pairs
   in a hash is arbitrary, and thus there is no
   way to control the order of the resulting
   items.

Adding items to the end of an array

Combining two arrays

Sometimes you'll want to add the items from one array to another.

To add the items from one array to another array:

1. Type **@combined**, where *combined* is the name of the array that will contain the items from both arrays.

2. Type **=** (the equals sign).

3. Type **(@first, @second)** where *first* is the name of the array whose elements should be at the beginning of the array and *second* is the name of the array whose items should follow.

4. Type **;** to finish the line. The @combined array now contains the items from @first followed by the items from @second.

✔ Tips

- You may add the items from as many arrays as you like. Simply separate each array name with a comma.

- If you want the resulting array to have the items from array2 at the *beginning* of the list, use **(@array2, @array)**.

- You may assign any combination of arrays or scalars to another array. The result is a list of the items in each array and the scalar items, in the order they appear within the parentheses.

- To add just a selection of the items from one array to another, you have to use a slice. For more information, consult *Getting multiple items from an array* on page 89.

```perl
1   #!/usr/local/bin/perl
2
3   require "subparseform.lib";
4   &Parse_Form;
5
6   @classes = ("Latin 305", "Advanced
      Greek Grammar");
7   $newclasses =
      $formdata{'newclasses'};
8   @newclasses = split(/,/, $newclasses);
9
10  @classes = (@classes, @newclasses);
11
12  print "Content-type: text/html\n\n";
13
14  print "<H2>You added:</H2><UL>";
15  foreach $item (@newclasses) {
16      print "<LI>$item";
17  }
18  print "</UL>";
19  print "<H2>Your complete list is
      now:</H2><UL>";
20  foreach $item (@classes) {
21      print "<LI>$item";
22  }
23  print "</UL>";
```

8: The visitor's new input is stored in the @new-classes array.

10: This line combines elements from the @classes and @newclasses arrays into the @classes array.

Figure 7.24 *The script now contains two foreach loops. The first goes through each element in the @newclasses array. The second gives the complete list of courses by iterating the elements of the newly combined @classes array.*

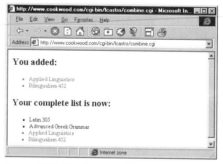

Figure 7.25 *The elements added from the second array now form part (at the end) of the original array.*

```
1   #!/usr/local/bin/perl
2
3   require "subparseform.lib";
4   &Parse_Form;
5
6   @classes = ("Latin 305", "Advanced
       Greek Grammar", "Applied Linguistics",
       "Virgil and the Iliad");
7
8   $removed = shift(@classes);
9
10  print "Content-type: text/html\n\n";
11  print "<H2>You removed $removed. Your
       complete list is now:</H2><UL>";
12
13  foreach $item (@classes) {
14      print "<LI>$item";
15  }
16  print "</UL>";
```

6:   Again, for simplicity's sake, I've created the
     base array manually. Hopefully, what the
     example lacks in usefulness, it makes up in
     clarity.

8:   Two things are going on here. In the right-
     hand expression, the shift function removes
     the first element from the @classes array.
     Then the removed element is stored in the
     $removed variable.

Figure 7.26 *The only reason I've stored the removed element in the $removed variable is so that I can print it out later. You don't need to store the result of the shift function for the array to be changed.*

Figure 7.27 *You can print and use the removed element to give extra information to your visitor. Notice that the array no longer contains the removed element.*

Removing the first item in an array

You can eliminate one or more individual items from the beginning of an array using the shift function.

To remove the first item in an array:

1. Type **shift (@array)** where *@array* is the name of the array from which you wish to remove the first item.

2. Type **;** to finish the line. The @array now contains one less item.

When you remove an item from an array, by default it disappears into the cyberether. If you're interested in using the removed item for another operation, you'll have to save it to a scalar variable.

To remove the first item in an array and store it in a scalar variable:

1. Type **$scalar**, where *scalar* is the name of the variable where you will store the element from the array.

2. Type **=**.

3. Type **shift (@array)** where *@array* is the name of the array from which you wish to remove the first item.

4. Type **;** to finish the line. The @array now contains one less item.

Removing the last item in an array

You can eliminate individual items from the end of an array using the pop function.

To remove the last item in an array:

1. Type **pop(@array)** where *@array* is the name of the array from which you wish to remove the last item.

2. Type **;** to finish the line.

When you remove an item from an array, by default it disappears into the cyberether. If you're interested in using the removed item for another operation, you'll have to save it to a scalar variable.

To remove an item from the end of an array *and* store it in a scalar variable:

1. Type **$scalar**, where *scalar* is the name of the variable where you will store the element from the array.

2. Type **=**.

3. Type **pop(@array)** where *@array* is the name of the array from which you wish to remove the last item.

4. Type **;** to finish the line.

```perl
1   #!/usr/local/bin/perl
2
3   require "subparseform.lib";
4   &Parse_Form;
5
6   @classes = ("Latin 305", "Advanced Greek
        Grammar","AppliedLinguistics","Virgil
        and the Iliad");
7
8   $removed = pop(@classes);
9
10  print "Content-type: text/html\n\n";
11  print "<H2>You removed $removed. Your
        complete list is now:</H2><UL>";
12
13  foreach $item (@classes) {
14      print "<LI>$item";
15  }
16  print "</UL>";
```

6: Again, for simplicity's sake, I've created the base array manually. Hopefully, what the example lacks in usefulness, it makes up in clarity.

8: Two things are going on here. In the right-hand expression, the pop function removes the last element from the @classes array. Then the removed element is stored in the $removed variable.

Figure 7.28 *The only reason I've stored the removed class in the $removed variable is so that I can print it out later. You don't need to store the result of the pop function for the array to be changed.*

Figure 7.29 *Again, I use the $removed_element variable so I can give visitors more information. Notice that the element no longer forms part of the array.*

Removing the last item in an array

```
1   #!/usr/local/bin/perl
2
3   require "subparseform.lib";
4   &Parse_Form;
5
6   @classes = ("Latin 305", "Advanced Greek
       Grammar","Applied Linguistics","Virgil
       and the Iliad");
7   $newclass = $formdata{'newclass'};
8   $ID = $formdata{'ID'};
9
10  print "Content-type: text/html\n\n";
11  print "<H2>You replaced $classes[$ID]
       with $newclass. ";
12
13  $classes[$ID] = $newclass;
14
15  print "Your complete list is now:
       </H2><UL>";
16
17  foreach $item (@classes) {
18      print "<LI>$item";
19  }
20  print "</UL>";
```

7:   The name of the new class is received from
     the visitor and stored in $newclass.
8:   The number of the class to be removed is
     received and stored in $ID.
11: Before replacing the element in the array, this
     line takes advantage of the old information to
     tell the visitor what they're getting rid of.
13: The value of $ID determines which element
     of the @classes array is substituted with the
     value of $newclass.

Figure 7.30 *Identifying an item in an array by its element number is the easiest way to replace it with an updated element.*

Figure 7.31 *Notice that the first time I reference classes[ID] (in line 11), the old value is printed. The second time, after the value has been changed in line 13, the new value is printed out (line 18).*

Replacing an item in an array

You can use the fact that array items are numbered to replace a particular item in an array.

To replace an item in an array:

1. Type **$array**, where *array* is the name of the array that contains the item to be replaced. (Notice that you use a dollar sign and not an at sign.)

2. Type **[n]**, where *n* is the number of the desired item in the array (the leftmost item is 0, the next item is 1, etc.)

3. Type **=** (the equals sign).

4. Type **scalar**, where *scalar* is either a scalar variable or a scalar constant.

5. Type **;** to finish the line.

✔ Tips

- You can also use this technique to add new array items in particular positions. For example, if @array has four elements (numbered 0–3), and you use **$array[4] = scalar**, the value of scalar will be assigned to the array in the 4 position. If you used **$array[6] = scalar** in this same example, the intermediate positions would be undefined (undef), while the 6 position would be set to the value of the scalar.

- For information about replacing several items in an array, see page 96. You can get information about changing all the elements in the array at once on page 87.

Replacing more than one item in an array

You can replace several items in an array simultaneously by assigning an array with the new items to a slice of the array marking the items that need to be replaced.

To replace more than one item in an array:

1. Type **@array**, where *array* is the name of the array that contains the items to be replaced.

2. Type **[**.

3. Type **n, m**, where *n* and *m* (and any others) are the index numbers of the desired items in the array (the leftmost item is 0, the next item is 1, etc.) The numbers should be separated with commas.

   Or type **@numbers**, where *numbers* is the name of the array that contains the index numbers that identify the desired items in the array referenced in step 1.

4. Type **]**.

5. Type **=**.

6. Type **(scalar_n, scalar_m)**, where *scalar_n* is the new value for the item numbered *n* and *scalar_m* is the new value for the item numbered *m*. Add additional scalar items if you've referenced additional positions in the array in step 3.

   Or, type **@replacement_array**, where *replacement_array* is the name of the array that contains the items you wish to substitute for the ones referenced in step 3.

7. Type **;** to finish the line.

```perl
1   #!/usr/local/bin/perl
2
3   require "subparseform.lib";
4   &Parse_Form;
5
6   @classes = ("Latin 305", "Advanced Greek
       Grammar","AppliedLinguistics","Virgil
       and the Iliad");
7   @newclasses = split(/,/,
       $formdata{'newclass'});
8   @IDs = split(/,/, $formdata{'ID'});
9
10  print "Content-type: text/html\n\n";
11  print "<P><B>You replaced: </B>";
12
13  foreach $number (@IDs) {
14     $number--;
15     print "<LI>$classes[$number]";
16  }
17
18  print "<P><B>with:</B> ";
19  foreach $course (@newclasses) {
20     if ($course ne " ") {
21        print "<LI>$course";
22        @newarray = (@newarray, $course);
23     }
24  }
25
26  @classes[@IDs] = @newarray;
27
28  print "<H2>Your complete list is now:</
       H2><UL>";
29  foreach $item (@classes) {
30     print "<LI>$item";
31  }
32  print "</UL>";
```

7: Lines 7 and 8 receive, split, and store input from the visitor.

13: Lines 13–16 contain a foreach loop that reduces each ID number by 1 (so that it will match the class' array index) and then prints out the classes that should be removed.

19: The beginning of the foreach loop that goes through each element in @newclasses.

20: An interior if conditional checks to see if each element is not empty, and if not, prints the course name, and then adds it to a new array (that will only contain the non-empty elements of the @newclasses array).

23: Notice that each block needs its own closing curly bracket (lines 23 and 24).

26: This is the line that actually substitutes the chosen old classes and replaces them with the new ones. Notice I've used the @IDs array, which contains the index numbers, to identify the desired elements in @classes.

29: Now that the @classes array contains the updated list, we can use a foreach block to print out each element.

Figure 7.32 *The ability to replace particular elements of an array with elements from another array makes arrays versatile and very powerful.*

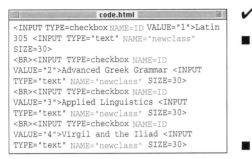

```
┌─────────────────────────────┐
│ ▓▓       code.html       ▓▓ │
├─────────────────────────────┤
│<INPUT TYPE=checkbox NAME=ID VALUE="1">Latin
│305 <INPUT TYPE="text" NAME="newclass"
│SIZE=30>
│<BR><INPUT TYPE=checkbox NAME=ID
│VALUE="2">Advanced Greek Grammar <INPUT
│TYPE="text" NAME="newclass" SIZE=30>
│<BR><INPUT TYPE=checkbox NAME=ID
│VALUE="3">Applied Linguistics <INPUT
│TYPE="text" NAME="newclass" SIZE=30>
│<BR><INPUT TYPE=checkbox NAME=ID
│VALUE="4">Virgil and the Iliad <INPUT
│TYPE="text" NAME="newclass" SIZE=30>
```

Figure 7.33 *An excerpt from the HTML file used to create the form shows the set of checkboxes are named* ID *while each text field is named* newclass. *These names are used to identify the incoming data in lines 8 and 7 respectively of Figure 7.32 on page 96.*

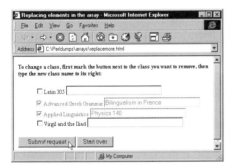

Figure 7.34 *By checking the box next to the old course, the ID is set to remove that item (and accept a new one). Typing in the new course creates the replacement element in the @newclasses array.*

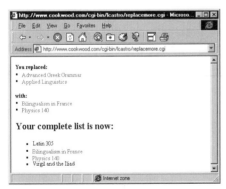

Figure 7.35 *The chosen old classes are replaced with the new ones. Printing out each stage of the script not only gives your visitor information but is also a good debugging tool (see page 216).*

✔ **Tips**

■ If you already know what elements you want to replace, your example will be a lot simpler than this one (line 26 contains the crucial code). I wanted to give the visitor the ability to *choose* which items to replace.

■ The tips at the bottom of page 95 apply here as well.

■ In this example, two items are replaced with an array that contains two items. If the replacement array contains more items than the items marked by the slice, the extra items are ignored. If there are more items to be replaced than there are replacement items, the original items are removed and the unmatched items are left undefined.

■ You can replace a slice of one array with a slice of another. Use **@array[m,n] = @otherarray[x,y]**.

Replacing more than one item in an array

Sorting arrays

You can change an array so that the items it contains are sorted in alphabetical, or ASCII order.

To sort arrays:

1. Type **sort** to sort in ASCII order.

    Or type **sort {$b cmp $a}**, to sort in reverse ASCII order.

    Or type **sort {$a <=> $b}**, to sort numerically in ascending order.

    Or type **sort ($b <=> $a}** to sort numerically in descending order.

2. Type **(@array)**, where *array* is the name of the array that contains the items that you wish to put in order.

✔ Tips

■ The sort function doesn't affect the array itself. If you want to save the results of the sorting action, you'll have to assign the result to an array (the same one or a different one) with **@array = sort(@array);**.

■ Another way to take advantage of the sort function is to use it in a larger expression, as in **print sort(@array);**. In this case, the array will be printed in ASCII order, but the original positions of the items will be maintained.

■ The ASCII order for numbers is not the same as going from lowest to highest numerically. For example, the numbers 1, 2, 3, 10, 12, 20, 35 are in ascending numerical order. The basic sort function would arrange them according to their ASCII values: 1, 10, 12, 2, 20, 35.

```
1   #!/usr/local/bin/perl
2
3   require "subparseform.lib";
4   &Parse_Form;
5
6   $class = $formdata{'class'};
7   @classes = split(/,/, $class);
8
9   print "Content-type: text/html\n\n";
10
11  print "<H2>You chose:</H2><UL>";
12
13  @classes = sort (@classes);
14
15  foreach $item (@classes) {
16      print "<LI>$item";
17  }
18
19  print "</UL>";
```

13: This line rearranges the elements of the @classes array in alphabetical (ASCII) order, and then stores the result back into the @classes array.

Figure 7.36 *The sort function puts items in ASCII order by default.*

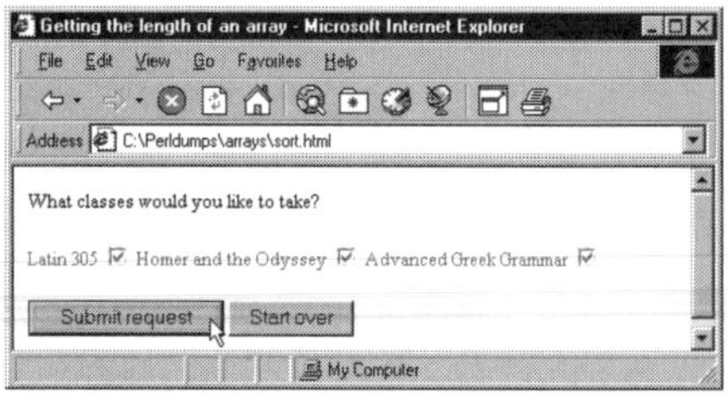

Figure 7.37 *The visitor chooses the classes they want to take...*

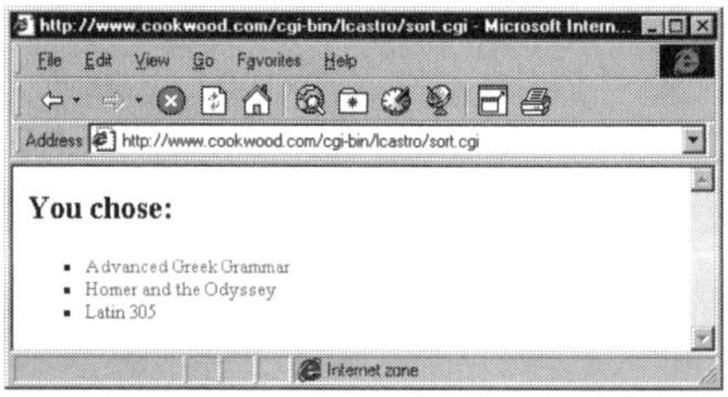

Figure 7.38 *...and the script confirms the choices in alphabetical order (cf. Figure 7.9 on page 86).*

```
1   #!/usr/local/bin/perl
2
3   require "subparseform.lib";
4   &Parse_Form;
5
6   $class = $formdata{'class'};
7   @classes = split(/,/, $class);
8
9   print "Content-type: text/html\n\n";
10
11  print "<H2>You chose:</H2><UL>";
12
13  @classes = sort (@classes);
14  @classes = reverse (@classes);
15
16  foreach $item (@classes) {
17      print "<LI>$item";
18  }
19
20  print "</UL>";
```

13: This line rearranges the elements of the @classes array in alphabetical (ASCII) order, and then stores the result back into the @classes array.

14: This line reverses the order of the elements in the @classes array (now they'll be in descending alphabetical order), and stores the result back in the @classes array.

Figure 7.39 *You have to store the result of the reverse function somewhere if you want to use it later in your script.*

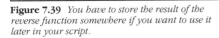

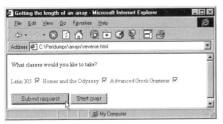

Figure 7.40 *Again, the visitor chooses which classes to take.*

Figure 7.41 *This time the confirmation shows the classes in reverse alphabetical order (cf Figure 7.38 on page 98).*

Reversing the order of an array's contents

You can completely reverse the order of the items in an array, putting the last item first, the second to last item second, and so on.

To reverse the order of the items in an array:

1. Type **reverse**.

2. Type **(@array)**, where *array* is the name of the array whose items you want to reverse the order of.

✔ Tips

■ The reverse function doesn't affect the array itself. If you want to save the results of the reversing action, you'll have to assign the result to an array (the same one or a different one) with **@array = reverse(@array);**.

■ Another way to take advantage of the reverse function is to use it in a larger expression, as in **print reverse(@array);**. In this case, the array will be printed in reverse order, but the original positions of the items will be maintained.

■ You can use the reverse function together with sort *(see page 98)* to reverse the chosen sort order.

Conditional Statements

A simple statement

$total = $price * $quantity;

Figure 8.1 *Here is a simple statement that multiplies the scalar $price by $quantity and assigns the result to $total.*

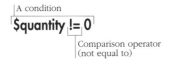

A condition

$quantity != 0

Comparison operator
(not equal to)

Figure 8.2 *A condition is either true or false. In this example, the value of the scalar variable $quantity is either not equal to 0 (in which case this condition would be true), or it is equal to 0 (in which case this condition would be false).*

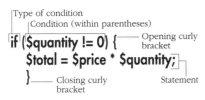

Type of condition
Condition (within parentheses)

if ($quantity != 0) {   Opening curly bracket
  $total = $price * $quantity;

} —— Closing curly bracket   Statement

Figure 8.3 *A conditional statement has three principal parts: the conditional word ("if") that determines how the condition will be analyzed; the condition itself, which is generally enclosed in parentheses; and a block, which begins with an opening curly bracket, then contains one or more statements, and ends with a closing curly bracket.*

So far, you've learned how to make definitive statements: multiply these two things together or add this thing to that array. In this chapter, you'll learn how to execute certain statements only under particular circumstances. For example, you may only want to multiply those two things together *if* one of them is not equal to 0. Or perhaps you want to add elements to an array *until* the array has seven elements.

A *conditional statement* generally contains three parts. First, we have the all important conditional word, such as *if* or *until*, that determines how the condition is interpreted. Notice the difference between "Multiply these two together *if* the quantity is not 0" and "Multiply these together *until* the quantity is not zero". As you can see, the choice of conditional words makes a good deal of difference.

Next, comes the condition itself, which in this example is "the quantity is not zero". When Perl encounters a condition, it has to decide whether it is true or false. In this case, if the value of $quantity is, say, 3, the expression is evaluated as true. If the value of $quantity is 0, the expression is false.

The last element in a conditional statement is a *block* of one or more statements that are executed depending on the true or false state of the condition. In this example, the statement "multiply the price by the quantity, and assign the result to the total" will only be executed if the condition (that the quantity is not zero) is true.

Comparing numbers

One typical way to create a condition is by comparing two numbers to see if they are equal, or not equal, or if one is bigger or smaller. The result of a comparison is either true or false.

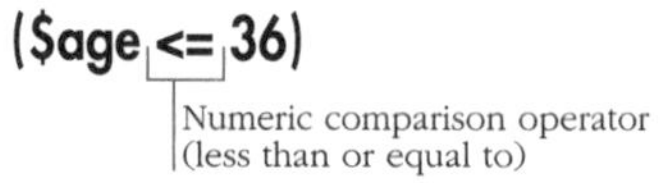

To compare numbers:

1. Type the first element in the comparison.

2. Type the numeric comparison operator:

Use **>** for greater than, **<** for less than, **>=** for greater than or equal to, **<=** for less than or equal to, **==** for equal to and **!=** for not equal to.

3. Type the second element in the comparison.

✔ Tips

■ There are separate comparison operators for numbers and strings. For more information on comparison operators for strings, consult *Comparing strings* on page 103.

■ If you use a numeric comparison operator on a string, Perl will convert the string into a number (stripping it of non-numeric symbols and characters and changing it to zero if it has no numbers at all). The results may not be what you expected. For comparing strings, use the string comparison operators *(see page 103).*

($age <= 36)

Numeric comparison operator
(less than or equal to)

Figure 8.4 *In this example, if the value of $age is 3 or 25 or anything else less than or equal to 36, the condition will be evaluated as true. If the value of $age is higher than 36, the condition is evaluated as false.*

Comparing numbers

($name eq "Ralph")

String comparison operator
(equivalent to)

Figure 8.5 *In this example, if the value of $name is exactly "Ralph", the condition is true. Otherwise, it is false.*

Comparing strings

While it's often useful to compare numbers to see which is bigger and which is smaller, with strings you usually want to know if they are the same or not. The result of a comparison is either true or false.

To compare strings:

1. Type the first string.

2. Type the string comparison operator:

Use **eq** for equal to, **ne** for not equal to, **gt** for greater than, **lt** for less than, **ge** for greater than or equal to, and **le** for less than or equal to.

3. Type the second string.

✔ Tips

■ Remember that case matters. "Zipper" is not equivalent to "zipper". In fact, it is greater than "zipper".

■ To decide whether a string is greater or less than another, Perl looks at the ASCII values of the characters that it contains. Therefore, *Z* is greater than (and *not equivalent* to) *z*. *Z* is of course greater than *A*, and all letters are greater than the digits 0–9 and many symbols (including the space). You can find an ASCII chart on this book's Web site *(see page 22)*.

■ Remember that since Perl expects strings with these operators, it will treat numbers as strings as well. For example, **42 gt 147** returns true (even though it's false if you consider the two operands as numbers) because the ASCII value of 4 is greater than the ASCII value of 1.

■ For comparing numbers, see page 102.

■ You can also use regular expressions with conditionals *(see page 137)*.

Comparing strings

Evaluating conditions without comparisons

While comparison operators are probably the simplest and most common way to construct a condition, they are not the only way. In fact, you can use any statement as a condition. Perl has a simple set of rules for deciding if a statement is true or false: if the statement is evaluated as 0, the empty string (""), or undefined, it is considered to be false. In all other cases, it is true.

For example, a condition like **($quantity)** will return true only if it is not empty, not undefined, and not equal to zero. This is a great way to test if a particular variable has had a variable assigned to it, and to execute further statements only if the assignment has already occurred.

Further, a function like **print "hello"** will return true if it was successful (able to print) and false if not.

✔ Tip

■ Note that if the condition contains an operation, the operation will always be executed. For example, if you use **if ($number++)**, the value of $number will be incremented by 1 regardless of whether the condition evaluates as true or false.

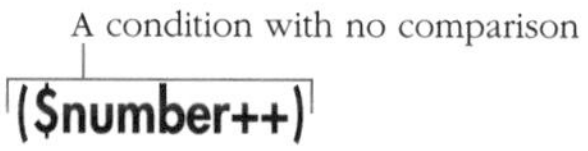

A condition with no comparison

($number++)

Figure 8.6 *In this example, the condition is true if the value of the expression is not empty, not undefined, and not equal to zero.*

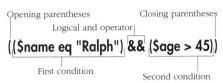

Figure 8.7 *With two comparisons and the logical and operator, the entire condition is true if and only if the value of both comparisons is true. In other words, the man in question must be named Ralph and must be older than 45.*

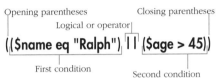

Figure 8.8 *If you use the logical or operator, only one of the comparisons needs to return true for the condition to be true. In this case, men older than 45, regardless of their name, or men named Ralph, regardless of their age, would match.*

Testing two or more comparisons at a time

While regular expressions let you make your conditions more flexible *(see page 137)*, you can also test more than one condition at a time.

To test two comparisons at a time:

1. Type **(** to begin the set of conditions.

2. Type **(condition1)**, where *condition1* is the first condition you want to test.

3. Type **&&** (this is the logical and operator) to test if both conditions are true.

   Or type **||** (the logical or operator) to test if at least one (but possibly both) of the conditions is true.

4. Type **(condition2)**, where *condition2* is the second condition.

5. Repeat steps 3–4 as necessary.

6. Type **)** to close the set of conditions.

✔ Tip

■ Don't forget the outer set of parentheses that encloses the two conditions and the operator.

Testing two or more comparisons at a time

Creating a basic conditional statement

You probably heard your first if statement from one of your parents: "*If* you don't eat your spinach, then you can't have dessert." Notice that there is an if, a condition, (you don't eat spinach), and something that will happen if the condition is true, (you won't get dessert). If statements in Perl aren't much different—except you can always have dessert.

To use if:

1. Type **if**.

2. On the same line, type **(** (an opening parenthesis).

3. Type the condition.

4. Type **)** (the closing parenthesis).

5. Still on the same line, type **{** (an opening curly bracket).

6. Now press Return, and on the next line, type the statement that should be executed if the condition in step 3 is true. Remember to end each statement on each line with a semicolon.

7. Repeat step 6 as many times as needed.

8. Type **}** (the closing curly bracket).

✔ Tips

- If you only have one short statement that will be executed if the condition is true, you can put the entire if block on one line.

- If the block contains only one statement, you can flip the order of the elements to more closely mirror English syntax: **print "You ate spinach, so you get dessert" if ($food eq "spinach");**.

```
1   #!/usr/local/bin/perl
2
3   require "subparseform.lib";
4   &Parse_Form;
5
6   $food = $formdata{'food'};
7
8   if ($food eq "spinach") {
9      print "Content-type: text/
         html\n\n";
10     print "You ate spinach, so you get
         dessert!\n";
11  }
```

8: If the value of $food, which the visitor inputs through the corresponding Web form, is *spinach*, then the rest of the statements in the if statement (lines 9–10) will be executed. Otherwise, they will be skipped.

9: The all-important MIME content line.

10: As long as the condition in line 8 is true, the program will execute this line, printing the phrase "You ate spinach, so you get dessert".

11: You must end an if statement with the final closing curly bracket.

Figure 8.9 *This if block contains two statements that will only be executed if the condition evaluates as true.*

Figure 8.10 *If the visitor types "spinach" in the field, the condition is true, both statements in the if block are executed, and both the MIME content line and the phrase "You ate spinach, so you get dessert'" are output to the browser.*

```
1   #!/usr/bin/perl
2
3   require "subparseform.lib";
4   &Parse_Form;
5
6   $food = $formdata{'food'};
7
8   print "Content-type: text/html\n\n";
9
10  if ($food eq "spinach") {
11    print "You ate spinach, so you get
          dessert!";
12  } else {
13    print "No spinach, no dessert!";
14  }
```

8: I've taken the MIME content line out of the if statement so that it is sent to the browser no matter what the outcome of the if.

12: The else clause begins after the closing curly bracket of the original if statement.

13: As long as $food is not spinach, the condition in line 10 is false and this line (13) will be executed, printing the line "No spinach, no dessert!".

14: You must end an else clause with a closing curly bracket.

Figure 8.11 *The else clause lets you add a statement that will be executed only if the condition is false. If the condition is true, the statements in the if block are executed as usual.*

Figure 8.12 *If the visitor types anything other than* spinach *(including nothing at all), the condition is false and the statement(s) in the else block are executed. In this case, that means the script outputs the sentence "No spinach, no dessert!" to the browser.*

Adding options for false conditions

In the example on the preceding page, if the visitor types anything except "spinach", the print statements are ignored resulting in a confused browser and an internal server error. Thankfully, you can add an "else" clause to an if block that lets you execute one group of statements if the condition is true and a different group if the condition is false (instead of giving up altogether). The statements in the else clause are only executed when the condition is *not* true.

To add options for when the condition is false:

1. Create an if statement as described on page 106.

2. After the final curly bracket (from step 8 on page 106), type **else**.

3. Type {.

4. Now press Return, and on the next line, type the statement that should be executed if the condition is false. Remember to end each statement (on each line) with a semicolon.

5. Type }.

✔ Tip

■ Although you could embed other if statements within an else clause, there is a better way to add multiple conditions *(see page 108)*.

Adding multiple, independent conditions

An if block with an else clause lets you control two outcomes: what should happen if the condition is true and what should happen if it's false. Perl also lets you add additional conditions that it will test after the if condition evaluates as false and before it executes the statements in the else clause.

To add multiple, independent conditions:

1. Create the if statement as described on page 106.

2. Type **elsif**. Notice that there is only one *e* in *elsif*.

3. Type **(condition)**, where *condition* is the expression that should be evaluated as true or false to determine if the following statements should be executed.

4. On the same line, type **{**.

5. Type the statements that should be executed if the condition in step 3 is true. Remember to type a semicolon at the end of each statement.

6. Type **}**.

7. Repeat steps 2–6 for each additional condition and statements.

8. Create an else clause as described in steps 2–5 on page 107, whose statement(s) will only be executed if *all* the preceding conditions are false.

✔ Tip

- Each condition is evaluated in order. Once Perl finds a true condition (or the else clause), the corresponding statements are executed and the rest of the block is ignored.

```
10  if ($food eq "spinach") {
11    print "You ate spinach, so you get
         dessert!";
12  } elsif ($food eq "broccoli") {
13    print "Broccoli's OK. Maybe you'll get
         dessert.";
14  } else {
15    print "No spinach, no dessert!";
16  }
```

9: Lines 1-9 are not shown. They are exactly the same as in Figure 8.11.

10: Supposing the user enters "broccoli" for $food, this first condition will be false and Perl will skip line 11 and look for an elsif.

11: Because the initial condition is false, this line is skipped.

12: The first additional condition follows the if's closing curly bracket. Now, Perl will look to see if $food is "broccoli". If so, the statements in this block are executed. If not, it jumps to the next elsif, if any, or to the else clause, (line 14).

13: If the visitor entered "broccoli" the elsif condition is true, and this statement is printed.

14: The elsif clause has its own closing curly bracket (shown here before the else). Don't forget it.

Figure 8.13 *If the condition in the initial if block is false, each elsif's condition is evaluated in order. If one turns out to be true, its statements are then executed and the rest of the if structure is ignored. If no conditions are true, the else block is executed.*

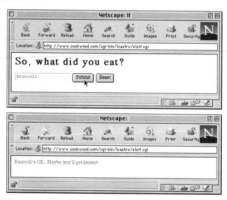

Figure 8.14 *If the visitor types "broccoli", the initial if condition is false, and the elsif is evaluated and found to be true. If they type "spinach" the result is the same as in Figure 8.10 on page 106. Anything else gets the result shown in Figure 8.12 on page 107.*

```
1   #!/usr/local/bin/perl
2
3   require "subparseform.lib";
4   &Parse_Form;
5
6   $food = $formdata{'food'};
7
8   print "Content-type: text/html\n\n";
9
10  unless ($food eq "spinach") {
11      print "No spinach, no dessert!";
12  }
```

10: With an unless block, the condition is evaluated and when it is *false*, the attached statements are executed. If it is true, the attached statements are skipped.

7: As long as the user does not enter a value of "spinach" for $food, this line is executed and the phrase is printed.

8: You must end an unless block with a closing curly bracket.

Figure 8.15 *The unless conditional works alone, without else or elsif.*

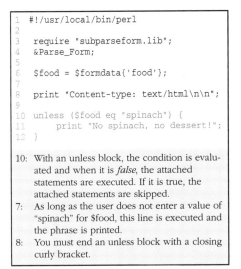

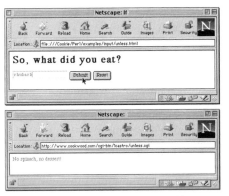

Figure 8.16 *Now the print statement will be executed only when the condition is false. In this case, the user entered "rhubarb"—which is certainly not "spinach"—so the phrase is indeed printed. Contrast this with Figure 8.12 on page 107.*

Using unless

Sometimes it's more important (and simpler) to know when a condition is false rather than when it's true. Although you could use an if statement and a convoluted, negative condition, Perl has another conjunction that makes this easy: *unless*. With unless, the attached statements are only executed if the condition is false.

To execute statements when the condition is false:

1. Type **unless**.

2. Type **(condition)**, where *condition* is the expression that should be evaluated as true or false to determine if the following statements should be executed.

3. Type **{** to begin the block.

4. Type the statements that should be executed if the condition in step 2 is *false*. Remember to type a semicolon at the end of each statement.

5. Type **}** to end the block.

✔ **Tip**

■ The unless block has neither an "else" nor an "elsunless". If you need to use multiple, independent conditions, you'll have to construct them using if, elsif, and else.

Repeating a block while a condition is true

So far we've used conditions to decide whether or not to execute one or more statements. Perl also has a number of constructs that let you execute one or more statements *as long as* a condition is true. Typically, one of the enclosed statements changes the values evaluated by the condition, although that's not required.

To repeat a block while a condition is true:

1. Type **while**.

2. Type **(condition)**, where *condition* is the expression that should be evaluated as true or false to determine if the following statements should be executed.

3. Type **{**.

4. Type the statements that should be executed *while* the condition in step 2 is true. Remember to type a semicolon at the end of each statement.

5. If desired, add a statement that modifies the value of the condition.

6. Type **}**.

✔ Tips

- While statements often have conditionals without comparison operators *(see page 104)*. The condition is true when it is defined, false when it is undefined or zero.

- You could also use **--$start** as the condition in this example. The first printed value of $start would be one less than the visitor entered (since the value is decremented before it is first printed), but you save a line of code.

```perl
1   #!/usr/local/bin/perl
2
3   require "subparseform.lib";
4   &Parse_Form;
5
6   $start = $formdata{'start'};
7
8   print "Content-type: text/html\n\n";
9   print "<P>Starting countdown...";
10
11  while ($start >= 0) {
12      print "$start... ";
13      --$start;
14  }
15  print "KABOOM!";
```

11: In English, this line says "while $start is greater or equal than 0 (that is, the condition is true), execute the following statements and then evaluate the condition again. If it is true, execute the statements and then evaluate the condition again. If it is false, skip the statements and exit the loop.

12: This statement prints the value of $start followed by three periods and a space.

13: The decrement operator subtracts one from the value of $start. This means that at some point (as long as you start with a non-negative number), the condition in line 11 will be false.

13: The while block ends with a curly bracket.

Figure 8.17 *Notice that the MIME content line is outside of the while statement. Once the Perl script is running, it just creates one page. All the results are output to the same page.*

Figure 8.18 *The statements within the while block (printing the value of $start and then decrementing it by one), are repeated as long as the condition remains true.*

Repeating a block while a condition is true

```
1   #!/usr/local/bin/perl
2
3   require "subparseform.lib";
4   &Parse_Form;
5
6   $start = $formdata{'start'};
7
8   print "Content-type: text/html\n\n";
9   print "<P>Starting countdown...";
10
11  until ($start <= 0) {
12      print "$start... ";
13      --$start;
14  }
15
16  print "KABOOM!";
```

11: In English, this line says, "until $start is less than or equal to 0 (that is, the condition evaluates true), execute the following statements and then evaluate the condition again. If it is still true, execute the statements and evaluate the condition again. Once it is zero or less, skip the following statements and exit the loop.

12: This statement prints the value of $start followed by three periods and a space.

13: The $start value is decremented by one. This makes it possible for the condition in line 11 to someday be true (as long as the visitor entered a starting value greater than 0).

14: The until block ends with a curly bracket.

Figure 8.19 *Aside from the type of condition used, the principal difference between this example and the one in Figure 8.17 is the condition itself.*

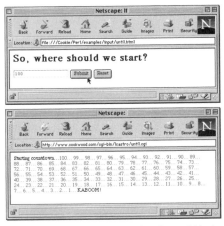

Figure 8.20 *The statements within the until block (printing the value of $start and then decrementing it by one), are repeated as long as the condition remains false.*

Repeating a block while a condition is false

You can also have Perl repeat a set of statements as long as a condition is false, or perhaps more precisely, *until* it is true.

To repeat a block while a condition is false:

1. Type **until**.

2. Type **(condition)**, where *condition* is the expression that should be evaluated as true or false to determine if the following statements should be executed.

3. Type **{**.

4. Type the statements that should be executed *until* the condition in step 2 is true. Remember to type a semicolon at the end of each statement.

5. If desired, add a statement that modifies the value of the condition.

6. Type **}**.

Executing the block at least once

With a while block, if the condition is false from the start, Perl will never get to the statements in the block. If you want Perl to execute the statements at least once, you can use a do block.

To execute the block once before testing the condition:

1. Type **do**.

2. Type **{**.

3. On the next line, type the statements that should be executed at least once, and more times if the condition in step 5 below is true.

4. Type **}**.

5. Type **while** or **until**, depending on whether you want to test if the condition is true or false, respectively.

6. Type **(condition)**, where *condition* is the expression that should be evaluated as true or false to determine if the statements in step 3 should be executed.

7. Type **;** (semicolon) to end the line.

```
1   #!/usr/local/bin/perl
2
3   require "subparseform.lib";
4   &Parse_Form;
5
6   $start = $formdata{'start'};
7
8   print "Content-type: text/html\n\n";
9   print "<P>Starting countdown...";
10
11  do {
12      print "$start... ";
13      --$start;
14  } while ($start > 0);
15
16  print "KABOOM!";
```

11: In English, this line says, "execute the following statements and then check to see if the value of $start is greater than 0 (that is, the condition is true in line 14). If it is, execute the statements again and check again, continuing in this manner until $start is not greater than 0.

12: This statement prints the value of $start followed by three periods and a space.

13: The $start value is decremented by one.

14: The do block ends with a curly bracket, and is followed by while or until and a condition, and then a semicolon.

Figure 8.21 *With a do block, the statements are always executed at least once, no matter how the condition evaluates.*

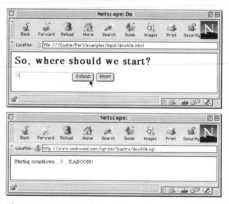

Figure 8.22 *Even if the visitor enters a number that is less than or equal to 0 (like 0 itself), the statements in the do block are executed at least once. Then the while conditional takes over and the loop is exited.*

```
1   #!/usr/local/bin/perl
2
3   require "subparseform.lib";
4   &Parse_Form;
5
6   $start = $formdata{'start'};
7
8   print "Content-type: text/html\n\n";
9   print "<P>Starting countdown...";
10
11  for ($i = $start; $i > 0; --$i) {
12      print "$i... ";
13  }
14
15  print "KABOOM!";
```

11: In English, this line says, "Set the value of $i (the typical counter variable) to the value of $start. Check to see if $i is greater than 0. If so, execute the statements in the block and then decrement $i and evaluate the condition again. If and when the condition returns false, skip the statements and exit the loop.

12: This statement prints the value of $start followed by three periods and a space.

14: The for block ends with a curly bracket.

Figure 8.23 *Notice that no statement is required within the block to modify the condition. The third argument of the for condition has already taken care of that.*

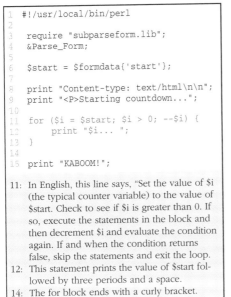

Figure 8.24 *The for block executes the statements for each value of $i until the condition is false.*

Repeating a block a given number of times

The for conditional makes it easy to repeat a block a given number of times by following the progress of a counter—a variable whose sole purpose in life is to count how many times the block has been executed. You first must set the initial state of the counter, then decide what condition should cause the statements to stop being executed, and then set the way the counter will be incremented.

To repeat a block a given number of times:

1. Type **for**.

2. Type **(**.

3. Type **$i=1**, where *i* is the name of the counter variable and *1* is its initial value.

4. Type **;**.

5. Type **condition**, where *condition* is the expression that should be evaluated as true or false to determine if the following statements should be executed. The condition generally takes into account the value of the counter variable.

6. Type **;**.

7. Type **$i++**, or any other expression that increments or decrements the value of the counter variable. (In the example, I use **--$i**.)

8. Type **)**.

9. Type **{**.

10. Type the statements that should be executed as long as the for block is repeated.

11. Type **}**.

Repeating a block for each item in an array

Perl has a special construction that lets you execute a block of statements for each element of an array. It's called foreach.

To repeat a block for each item in an array:

1. Type **foreach**.

2. Type **$element**, where *element* is the name of the variable to which each successive item from the array will be assigned.

3. Type **(@array)**, where *array* is the name of the array.

4. Type **{**.

5. Type the statements that should be evaluated for each item in the array specified in step 3.

6. Type **}**.

✔ Tips

■ Typically, you use the name of the array in step 3 for the scalar variable in step 2. But it's not required.

■ Note that if your statements perform some calculation on each item in the array, the array itself will be updated to reflect the new values *(see page 87)*.

```
1   #!/usr/local/bin/perl
2
3   require "subparseform.lib";
4   &Parse_Form;
5
6   print "Content-type: text/html\n\n";
7
8   $name = $formdata{'name'};
9   @prey = split (/,/, $formdata{'prey'});
10
11  foreach $creature (@prey) {
12    print "<P>$name likes to eat
         $creature.";
13  }
```

9: With menus and checkboxes, it's possible to mark more than one option. The split function separates the incoming data using the comma as a delimiter. Then the individual elements are saved in the @prey array.

11: In English, this lines says "take the first element in the @prey array, assign it to the $creature variable and use it in the following statements. Then take the next element and do the same thing. Repeat for each element in the array.

12: This statement prints the value of $start and the current value of $creature. It will be repeated each time the foreach statement gets the next element in the array.

13: The for block ends with a curly bracket.

Figure 8.25 *The foreach loop is essential for working with arrays.*

Figure 8.26 *Since the visitor chose Moles and Birds in the form, these are the elements of the @prey array.*

Repeating a block for each item in an array

```
11  while ($start > 0) {
12    if ($start - int $start) {
13        $start = int $start;
14    }
15      print "$start... ";
16      --$start;
17  }
18  print "KABOOM!";
```

10: Lines 1–10 are the same as in Figure 8.17.

12: The nested if conditional block is only evaluated if the outside while conditional is true. In this example, the condition subtracts the integer portion of $start from $start to see if the visitor entered a decimal.

13: If the visitor has entered a decimal portion of a number (that is, the condition is true), this line strips the decimal portion by subtracting the integer value of $start from $start itself.

14: The nested conditional still requires its own closing curly bracket.

15: The rest of the outside while conditional continues as before.

Figure 8.27 *A nested conditional block lets you test for additional characteristics or problems in your incoming data.*

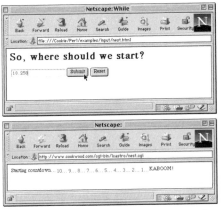

Figure 8.28 *If the visitor enters a decimal number in the form, the script strips the decimal portion so that it can do a normal countdown. (10.258, 9.258, 8.258... just doesn't have the same ring to it.)*

Nesting conditional statements

Often, the only way to test your incoming data completely is to use more than one kind of conditional. You can nest one inside the other without much extra trouble.

To nest conditional statements:

1. Create the first conditional statement, following the steps on pages 106–114.

2. Within the statement area of the first conditional statement, create the second conditional statement.

✔ Tips

■ Probably the trickiest part of nesting conditionals is making sure you have enough closing curly brackets. Make sure you have one closing curly bracket for each opening curly bracket. If you don't, the script won't run.

■ It's typical practice to combine closing brackets all on one line, where applicable. That's OK too, as long as you have the same number of opening brackets as you do closing brackets.

■ Perl has three extra functions that let you leave nested conditionals early, as it were: **next**, **last**, and **redo**. They're a bit beyond the scope of this book—although I wanted you to know that they exist.

Subroutines

Subroutine is one of those words that sounds so completely technical and uninviting. Just the same, subroutines are extremely useful time-saving devices that you'll want to use throughout your script.

A subroutine is like a mini-program inside your script that completes a certain, specific function that you might have to perform several times. Saving the process in a subroutine lets you perform the entire process as many times as needed without having to type it over each time.

Typical subroutines for CGI Perl scripts do common tasks such as parsing forms and printing out HTML headers and footers.

Creating a simple subroutine

A subroutine is just a block of statements that will be executed when the subroutine is called. For example, you could create a subroutine that prints out the content line that tells your visitor's browser to expect a Web page *(see page 34)*. Then, whenever you want to create Web output, you can call the subroutine to print that line.

To create a subroutine:

1. Type **sub**. The sub function defines the subroutine.

2. Type **name**, where *name* identifies the subroutine for later use.

3. Type {.

4. Now press Return, and on the next line, indented, type the statement(s) that should be executed when the subroutine is called. Remember to end each statement (on each line) with a semicolon.

5. Type }.

✔ Tips

■ Although it seems like you should have to place a subroutine *before* the line that uses it, you don't. It doesn't really matter where in your script you put a subroutine, and in fact the convention is to leave them until the very end, or to store them in a separate file altogether *(see page 124)*.

■ The convention is to use all lowercase letters (and an underscore if desired) for subroutine names.

■ Since the idea of a subroutine is to save you time, you might as well invent names that are short and sweet.

```
1  #!/usr/local/bin/perl
2
3
4  sub mime {
5      print "Content-type: text/
   html\n\n";
6  }
```

4: The sub function creates a subroutine called *mime* and gets ready to define it with the statements listed after the opening curly bracket.

5: This is a simple print statement. When the subroutine is invoked, the program will print "Content-type: text/html" followed by two line breaks, which is precisely the initial information that is required when sending a Web page to a browser.

6: The closing curly bracket completes the definition of the subroutine named *mime*.

Figure 9.1 *By putting a common task like printing out the MIME content line in a subroutine, you save typing time and minimize the possibility of typographical errors. As long as you've created the subroutine properly this time, it will always work correctly in the future. Whereas, if you type this line a zillion times, you're apt to make a mistake at some point.*

```
1   #!/usr/local/bin/perl
2
3   &mime;
4   print "<HTML><HEAD><TITLE>A new page</
    TITLE></HEAD><BODY>";
5   print "This page wholly created with CGI
    and Perl!";
6   print "</BODY></HTML>";
7
8   sub mime {
9       print "Content-type: text/
    html\n\n";
10  }
```

3: This line calls (executes) the subroutine. Therefore, the line "Content-type: text/html" will be sent to the browser followed by two newlines (line 9).

4: This is a simple print statement that prints the header portion of the Web page.

5: Here is another simple print statement that prints out the content of the Web page, in this case a fairly inane sentence: "This page wholly created with CGI and Perl".

6: The final print statement outputs the end of the HTML page code.

Figure 9.2 *Typically a subroutine goes at the end of the script, but it doesn't really matter where it is.*

Figure 9.3 *By using a subroutine to create the MIME content line, you can be sure that you haven't made any typographical errors.*

Using a simple subroutine

Some subroutines are relatively independent and require no additional information before being processed. For example, the subroutine created in Figure 9.1 on page 118 doesn't require any input (officially called *arguments*). These subroutines can still use variables defined within the rest of the script, but they don't actually work on those variables or change their values.

To use a simple subroutine (with no arguments):

1. Type **&name**, where *name* is the label for the subroutine that you defined in step 2 on page 118.

2. Type **;** to complete the line.

✔ **Tip**

■ Sometimes you'll see programmers leave out the ampersand (&) and use empty parentheses when calling a simple subroutine, like so: **name()**. That's fine too—as long as you're using Perl 5 or later *(see page 18)*.

Using a simple subroutine

Creating a subroutine that takes input

Sometimes you'll want to apply the subroutine to some piece of data. For example, imagine that you want to create a subroutine that prints out the first part of an HTML page, but you want to be able to tell it what the title of the page should be. You can pass the title to the subroutine, have the subroutine insert the title, and then print it out with the rest of the HTML page. (Any data passed to the subroutine is called an *argument*.)

Subroutines transfer all the data that is passed to them into the special underscore array, written as @_. You can then use each individual element of this array in your subroutine and perform operations on them as desired.

Remember that the elements of the @_ array are $_[0], $_[1], and so on. For more information on accessing individual elements of an array consult *Getting a particular item from an array* on page 84.

To create a subroutine that takes input:

1. Create the subroutine as described on page 118.

2. In the statements, use $_[0] to refer to the first argument passed to the subroutine, $_[1] to refer to the second argument passed to the subroutine, and so on.

✔ Tip

■ If the subroutine is only going to have one argument, you can also refer to it with the entire array: @_ instead of $_[0]. The result is the same.

```
1   #!/usr/local/bin/perl
2
3   &mime;
4   &header("This is the page title");
5
6   print "This is more of that page wholly
        created by CGI and Perl!";
7
8   &footer;
9
10  sub header {
11      print "<HTML><HEAD><TITLE>";
12      print "$_[0]";
13      print "</TITLE></HEAD><BODY>"
14  }
15
16  sub footer {
17      print "</BODY></HTML>";
18  }
19
20  sub mime {
21      print "Content-type: text/
        html\n\n";
22  }
```

10: The sub function names the subroutine. This one is called "header".
11: This line prints the opening HTML tags.
12: The variable $_[0] will get its value from the argument passed to the subroutine. Therefore, whatever argument is used will be printed here.
13: This line prints the closing TITLE tag, the closing HEAD tag and then the opening BODY tag—basically everything you need to complete the header.

Figure 9.4 *Using a subroutine to generate all the repetitive HTML code can save you lots of time.*

```
1   #!/usr/local/bin/perl
2
3   &mime;
4   &header("This is the page title");
5
6   print "This is more of that page wholly
        created by CGI and Perl!";
7
8   &footer;
9
10  sub header {
11      print "<HTML><HEAD><TITLE>";
12      print "$_[0]";
13      print "</TITLE></HEAD><BODY>"
14  }
15
16  sub footer {
17      print "</BODY></HTML>";
18  }
19
20  sub mime {
21      print "Content-type: text/
        html\n\n";
22  }
```

3:   This is the same subroutine that we saw in
     Figure 9.2.
4:   This line calls the header subroutine and
     passes it the desired title for the generated
     page ("This is the page title").
10: The header subroutine is defined on lines
     10–14. For more details, see Figure 9.4.
12: The variable $_[0] gets its value from the
     argument passed to the subroutine (in line 4).
     Therefore, this line prints the phrase "This is
     the page title".

Figure 9.5 *If the subroutine has only one argument
as in this example, you access it with $_[0].*

Figure 9.6 *The title in the title bar of the generated
page comes from the argument of the header
subroutine.*

Calling a subroutine that takes input

Once you have set up a subroutine to process
the arguments *(see page 120)*, you're ready to
pass the actual data to the subroutine.

To call a subroutine that takes input:

1. Type **&name**, where *name* identifies the
   subroutine.

2. Type **(**.

3. Type **argument**, where *argument* is the
   array or scalar that you want to process
   with the subroutine.

4. Repeat step 3 for each argument you
   want to process, separating each one
   with a comma.

5. Type **)**.

6. Type **;** to complete the sentence.

✔ Tips

■ Again, *argument* is just another word for
  the data that some function (like a subroutine) processes.

■ If you use an array in step 3, its individual
  elements become the arguments.

Calling a subroutine that takes input

Using a subroutine's return value

When you call a subroutine, it generally executes all of the statements that it contains. If you're just printing an HTML header or some other static code, executing a series of statements may be all you're interested in. Like other functions, however, a subroutine not only completes one or more operations, it also has an intrinsic final value, called a *return value*, which you can store for later use *(see page 27)*. The default return value is the value of the last expression evaluated in the block.

To store a subroutine's return value:

1. Type **$scalar** or **@array**, depending on whether the subroutine will have one or more return values.

2. Type **=**.

3. Type **&subroutine** or **&subroutine (argument)** to call the subroutine whose return values you want to save.

✔ Tips

■ You can also use a subroutine's value directly in an expression, as if it were a scalar or array. For example, you could use **$scalar = &subroutine + 5;**.

■ Make sure you know what the return value of the last expression in your subroutine is. For example, if the last statement in your subroutine block is a print statement, since the return value of a print statement is 1, the value of the subroutine will also be 1.

■ For information on setting the return value manually, see page 123.

```
1   #!/usr/local/bin/perl
2
3   &mime;
4   &header("This is the page title");
5
6   print "<P>This is more of that page
       wholly created by CGI and Perl!";
7   $which = &which;
8   print "<P>You\'rebrowsingthispagewith
       $which";
9
10  &footer;
11
12  sub which {
13      $browser = $ENV{'HTTP_USER_AGENT'};
14      if ($browser =~ /MSIE/) {
15          $browser = "Explorer";
16      } elsif ($browser =~/Mozilla/) {
17          $browser = "Netscape";
18      } else {
19          $browser = "something besides
             Netscape and Explorer";
20      }
21  }
```

7: The return value of the which subroutine is stored in the $which variable.

8: This line prints the sentence shown followed by the value of the which variable.

12: The which subroutine uses the HTTP_USER _AGENT environment variable *(see page 62)* to see which browser the visitor is using. Depending on which condition evaluates as true, the last expression evaluated will give the name of the browser being used. That last expression (for example, $browser = "Netscape") becomes the return value for the subroutine. Thus, in line 7, the $which variable gets the name of the browser used.

22: The other subroutines are not shown, but they're still there!

Figure 9.7 *You can effectively use the return value of a subroutine in other expressions.*

Figure 9.8 *The return value of the subroutine is printed, along with the descriptive statement.*

Using a subroutine's return value

```
1   #!/usr/local/bin/perl
2
3   &mime;
4   &header("This is the page title");
5   print "<P>This is more of that page
        wholly created by CGI and Perl!";
6
7   $capped_which = &cap(&which);
8
9   print "<P>You\'rebrowsingthispagewith
        $capped_which";
10  &footer;
11
12  sub cap {
13      $captext = $_[0];
14      $captext =~ tr/a-z/A-Z/;
15      return $captext;
16  }
```

7: The &cap subroutine is performed on the return value of the &which subroutine. The return value of the cap subroutine is then saved in the $capped_which variable.

9: The result is printed.

13: The argument of the &cap subroutine in line 8 (namely the return value of the &which subroutine) is temporarily stored in $captext.

14: The value of $captext is capitalized and then stored back in $captext.

15: The new value of $captext is manually set as the return value for this subroutine. Notice that the return value for line 14 is not the capitalized text (that we want), but rather the number of characters substituted by the tr operator. For more on tr, see the Web site.

17: The other subroutines are not shown, but they're still there!

Figure 9.9 *If the last expression evaluated has a return value different from the one you need, you'll have to set the return value manually.*

Figure 9.10 *The return value from the which subroutine is capitalized by the cap subroutine.*

Figure 9.11 *If you don't manually set the return value for the cap subroutine, you'll get the return value of the tr operator, which returns the number of characters that it changed.*

Setting the return value manually

There are many instances in which the last expression evaluated is not the value you're most interested in. Sometimes, for example, you just want to know whether or not the subroutine has executed successfully, or perhaps, which one of its conditional outcomes it has arrived at. You can prescribe a return value manually for the subroutine with the return function.

To set a subroutine's return value manually:

1. Create the subroutine as described on page 118 or page 120.

2. After the last statement in the subroutine, and on its own line, type **return**.

3. Then type **value**, where *value* is the desired return value for the subroutine.

4. Type **;** to end the sentence.

✔ Tips

■   The value you use in step 3 can be a scalar or array variable that you've created or calculated in the subroutine, or it can be a constant.

■   If you have a series of conditional blocks, you may need to create a return statement for each branch of the condition.

■   The return function not only assigns the return value for the subroutine, it also causes the subroutine to exit, skipping all statements that follow.

■   For more details on the difference between the result of a function and its return value, consult *Result vs. Return value* on page 27.

Setting the return value manually

Storing subroutines in a separate file

There are some subroutines that you will want to call again and again from almost every CGI script that you write. For example, you'll almost always need some kind of form-parsing subroutine. Instead of tacking such a subroutine onto the end of every script, you can save it in its own file—often called a *library*—and then call it from each script in which it's necessary.

To store subroutines in a separate file:

1. Create a separate text file as described on page 30. You may omit the shebang line described on page 32.

2. Create the subroutine as described on page 118 or page 120.

3. On the very last line of the file, type **1;**. When you call the subroutine, this value will return true, and Perl will know that the external file was accessed successfully.

4. Save the file as usual (in text-only format).

✔ Tips

■ Files that contain subroutines (but no main script) often carry the extension .lib (for *library*), though it is not essential.

■ You can create one external file that contains several subroutines as shown in this example.

■ External files with subroutines do not need to be executed and therefore need neither the shebang line *(see page 32)* nor extra permissions *(see page 39)*.

```
1   sub cap {
2      $captext = $_[0];
3      $captext =~ tr/a-z/A-Z/;
4      return $captext;
5   }
6
7   sub which {
8      $browser = $ENV{'HTTP_USER_AGENT'};
9      if ($browser =~ /MSIE/) {
10        $browser = "Explorer";
11     } elsif ($browser =~/Mozilla/) {
12        $browser = "Netscape";
13     } else {
14        $browser = "something besides
                      Netscape and Explorer";
15     }
16  }
17
18  sub header {
19    print "<HTML><HEAD><TITLE>";
20    print "$_[0]";
21    print "</TITLE></HEAD><BODY>"
22    }
23
24  sub footer {
25    print "</BODY></HTML>";
26  }
27
28  sub mime {
29    print "Content-type: text/html\n\n";
30  }
31
32  1;
```

3:   Lines 1–30 contain the subroutines we've been using in this chapter. Notice that no shebang line *(see page 32)* is needed.

32: This line ensures that when the external file is called with the require function *(see page 125)*, the function will return true (1), and Perl will know that the external file has been accessed successfully.

Figure 9.12 *Don't forget to add the last line. It looks unimportant, but without it, Perl won't know the file was accessed successfully and won't let you call any of the subroutines that it contains.*

Figure 9.13 *Save the file as text-only. Often, external files with subroutines are given the .lib extension, but it's not required.*

```
1   #!/usr/local/bin/perl;
2
3   require 'subroutines.lib';
4
5   &mime;
6   &header("This is the page title");
7
8   print "<P>This is more of that page
       wholly created by CGI and Perl!";
9   $capped_which = &cap(&which);
10
11  print "<P>You\'re browsing this page with
       $capped_which";
12
13  &footer;
```

3:   Lines 3 makes the subroutine library file and
     the subroutines it contains accessible to this
     script.

5:   Now when we call the &mime subroutine, for
     example, Perl will look for it in this script,
     and if it doesn't find it, it will check the
     subroutines.lib file (where it *will* find it).
     Then, the subroutine is executed as usual.

Figure 9.14 *This script is virtually identical to the one shown in Figure 9.9 on page 123. However, it's neater, and the subroutines can also be accessed from other scripts.*

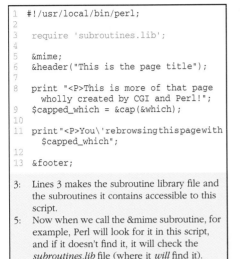

Figure 9.15 *The location of the subroutines is completely invisible to the visitor. This result is exactly the same as when the subroutines were in the main script itself (cf. Figure 9.10 on page 123).*

Calling subroutines from an external file

Saving subroutines in an external file makes it easy to use them in your other Perl scripts without having to type them out each time. From the Perl script, you have to first make the file that contains the subroutine (often called a *library*) available to the script and then you call the subroutine as usual.

To call subroutines from an external file:

1. In the main script, type **require 'file-name.lib'** where *filename.lib* is the name of the external file that contains the desired subroutine.

2. Type **;** to complete the line.

3. Type **&subroutine** or **&subroutine (arguments)** as usual to call the subroutine. For more details, consult *Using a simple subroutine* on page 119 or *Calling a subroutine that takes input* on page 121, respectively.

✔ Tips

■ You can also use a scalar variable or an expression as the argument for the require function.

■ Once the main script accesses the external file with the require function, the subroutines in the external file remain available for the duration of the main script. In other words, you can call the subroutines in the external file as many times as you need.

Calling subroutines from an external file

Working with Hashes

Figure 10.1 *The visitor enters data in the form.*

```
1  #!/usr/local/bin/perl
2
3  require "subparseform.lib";
4  &Parse_Form;
5  print "Content-type: text/html\n\n";
6
7  foreach $key (keys %formdata) {
8    print "<P>You entered
       <B>$formdata{$key}</B> in the
       <B>$key</B> field."
9  }
```

3:   The &Parse_Form subroutine creates a hash out of each field name and input.

7:   Lines 7–9 print out the field name (key) and visitor input ($formdata{key}—which represents the value) from the form.

Figure 10.2 *The script converts the visitor input into a hash that you can process or print.*

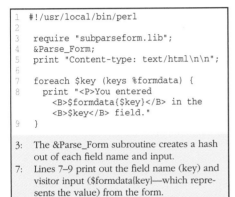

1st pair: key is "first", value is "Llumi"

%formdata = ("first", "Llumi",

"age", 4, "prey", "mole"); 3rd pair: key is "prey", value is "mole"

2nd pair: key is "age", value is 4

Figure 10.3 *This is just a representation of* assigning *the values to the hash, something that a form-parsing subroutine takes care of.*

The visitor entered mole in the prey field.

The visitor entered Llumi in the first field.

The visitor entered 4 in the age field.

Figure 10.4 *The data gathered from the form is printed out by the script.*

A *hash* is little more than a special kind of array that contains pairs of associated elements—the *key* and the *value*. In fact, hashes are often called *associative arrays*. While the order of the elements within a pair is crucial (the key, *then* the value), the order of the pairs themselves is not. Unlike array elements, values in a hash are identified by a key (and vice versa), not by an index number. Hash variables begin with a percent sign (%)—perhaps the two circles on either side of the slash suggest a pair of linked values.

Hashes are particularly important in Perl CGI scripts because most form-parsing subroutines store data gathered from a Web form in a hash. The key in each pair is generally the field name (from the NAME attribute in the corresponding form tag in the HTML file) while the value in the pair corresponds to the data the visitor types in (or to the VALUE attribute). You can then use the field names (keys) to identify, access, and process the corresponding input data (values).

Hashes are also important in Perl CGI scripts for storing environment variables. For details, see Chapter 4, *Environment Variables*.

You've already learned how to manually enter a list of paired items into a hash *(see page 71)*. In this chapter you'll learn how to create hashes in other ways, and to manipulate them once they're set up.

Unfortunately, there's simply not enough room to show both the HTML and all the Perl scripts involved. You can find all the files used at the Web site *(see page 22)*.

Getting a value by using a key

Hashes are made up of pairs of elements, each with the key first and the value second. You can use the key to access the corresponding value and then use that value in a larger expression.

To get a value by using a key:

1. Type **$hash**, where *hash* is the name of the hash that contains the desired item. (Yes, that's a dollar sign—not a percent sign—since you're accessing *one* piece of data from the hash.)

2. Type **{key}**, where *key* is the label that corresponds to the value you want to get.

✔ Tips

- Yes, those are curly brackets and not parentheses. It makes a difference.

- If you're using a constant string for the key—for example, a field name— you should enclose it in single quotation marks: **$formdata{'field_name'}**.

- Although hashes begin with a percent sign (%), when you want to access an individual item, you preface the hash name with a dollar sign ($). Remember: individual pieces of data are scalars, even if they come from hashes.

- Getting a value from a hash doesn't affect the hash. The value (and the key) remain parts of the hash.

- To assign a value from a hash to a scalar variable, use **$scalar = $hash{key};**.

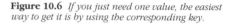

```
code.html
First name:
<INPUT TYPE="text" NAME="first">
```

Figure 10.5 *The value of the NAME attribute in the form element in the HTML code will be the key that you use to access the data entered in that field by the visitor.*

```
1   #!/usr/local/bin/perl
2
3   require "subparseform.lib";
4   &Parse_Form;
5
6   $name = $formdata{'first'};
7
8   print "Content-type: text/html\n\n";
9   print "You entered a first name of
        <B>$name</B>";
```

4: The Parse_Form subroutine *(see page 66)* stores the field names and visitor input in a hash.

6: The value that corresponds to the key named 'first' is stored in the scalar variable $name.

9: The $name variable is printed (along with some explanatory filler).

Figure 10.6 *If you just need one value, the easiest way to get it is by using the corresponding key.*

Figure 10.7 *What we're interested in is the data the visitor inputs into the First name field (officially called 'first'). The visitor types* Llumi.

Figure 10.8 *The script outputs the corresponding value. (Llumi is my mischievous black cat.)*

Getting a value by using a key

```
========= code.html =========
First name:<INPUT TYPE="text" NAME="first">
Last name:<INPUT TYPE="text" NAME="last">
```

Figure 10.9 *Here is an excerpt of the HTML code displaying the NAME attribute for each field. The NAME attribute becomes the* key *in the hash.*

```
1   #!/usr/local/bin/perl
2
3   require "subparseform.lib";
4   &Parse_Form;
5
6   @name = @formdata{'first', 'last'};
7
8   print "Content-type: text/html\n\n";
9   print "You entered a full name of
        <B>@name</B>";
10
```

4: The Parse_Form subroutine *(see page 66)* stores the field names and visitor input in a hash.
6: The values that corresponds to the keys named 'first' and 'last' are stored in the @name array.
9: The elements in the @name array are printed with some explanatory information.

Figure 10.10 *A slice lets you get several values (in this case, first and last names) at once from a hash.*

Figure 10.11 *Now we're interested in the data that the visitor inputs into both the First and Last name fields (officially called 'first' and 'last', respectively). The visitor types* Woody *and* Monster.

Figure 10.12 *When you print an array in quotation marks, each of its elements is printed, separated by a space.*

Getting several values using keys

If you need more than one value and you already know the corresponding keys, you can use the keys to access the values. This is called taking a *slice* of the hash.

To get several values using keys:

1. Type **@hash**, where *hash* is the name of the hash that contains the desired items. (You use @ because the result will be several values, not just one.)

2. Type **{key1, key2}**, where *key1* and *key2* (and any others) are the keys that correspond to the desired values from the hash.

    Or type **{@array}**, where *@array* is an array that contains the keys that correspond to the desired values from the hash.

✔ Tips

■ Preface the hash name with @—and not % or $—since you're accessing *several* pieces of data.

■ To get *all* the values from a hash, consult *Getting all of a hash's values* on page 130.

■ Getting values from a hash does not alter the hash itself.

■ If desired, you can use a scalar variable to call the key names in step 2.

■ If you use scalar constants (strings) to specify the keys, you must delimit them with single quotation marks.

■ You can store the acquired values in another array with **@values_array = @hash{key1, key2};**.

Getting all of a hash's values

Sometimes it's useful to print or process all of the values of a hash. Perl has a special function, **values**, that makes this easy.

To get all of a hash's values:

1. Type **values**.

2. Type **(%hash)**, where hash is the name of the hash that contains the desired values.

✔ Tips

■ You can create an array with each of the values in a hash using **@array = values(%hash);**.

■ You could (and most programmers would) combine lines 6 and 11 in the example to read **foreach $value (values(%formdata))** {. I've separated out the lines so you can see more clearly what the **values** function does.

```
1   #!/usr/local/bin/perl
2
3   require "subparseform.lib";
4   &Parse_Form;
5
6   @values = values(%formdata);
7
8   print "Content-type: text/html\n\n";
9   print "<H2>Values:</H2><UL>";
10
11  foreach $value (@values) {
12    print "<LI>$value";
13  }
14  print "</UL>";
```

6:   The values function gets all of the values from the %formdata hash (created by the Parse_Form subroutine). These values are stored in the @values array.

9:   This simple print statement formats and prints a header for the list of values.

11: A simple foreach loop prints each value in the @values array.

Figure 10.13 *You'll usually do more interesting things with the values than simply print them out. Once you have them, you can use them to access the keys, for example.*

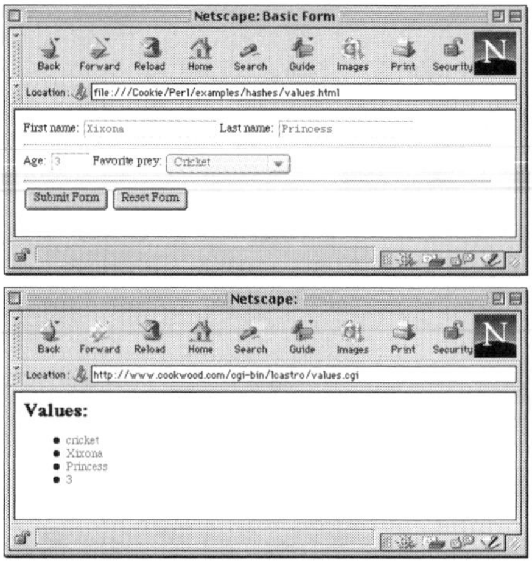

Figure 10.14 *Each of the values the visitor entered in the form is printed out in list form in the browser.*

```
                code.html
First name:<INPUT TYPE="text" NAME="first">

Last name:<INPUT TYPE="text" NAME="last">

<HR>Age:<INPUT TYPE="text" NAME="age" SIZE=5>
Favorite prey:
<SELECT NAME="prey">
<OPTION VALUE="mouse">Mouse
<OPTION VALUE="mole">Mole
<OPTION VALUE="bird">Bird
<OPTION VALUE="cricket">Cricket
<OPTION VALUE="Liz's hands">Liz's hands
</SELECT>
```

Figure 10.15 *In the HTML code for the form, the NAME attribute for each field determines the key in the %formdata hash.*

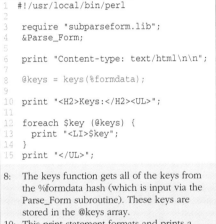

```
1   #!/usr/local/bin/perl
2
3   require "subparseform.lib";
4   &Parse_Form;
5
6   print "Content-type: text/html\n\n";
7
8   @keys = keys(%formdata);
9
10  print "<H2>Keys:</H2><UL>";
11
12  foreach $key (@keys) {
13    print "<LI>$key";
14  }
15  print "</UL>";
```

8:   The keys function gets all of the keys from the %formdata hash (which is input via the Parse_Form subroutine). These keys are stored in the @keys array.

10: This print statement formats and prints a header for the list of keys.

12: A foreach loop prints each key in the @keys array *(see page 114)*.

Figure 10.16 *You'll usually do more interesting things with the keys than simply print them out. See, for example, page 132.*

Figure 10.17 *Each of the keys (the names of the fields in the form) is printed out in list form in the browser.*

Getting all of a hash's keys

Sometimes it's useful to print or process all of the keys of a hash. Perl has a special function (keys) that makes this easy.

To get all of a hash's keys:

1. Type **keys**.

2. Type **(%hash)**, where hash is the name of the hash that contains the desired keys.

✔ Tips

■ You can create an array with each of the keys in a hash using **@array = keys(%hash);**.

■ The **keys** function is typically used in a foreach loop to go through each key-value pair in a hash. For more details, see page 133.

■ Once you get the array of keys by using the **keys** function, you can use the **sort** function on that array to sort the values in the hash.

■ You could (and most programmers would) combine lines 6 and 11 in the example to read **foreach $key (keys(%formdata)) {**. I've separated out the lines so you can see more clearly what the **keys** function does.

Getting each key and value in a hash

There are two principal ways to access a hash's keys and values at the same time.

Perl's each function goes through each key and value in a hash sequentially. Each time you use the each function, it returns the next pair of items.

To get the first key and value:

Type **each (%hash)**, where *hash* is the name of the hash that contains the desired keys and values.

To get the *next* key and value:

Use **each (%hash)** again later in your script.

✔ **Tip**

- Each time you use **each (%hash)**, you get the next key-value pair in the hash. You can use a loop statement (like while or foreach) to go through each pair in the hash without having to type the each function successive times. Each time you use the each function is executed, the *next* key-value pair is accessed.

```
1   #!/usr/local/bin/perl
2
3   require "subparseform.lib";
4   &Parse_Form;
5
6   print "Content-type: text/html\n\n";
7
8   while (($key, $value) =
        each (%formdata)) {
9       print "<P>The key is $key and the value
          is $value";
10  }
```

8: The condition assigns the first key-value pair from %formdata to the scalar variables $key and $value. If the assignment is successful, the condition evaluates as true and the statements in the while block are executed. Using each means that the next time the condition is evaluated, the *subsequent* key-value pair will be assigned to the scalar variables. This will continue until there are no more pairs, at which time the condition evaluates as false, and the block is exited.

9: When the condition is true, the $key and $value are printed.

Figure 10.18 *The each function gets each key-value pair in the hash, one after the next.*

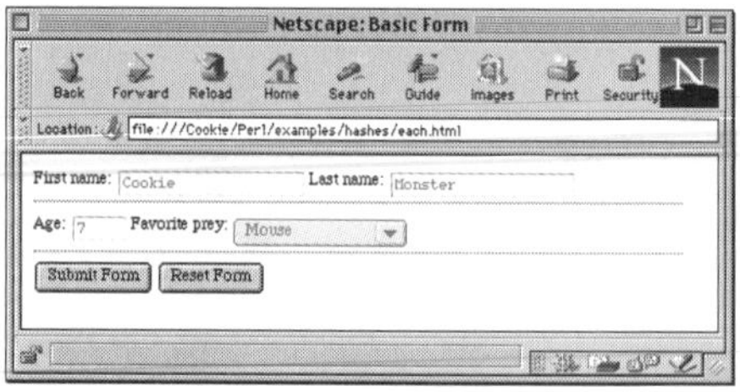

Figure 10.19 *The visitor enters the data.*

Figure 10.20 *Combining the while block with the each function is an easy and quick way to go through and operate on (or print out, as shown here), each key-value pair in a hash.*

```
1   #!/usr/local/bin/perl
2
3   require "subparseform.lib";
4   &Parse_Form;
5
6   print "Content-type: text/html\n\n";
7
8   print "<TABLE><TR><TH>Keys:
      <TH>Values:";
9
10  foreach $key (keys %formdata) {
11    print "<TR><TD>$key
        <TD>$formdata{$key}";
12  }
13  print "</TABLE>";
```

8: This lines adds some pretty HTML code to set up the table and the header cells.

10: Notice that the "array" for the foreach loop is actually an expression: the array created when you get the keys from %formdata.

11: The print statement includes <TD> tags for placing the keys and values in cells. The variable $key will contain the key, and then it is also used in $formdata{$key} to access the value *(see page 128)*.

13: Without the closing </TABLE> tag, the table won't appear.

Figure 10.21 *Again, you may want to do something more interesting than print out the keys and values in a table. You can use whatever statements you like in the foreach loop.*

Figure 10.22 *The foreach loop takes the script through each of the key-value pairs in the hash, printing out each one.*

You can also use the keys function *(see page 131)* combined with a foreach loop *(see page 114)* to go through each key-value pair in a hash.

To use the keys function to get key-value pairs:

1. Type **foreach**.

2. Type **$key**, where *key* is the name of the scalar that will hold each individual key as you go through the loop. (It doesn't have to be called "key".)

3. Type **(keys %hash)**, where *hash* is the name of the hash that contains the desired key-value pairs. If you use the Parse_Form subroutine in this book, you'll want to use **(keys %formdata)** here. The word "keys" is the name of the function and must be typed as is.

4. Type **{**.

5. Type the statements that should be executed each time the script gets the next key-value pair from the hash. You can use **$hash{$key}** to access each value from the hash.

6. Type **}**.

✔ Tips

■ For more information on foreach loops, consult *Repeating a block for each item in an array* on page 114.

■ For more information on the keys function, consult *Getting all of a hash's keys* on page 131.

Getting each key and value in a hash

Removing key-value pairs

Sometimes you'll want to get rid of a key-value pair altogether—perhaps because the data is obsolete as in the case of a hash with user names and passwords.

To remove a key-value pair:

1. Type **delete**.

2. Type **$hash**, where *hash* is the name of the hash that contains the key-value pair that you want to eliminate.

3. Type **{key}**, where *key* is the key that identifies the value (and thus the entire pair) that you want to eliminate.

4. Type **;** to finish the line. The referenced key-value pair is permanently removed from the hash.

✔ Tips

- If the key is a string, you should enclose it in single quotes: **delete $formdata{'first'};**

- You can assign the result of the **delete** function to a scalar variable: **$value = delete $hash{key}**. The result is the value that corresponds to the key used (in the example in Figure 10.24, $value would be set to "Princess").

```
1  #!/usr/local/bin/perl
2
3  require "subparseform.lib";
4  &Parse_Form;
5
6  print "Content-type: text/html\n\n";
7  print "<TABLE><TR><TH>Keys:
      <TH>Values:";
8
9  delete $formdata{'last'};
10
11 foreach $key (keys %formdata) {
12   print "<TR><TD>$key
        <TD>$formdata{$key}";
13 }
14 print "</TABLE>";
```

9: The delete function removes the key-value pair identified by the key 'last' from the hash.

Figure 10.23 *Again, you may want to do something more interesting than print out the keys and values in a table. You can use whatever statements you like in the foreach loop.*

Figure 10.24 *The deleted key-pair value no longer appears in the list. Notice that both the key and the value are removed.*

```
1    #!/usr/local/bin/perl
2
3    require "subparseform.lib";
4    &Parse_Form;
5    print "Content-type: text/html\n\n";
6
7    if (exists $formdata{'sales'}) {
8      print "You came to this script from the
         Sales page";
9    }
10   elsif (exists $formdata{'first'}) {
11     print "You came to this script from the
         general info page";
12   }
13   else {
14     print "I don't know how you accessed
         this script";
15   }
```

7:   The condition tests to see if there is a key
     equal to *sales*. In other words, did the form
     that accessed this script have a field with the
     NAME attribute equal to *sales*? If so, line 8 is
     executed.

10: This condition tests to see if there is a key
     equal to *first*. If so, the statements in this elsif
     statement (line 11) is executed.

13: If neither of the first two conditions are true,
     the else block gives a generic response.

Figure 10.25 *This example simply prints a message depending on the result of the exists function. A more practical use would be to direct the script to a particular subroutine (see page 117).*

Figure 10.26 *The form from which we accessed the script contains the 'first' but not the 'sales' field. Thus, only line 11 is output.*

Checking to see if a key exists

If you don't want to list all the keys in a hash to see if the one you're after appears, you can simply check to see if your key is part of the hash.

To check to see if a key is part of the hash:

1. Type **exists**.

2. Type **$hash**, where *hash* is the name of the hash that may or may not contain the key in question.

3. Type **{key}**, where *key* is the key that you are looking for in the hash.

✔ Tips

- If the key does exist in the hash, the **exists** function returns a value of 1 (true). If the key does not exist, the value returned is 0 (false). You can use the **exists** function effectively in if statements *(see page 106)*.

- The **exists** function returns true as long as the key exists in the hash—even if the corresponding value is undefined or empty.

Checking to see if a key exists

Analyzing Data

Once you receive a chunk of incoming information from a Web visitor, you'll want to see what it contains. Perl has three operators that let you look inside incoming data and then act accordingly: match, substitute, and split.

The **match** operator just checks to see if a variable *contains* the specified data *(see page 138)*. Then you can set up a conditional to do one thing if the data's there, and another if it's not.

The **substitute** operator not only looks to see if a variable contains the specified data but, once it finds such data, lets you change it into something else *(see page 139)*.

The **split** function lets you search for the delimiter in a string of values in order to divide that string into its individual components *(see page 141)*. This is useful when analyzing data from checkboxes and menus.

What can you look for? Perl is a powerful language for analyzing Web data because you can not only look for straightforward values such as "Smith" and "Hartford, CT" but also generalized patterns that will match a wider range of possibilities. For example, **/^\d{5}-\d{4}$/** would match *any* nine-digit zip code, as long as it was made up of five digits, a dash, and four more digits.

If that string of funny looking characters gives you pause, relax. This chapter not only explains how to set up the three operators, but also how to construct (and understand) the patterns at their core.

Finding something

Finding something with Perl's matching operator is a lot like using the Find command in your word processor: you want to know if the given text is present but you don't plan to change that text.

To find something:

1. Type **$scalar** where *scalar* is the variable that contains the string that you want to search.

2. Type **=~ m/**.

3. Type the pattern that describes what you're looking for *(see pages 142–158)*.

4. Type **/**.

5. If desired, type **i** to *i*gnore whether the letters are upper or lowercase during the search.

✔ Tips

- Note that the match returns true as long as the variable *contains* the pattern. Generally, it doesn't matter if it also contains non-matching data.

- If your pattern itself contains a lot of forward slashes, you can use some other delimiter so as not to confuse the slashes in your pattern with the slashes in the matching operator. For example, you could use **m#pattern#**.

- As long as you use slashes to delimit the pattern, you can omit the *m*. So, **$scalar =~ /pattern/** is the same as **$scalar =~ m/pattern/**.

```
1   #!/usr/local/bin/perl
2
3   print "Content-type: text/html\n\n";
4
5   $browser = $ENV{'HTTP_USER_AGENT'};
6
7   if ($browser =~ m/MSIE/) {
8     print "You're using IE";
9   } elsif ($browser =~ m/Mozilla/) {
10    print "You're using Netscape";
11  } else {
12    print "You're using something else";
13  }
```

5: The visitor's browser information is automatically saved in the HTTP_USER_AGENT environment variable *(see page 62)*.

7: This line asks if the scalar variable $browser contains the sequence of letters MSIE (which happens to be the identifying code for Explorer).

9: If the first condition fails (that is, the visitor isn't using Internet Explorer), the second condition sees if $browser contains *Mozilla* (Netscape's code name). If it does, we know the visitor is using Netscape.

Figure 11.1 *In this example, I've used the simplest of search patterns: words. Don't get hung up on the search patterns yet, focus on the syntax of the match operator. We'll get to constructing search patterns on page 142.*

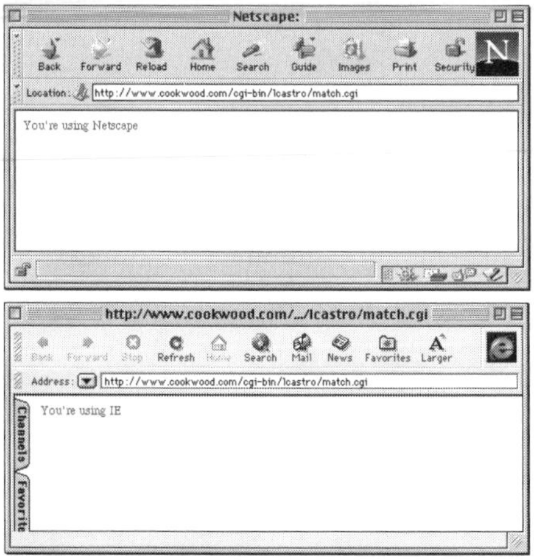

Figure 11.2 *You'll probably want to do more with the information about your visitor's browser than just parrot it back to them.*

```
1   #!/usr/local/bin/perl
2
3   require "subparseform.lib";
4   &Parse_Form;
5   print "Content-type: text/html\n\n";
6
7   $comments = $formdata{'comments'};
8
9   if ($comments =~ /<IMG[^>]*>/) {
10    print "<P>Sorry, images are not
          permitted. Please limit your
          comments to text.";
11    $comments =~ s/<IMG[^>]*>//g;
12  }
13  print "<P>Your text comments were
        <P><B>$comments" if $comments;
```

9: The condition uses the match operator to see if the submitted comments ($comments) contains an IMG tag. If it does find one, it prints an error message.

11: In this line, we use the substitute operator to look to see if $comments contains an IMG tag. If it finds one, it replaces it with nothing (the contents of the second two slashes). The final *g* ensures that all substitutions (and not just the first one) are made.

Figure 11.3 *Don't try to analyze that ugly looking search pattern in line 9 yet. We'll start with those on page 142. For now, I want you to learn how to set up the substitution operator.*

Figure 11.4 *Images can sometimes either bog down or offend. This little script gets rid of all images that your visitor might try to enclose.*

Finding and replacing

As in a word processor, you can either just find, or you can find and replace. That is, you can *change* the matched strings that you find.

To find and replace:

1. Type **$scalar** where *scalar* is the name of the variable that contains the original text and that will be used to store the changed text.

2. Type **=~ s/**.

3. Type the pattern that describes the text you're looking for *(see pages 143–157)*.

4. Type **/**.

5. Type the text with which you want to replace the text found in step 3.

6. Type **/**.

7. If desired, type **i** to *i*gnore the case of the letters that you're searching.

8. If desired, type **g** to replace *all* occurrences of the text described in step 3 (that is, globally). Otherwise, only the first match will be replaced.

✔ Tip

■ That little *s* in step 2 stands for *substitute*. It's not optional.

Finding and replacing

Seeing and using what was found

When using the match and substitution operators, it's not always obvious, especially with more general search patterns, what exactly was matched. Also, if the pattern appears more than once in the search string, you might want to know which occurrence triggered the match.

After a match, Perl sets the values of three special variables. **$&** will contain the data that the pattern matched, **$`** will contain any text that preceded the matched text, and **$´** will contain any text that came after the matched text in the searched string.

You can use these variables in your scripts and even in the replacement section of the substitution operator.

✔ **Tip**

■ If you've used parentheses in your pattern, Perl also remembers what the contents of each set of parentheses matched and stores this data for later use. For more details, consult *More on using what you already matched* on page 158.

```
1   #!/usr/local/bin/perl
2
3   print "Content-type: text/html\n\n";
4   $browser = $ENV{'HTTP_USER_AGENT'};
5
6   if ($browser =~ /MSIE/) {
7     print "You're using IE";
8   } elsif ($browser =~ /Mozilla/) {
9     print "You're using Netscape";
10  } else {
11    print "You're using something else";
12  }
13
14  print "<HR><FONT SIZE=+1>";
15  print "<P>The environment variable
        was $browser";
16  print "<P>\$& is $&";
17  print "<P>\$` is $`";
18  print "<P>\$' is $'";
19  print "</FONT>";
```

16: The $& variable contains exactly what matched, if anything.

17: The $` variable contains the portion of the $browser variable that didn't match that was to the left of the matching section.

18: The $' variable contains the portion of the $browser variable that didn't match that was to the right of the matching section.

Figure 11.5 *You won't normally want to print each variable out—unless you're showing someone how the variables work.*

Figure 11.6 *In this example, we were looking for MSIE in the environment variable, which is printed out just below the horizontal rule. The $& variable shows that MSIE was indeed found. $` displays the text from the beginning of the environment variable to the matched part. The $' variable shows the piece of the environment variable that didn't match starting from the matching part and going until the end of the string.*

```
1  #!/usr/local/bin/perl
2
3  require "subparseform.lib";
4  &Parse_Form;
5
6  $spouse = $formdata{'spouse'};
7  @qualifications = split(/,/,
     $spouse);
8
9  print "Content-type: text/html\n\n";
10
11 print "<FONT SIZE=+1><UL><B>You
     chose:</B>";
12
13 foreach $item (@qualifications) {
14     print "<LI>$item";
15 }
16
17 print "</UL></FONT>";
```

7: This line takes the scalar variable $spouse
    and divides its contents—using the comma as
    a delimiter—into individual elements of the
    array @qualifications.

13: You would not be able to list the qualifica-
    tions separately if they were still only part of
    a single scalar variable.

Figure 11.7 *Generally, the regular expression you
use with the split function is a single character—the
delimiter of the multiple values contained in the scalar variable.*

Figure 11.8 *The form-parsing subroutine stores all
of the checkbox values in a single scalar variable.
With the split function, you can convert the multiple
values in the scalar variable into individually accessible values in an array variable.*

Splitting a value into pieces

Splitting a scalar variable into pieces is particularly useful when parsing the incoming
information from a form. It can also be used
to divide the multiple values from a menu or
from check boxes *(see page 86).*

To split a scalar into pieces:

1. Type **@new** where *new* is the name of
    the array variable that will contain the
    split pieces.

2. Type **=**.

3. Type **split(**.

4. Type **/pattern/** where *pattern* is the reg-
    ular expression that describes the
    element that divides the pieces. For infor-
    mation on creating regular expressions,
    see pages 142–158.

5. Type **, $old**, where *old* is the name of the
    scalar variable that contains the string
    you want to split. Don't forget the comma.

6. Type the closing parenthesis **)**.

7. Type a semicolon **;** to finish the line.

✔ Tips

■ If you don't specify the element that
  divides the pieces, Perl automatically
  uses the regular expression **/\s+/** and
  thus, will divide the string into word
  shaped pieces.

■ The split function is often used in form-
  parsing subroutines to divide the long
  stream of input data from a stream into
  intelligible chunks *(see page 66).*

Constructing search patterns

Suppose you need a new Web page coder for your design firm. You could put an ad in the classifieds that asks for "Web designer" and you'd probably get quite a few responses. However, instead of wading through piles of resumes, it might behoove you to be more specific with your response so that the folks who apply more closely reflect your needs. On your second try, you might require knowledge of HTML, Perl, and JavaScript, and three years experience doing Web page coding. This time, you'd get fewer responses but they'd (hopefully) be closer to what you need.

When you analyze incoming data from a Web site, you need to take a similar tack. You use patterns to analyze data and make sure that it's what you're looking for. Instead of asking for four years experience, you might require that the data begin with an opening parentheses, be followed by three digits, then have a closing parentheses, a space, three more digits, a dash, and finally four more digits. If the data matched that description, you could be pretty sure that it's a telephone number.

Those patterns are obliquely called *regular expressions*, which is sometimes abbreviated into the nicely shorter, but even more obtuse *regex*. For example, the pattern that matches any telephone number like *(280) 421-9876* looks likes this: **/^((\(\d{3}\))? *\d{3}(-|)\d{4},? *)+$/**. Pretty scary looking, huh? The trick is to look at each element individually and not get overwhelmed by the multitude of symbols. The rest of this chapter will teach you how to read and construct your own regular expressions (which I often call search patterns).

Jeffrey E. F. Friedl has written an excellent if somewhat advanced book on regular expressions, titled *Mastering Regular Expressions*, and published by O'Reilly and Associates.

Constructing search patterns

Tips for constructing search patterns

A lengthy string of funny looking characters and symbols can be a bit daunting. And the truth is that creating a search pattern that matches what you want it to while filtering out the dreck can be tricky indeed. Here are some tips.

Those forward slashes

Although the forward slashes are part of the match or substitute operators, and not part of the pattern itself, I use them to visually delimit the search patterns in this book.

Combine general and specific components

Perl lets you be as specific or as general as you need. The pattern **/Mozilla/** will match only those characters in that order, while **/.*/** will match *any* quantity of *any* character (including nothing). Often, the most powerful and useful patterns come from combining specific and general components. For example, **/.*Mozilla.*/** would match "Mozilla", "Mozilla, Netscape 4", and "MSIE, Mozilla Compatible", among others.

Spaces

You may want to add spaces between all those chunks of expressions. But don't. Just put one piece right up alongside the next one and have faith that Perl will know what goes where. Spaces are counted like any other character.

Special symbols

When deciphering other folks' regular expressions, keep in mind that the symbols [,], (,), *, ., ^, -, |, \, and ? all have special meanings (which are explained throughout this chapter).

Matching a single character

To match any individual character, whether it be a letter or number, or some special symbol, you simply state that particular character. To match *any* single character (except a newline), you use the period (.).

To match a specific character:

Type the character you want to match.

To match any character:

Type a **.** (period).

✔ Tips

■ Some symbols—like period (.) described above—have a special meaning when used within a pattern. To look for the symbol itself (and not use its special meaning), precede it with a backslash. So, to search for a period, you'd have to use **/\./**. It's easy to see how patterns can quickly look so incomprehensible.

■ To match optional or multiple occurrences of single characters, consult *Choosing how many to match* on page 151.

■ The wildcard symbol (.) is particularly useful when combined with the quantifiers to match a whole string of unspecified characters next to the determining constant text that you're searching for. For more on quantifiers, consult *Choosing how many to match* on page 151.

```
1   #!/usr/local/bin/perl
2
3   require "subparseform.lib";
4   &Parse_Form;
5   print "Content-type: text/html\n\n";
6
7   $phrase = $formdata{'phrase'};
8
9   if ($phrase =~ /e/) {
10    print "<P>Sorry, that sentence did in
         fact have an e. I told you: it's
         harder than it seems.";
11  } else {
12    print "<P>Congratulations, that
         sentence had no e. Quite a feat!";
13  }
```

9: Here's the simplest of regular expressions, a single character. This line checks to see if there are any letter e's in the variable $phrase. If so, line 10 is executed. If not, Perl skips to line 12.

Figure 11.9 *In this example the regular expression is used by the matching operator.*

Figure 11.10 *This simple script looks through the entered phrase to see if it contains any letter e.*

```
1   #!/usr/local/bin/perl
2
3   require "subparseform.lib";
4   &Parse_Form;
5   print "Content-type: text/html\n\n";
6
7   $phrase = $formdata{'phrase'};
8
9   $phrase =~ s/damn/hoot/;
10
11  print "<P>Your more proper sentence is
      <P><B>$phrase";
```

9:   The regular expression /damn/ tries to find
     the letters *d, a, m, n,* in that order, with no
     intervening characters or spaces. (This line
     then substitutes the first occurrence of those
     letters with the letters *h, o, o, t.* For more
     details about substituting, see page 139.)

Figure 11.11 *Although* damn *may look like a word
(OK, and it is a word), for understanding regular
expressions, you're better off looking at it as a
sequence of characters.*

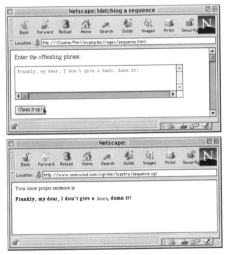

Figure 11.12 *Notice that only the first occurrence of
the* damn *sequence is replaced. To replace both
occurrences, you'd have to append a* g *to the end of
line 9 in Figure 11.11 (see page 139).*

Matching a string of characters

Often, you'll want to match a whole series of
characters, in order. This series of characters
might be a word or even a whole sentence,
but doesn't have to be.

To match a string of characters, in order:

Type the string of characters in the order in
which they should appear in the search
string.

✔ Tips

■   The series of characters must appear one
    after the other in the search string in the
    same order and without extra intervening
    characters or spaces to qualify as a
    match. Therefore, **/lemon/** won't find a
    match in *purple monkey*, even though
    purple monkey contains the five letters
    searched for in the proper order (since
    there's an extra space). And **/candle
    grip/** doesn't match *perl and cgi*, even
    though the letters are the same because
    they're not in the same order.

■   You can use the period (**.**) as a wildcard
    for any character *(see page 144)* in com-
    bination with any other characters. For
    example, **/p.p/** matches *pap, pep, pip,*
    and *pop,* as well as *p2p, p%p, p p,*
    among many others.

■   The pattern may appear surrounded by
    other letters (that is, part of another
    word, for instance) and still qualify as a
    match. For example, **/water/** matches
    both *watermelon* and *Goldwater,* as well
    as just *water.* For details on limiting
    searches to free-standing words, consult
    Limiting the location on page 149.

Matching a character from a group

You can also specify a group or *class* of characters that you want to search for in the search string. If any one character in the group is in the search string, the match will be successful.

To match a character from a group:

1. To begin the class definition, type **[**.

2. Type the characters in the class.

3. Type **]**.

✔ Tips

- Only one of the characters has to be present in the search string for the match to be successful.

- The order of individual characters doesn't matter.

- You can specify a range of characters with the hyphen. For example, **[a-z]** is an abbreviated way of saying "any lowercase letter from *a* to *z*"; **[0-3]** would match 0, 1, 2, or 3.

- You can specify more than one range at a time. No spaces are necessary between ranges. Therefore, **[a-zA-Z]** would match any letter in the English alphabet, lower or uppercase.

- You can add the hyphen to the class by preceding it with a backslash. So, **[a\-z]** would match the letter *a*, the hyphen, and the letter *z* (but not the letters *b*, *c*, and so on).

```
1   #!/usr/local/bin/perl
2
3   require "subparseform.lib";
4   &Parse_Form;
5   print "Content-type: text/html\n\n";
6
7   $number = $formdata{'number'};
8   %catalan = (1, "un", 2, "dos", 3, "tres",
       4, "quatre", 5, "cinc");
9   %spanish = (1, "uno", 2, "dos", 3,
       "tres", 4, "cuatro", 5, "cinco");
10  %french = (1, "un", 2, "deux", 3,
       "trois", 4, "quatre", 5, "cinc");
11
12  if ($number =~/^[1-5]$/) {
13    print "<P>You chose the number $number.
       That number translated into Catalan is
       <B>$catalan{$number}</B>. In French,
       it's <B>$french {$number}</B>. In
       Spanish, it's
       <B>$spanish{$number}<B>.";
14  } else {
15    print "<P>Sorry, you didn't choose a
       number between 1 and 5. Try again.";
16  }
```

12: The regular expression searches for any number in the range of 1 to 5. The caret and the dollar sign are explained on page 149.)

Figure 11.13 *Regular expressions are ideal for checking to see that incoming data satisfies the necessary criteria. (Here we want to make sure the visitor entered a number from 1 to 5 since that's all the translations that we have.)*

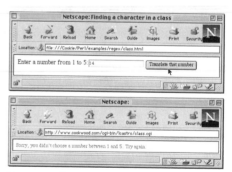

Figure 11.14 *If the visitor does not enter the data properly, they get an explanatory message (instead of throwing the server into a tizzy).*

Figure 11.15 *As long as the visitor does follow instructions (entering the number 4, here), the main part of the script is executed.*

```
1   #!/usr/local/bin/perl
2
3   require "subparseform.lib";
4   &Parse_Form;
5   print "Content-type: text/html\n\n";
6
7   $zip = $formdata{'zip'};
8
9   if ($zip =~/[^0-9\-]/) {
10    print "Your zipcode should only
          contain the numbers or the dash.
          Try again.";
11  } else {
12    print "You entered $zip for your
          zipcode";
13  }
```

9:   The regular expression tries to find anything
     that is *not* a number or a dash. If it does find
     such an offending character, it prints an error
     message (line 10).

Figure 11.16 *To make sure the incoming data contains no extraneous characters, that is, anything that's not a digit or a hyphen, use a negated class.*

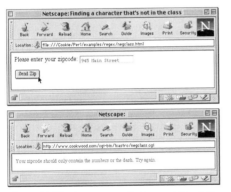

Figure 11.17 *Never assume that your visitors will follow your instructions. Instead, use regular expressions to check all incoming data. Then, if you have to reject data, make sure you explain to your visitor what the problem is.*

Matching a character that's not in the group

Sometimes you'll want to match a character that is not part of a specified group or class. You can search for those characters that don't belong to the group by preceding the class with a caret.

To match a character that's not in the group:

1. Begin the class definition with **[**.

2. Type **^** (that's Shift+6 on most keyboards).

3. Type the members of the class.

4. Type **]**.

✔ Tips

■ For more information on constructing classes, consult *Matching a character from a group* on page 146.

■ If the caret appears anywhere except as the first character in the class, it will be considered one of the members of the class. Therefore, **[^a-z]** would match any character that is *not* a lowercase letter, but **[A-Z^a-z]** would match any letter—including lowercase ones—or the caret.

■ Negated classes are tricky. While **[^a-z]** matches any character that's not a lowercase letter, it would still match *a1*, despite the presence of the *a*. Why? Because it is satisfied by matching the 1—which is not a lowercase letter.

■ When you use the negative caret, you're requiring that the search find you *something* that's not in the class. Finding nothing is not enough.

Using class shorthands

Although you can spell out your own classes as described on pages 146–147, Perl also understands a set of abbreviations for specifying common classes.

To use a class shorthand:

Type **\d** to match any digit. The longhand equivalent is [0-9].

Or type **\D** to match any character that is not a digit. The longhand equivalent is [^0-9].

Or type **\w** to match any upper or lowercase letter, digit or the underscore. The longhand equivalent is [a-zA-Z0-9_].

Or type **\W** to match any character that is not an upper or lowercase letter, a digit, or the underscore. The longhand equivalent is [^a-zA-Z0-9_].

Or type **\s** to match any space, tab, newline, return, or formfeed. The longhand equivalent is [\t\n\r\f].

Or type **\S** to match any character that is not a space, tab, newline, return, or formfeed. The longhand equivalent is [^ \t\n\r\f].

✔ Tips

■ Each of these abbreviations matches a *single* character. If you want to match more than one character of the given class, you'd have to specify that explicitly *(see page 151)*.

■ You don't need to enclose class abbreviations in straight brackets. They won't work correctly if you do.

■ Notice that \w is the class of characters that are valid in Perl variable names.

```
1   #!/usr/local/bin/perl
2
3   require "subparseform.lib";
4   &Parse_Form;
5   print "Content-type: text/html\n\n";
6   $phone = $formdata{'phone'};
7
8   if ($phone =~ /\(\d\d\d\) \d\d\d-
       \d\d\d\d/) {
9     print "You entered a phone number of
         $phone";
10  } else {
11    print "Please enter the phone number in
         the form <P>(123) 456-7899<P>";
12  }
```

8:   The regular expression tries to find a pattern that matches opening parentheses (which is backslashed), digit, digit, digit, closing parentheses (also backslashed), space, digit, digit, digit, dash, digit, digit, digit, digit.

Figure 11.18 *Using \d (the class shorthand) instead of [0-9] saves a lot of typing.*

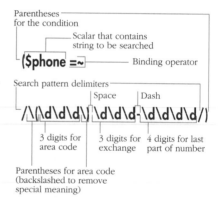

Figure 11.19 *Regular expressions can start to look pretty complicated. Here's a full description of line 8 from Figure 11.18.*

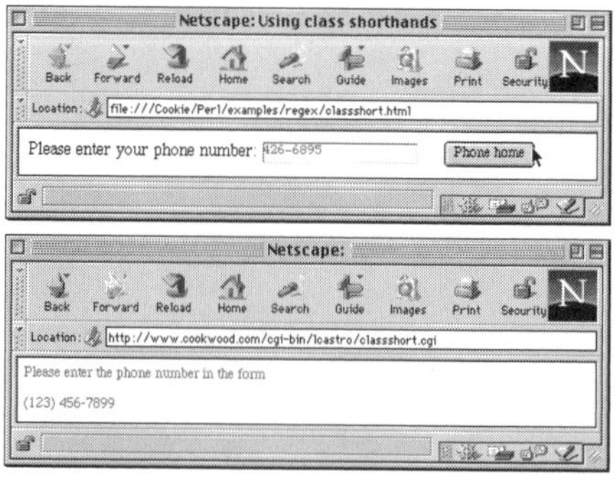

Figure 11.20 *If the number entered does not fit the desired pattern, the visitor gets an error and more information.*

Using class shorthands

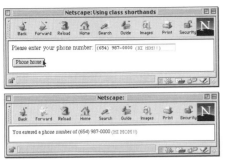

Figure 11.21 *With the script from Figure 11.18 on page 148, visitors can add extra data (as long as they also add a correctly formatted telephone number). Although this example is pretty innocuous, a visitor could do a fair bit of damage.*

```
1   #!/usr/local/bin/perl
2
3     require "subparseform.lib";
4     &Parse_Form;
5     print "Content-type: text/html\n\n";
6
7     $phone = $formdata{'phone'};
8
9     if ($phone =~ /^\(\d\d\d\) \d\d\d-
      \d\d\d\d$/) {
10      print "You entered a phone number of
        $phone";
11    } else {
12      print "Please enter the phone number in
        the form <P>(123) 456-7899<P>";
13    }
```

8:   The caret and the dollar sign ensure that the telephone number will only match if it is the only thing entered (that is, it's at the beginning and at the end of the entered string).

Figure 11.22 *Limiting the possible location of a match ensures that the visitor can only enter a properly formatted telephone number with no extra goodies.*

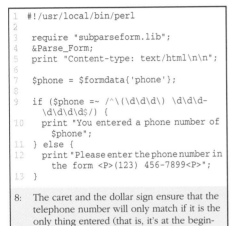

Figure 11.23 *Now when the visitor tries to be cute, they are rebuffed.*

Limiting the location

If you're looking for *wine*, you don't want to find *swine*. If you're looking for a three digit number, you probably don't want to find it *within* a four digit number. By limiting, or *anchoring*, the location of the found string to the beginning and/or end of a line, or to the beginning or end of a word, you can better control the results.

To require an element to appear at the beginning of the search string:

1. Type ^ as the very first character in the regular expression.

2. Type the element.

To require an element to appear at the very end of the search string:

1. Type the element.

2. Type **$**.

To require an element to appear at the beginning of a word:

1. Type **\b**.

2. Type the element.

To require an element to appear at the end of a word:

1. Type the element.

2. Type **\b**.

To require an element *not* to appear at the beginning of a word:

1. Type **\B**.

2. Type the element.

To require an element *not* to appear at the end of a word:

1. Type the element.

2. Type **\B**.

✔ Tips

■ So, to search for a string that contains a single element, you could use **/^element$/**.

■ And to search for a free-standing word, you could use **/\bword\b/**. Such a regular expression would match *word* but not *sword*, nor *wordy*.

Choosing how many to match

By default, Perl will search for only one of each element that you add to a regular expression. That is, **/a/** will match any search string that contains at least one *a;* **/baby/** will match any search string that contains at least one instance of the string *baby*; and **/[a-z]/** will match any search string that contains at least one lowercase letter. However, if you wanted to search for strings with, say, 3 *a*'s or two instances of *baby*, or individual words (combinations of the letters from a-z), you'd need to find more than one of the specified element. Perl has a number of *quantifiers* that let you do just that.

Perhaps the most important thing to remember about a quantifier is that it applies only to the individual element directly preceding it—even if that's just a single character. This is hard to remember when you're used to seeing words, like say, *fish,* as a single unit. But if you add the quantifier after the *h*, as in **/fish*/**, it applies only to the *h*, not to the entire *fish*.

You can make a quantifier affect more than one character by using parentheses. The parentheses group characters or strings as if they were one element. Therefore, in **/(fish)*/** the * quantifier affects the entire *fish*, not just the *h*.

A class is considered an independent unit. You don't need to add parentheses around it for the quantifier to apply to the whole class. So, **/[a-z]*/** matches the same as **/([a-z])*/**, and is much prettier to boot. (Although the parentheses have yet another purpose which you won't achieve if you leave them out. For more details, consult *More on using what you already matched* on page 158.)

Suppose part of the string you're looking for contains an element that might or might not be present. To have your string match whether that element *is there or not,* you use the ? quantifier.

To include optional elements:

1. Type the element that can either be present or not.

2. Type **?**.

✔ Tips

■ The ? quantifier will only match one of the elements. If there is a string of similar elements in a row, only the first will be matched by the element quantified with ?.

■ The ? quantifier only affects the element immediately preceding the ?. To have the ? affect an entire phrase, enclose that phrase in parentheses.

```
1   #!/usr/local/bin/perl
2
3   require "subparseform.lib";
4   &Parse_Form;
5   print "Content-type: text/html\n\n";
6
7   $phone = $formdata{'phone'};
8
9   if ($phone =~ /^(\(\d\d\d\))? ?
    \d\d\d-\d\d\d\d$/) {
10      print "You entered the phone
    number <B>$phone</B>";
11  } else {
12      print "Please enter the phone
    number in the form <P>(123) 456-
    7899<P>(The area code is
    optional.)";
13  }
```

8: There are two optional elements in this regular expression. The first question mark applies to the area code and surrounding parentheses. The second applies to the space between the area code and the number.

Figure 11.24 *The question mark applies to the element immediately preceding it. Enclose elements in parentheses where necessary (as here).*

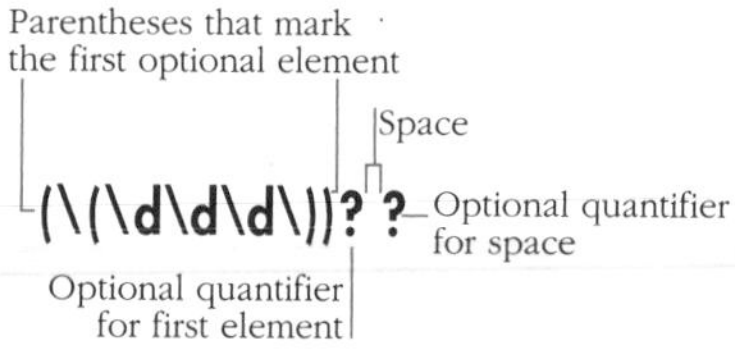

Parentheses that mark
the first optional element

Space

`(\(\d\d\d\))? ?` Optional quantifier for space

Optional quantifier
for first element

Figure 11.25 *Adding quantifiers (and necessary parentheses) make regular expressions even more bizarre looking. Taking them apart makes them easier to understand.*

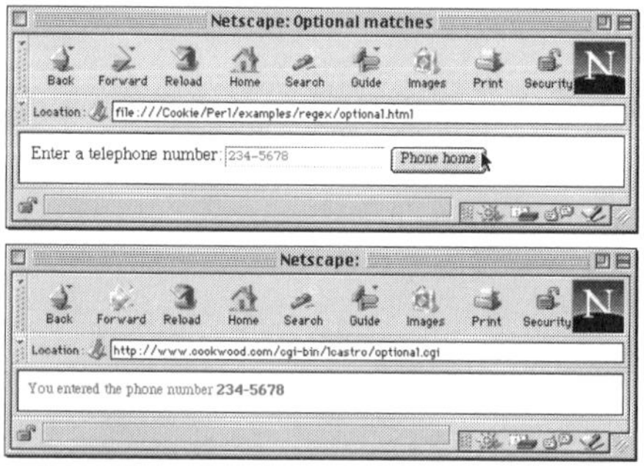

Figure 11.26 *Now the script accepts numbers with an area code as well as those without it.*

```
1   #!/usr/local/bin/perl
2
3   require "subparseform.lib";
4   &Parse_Form;
5   print "Content-type: text/html\n\n";
6
7   $phone = $formdata{'phone'};
8
9   if ($phone =~ /^((\(\d\d\d\))? ?
    \d\d\d-\d\d\d\d,? ?)+$/) {
10      print "You entered the phone
        number(s) <B>$phone</B>";
11  } else {
12      print "Please enter the phone
        number(s) in the form <P>(123) 456-
        7899<P>(The area code is
        optional.)";
13  }
```

8: I've enclosed the expression from
    Figure 11.24 on page 152 in parentheses and
    added a plus sign to allow visitors to enter
    one or more telephone numbers. Notice that
    I've also added an optional comma and
    optional space after the telephone number.

Figure 11.27 *Parentheses are crucial in determining what a quantifier applies to. Without the parentheses, the quantifier applies only to the single character immediately preceding it.*

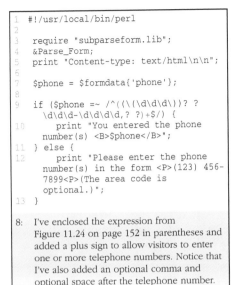

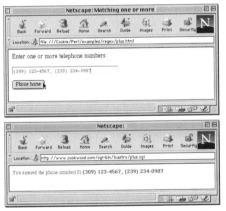

Figure 11.28 *Now the script will accept more than one telephone number, but will still require that at least one number be entered and that each number to be properly formatted.*

Let's make our example fit even more situations. Say we want to let visitors enter more than one telephone number but we still want to make them enter at least one. The solution is to surround the previous regular expression with parentheses and add the plus (+) quantifier. The plus quantifier requires that at least one, but possibly more, of the element be present.

To match one or more elements:

1. Type the element that you want there to be at least one of (up to an unlimited number) in the search string.

2. Type **+**.

✔ Tips

■ I've also added an optional comma and space after the telephone number in case the visitor feels compelled to separate the phone numbers in some way.

■ The match will fail if there is not at least one of the elements in the search string.

■ It doesn't matter how many of the elements are in the search string (as long as there is at least one).

There's still something that might trip up our visitors in our phone example. If they put an extra space between the area code and the phone number, they'll get an error message. In order to accept data with extra characters (like spaces in this example) as long as it fulfills the rest of the formatting requirements, you use the asterisk quantifier. The asterisk lets you match elements if they're present, but not worry too much if they're not. I describe such elements as *multiple optional*.

To include multiple optional elements:

1. Type the element that you want to search for in the search string.

2. Type *****. The match is successful whether the element is present or not.

✔ Tip

■ At first glance, a quantifier that matches whether something is there or not seems pretty useless. Nothing could be farther from the truth. It offers you the flexibility to accept minor variances in an otherwise rigid pattern.

```
1  #!/usr/local/bin/perl
2
3  require "subparseform.lib";
4  &Parse_Form;
5  print "Content-type: text/html\n\n";
6
7  $phone = $formdata{'phone'};
8
9  if ($phone =~ /^((\(\d\d\))? *
   \d\d\d-\d\d\d\d,? *)+$/) {
10   print "You entered the phone
     number(S) <B>$phone</B>";
11 } else {
12   print "Please enter the phone
     number(s) in the form <P>(123)
     456-7899<P>(The area code is
     optional.)";
13 }
```

8: The first asterisk allows an unlimited number of spaces (or none) after the area code. The second asterisk allows an unlimited number of spaces (or none) after each telephone number.

Figure 11.29 *Asterisks make the most sense when they're part of a larger regular expression.*

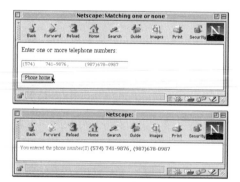

Figure 11.30 *Here the visitor has gone crazy, adding lots of extra spaces between the first area code and its number and again after the comma. Then she left off the space after the second area code. This script accepts all of that, as long as the rest of the pattern matches properly. Note that the spaces are lost in the displayed result since HTML doesn't recognize extra spaces.*

```
1   #!/usr/local/bin/perl
2
3   require "subparseform.lib";
4   &Parse_Form;
5   print "Content-type: text/html\n\n";
6
7   $phone = $formdata{'phone'};
8
9   if ($phone =~ /^((\(\d{3}\))? *\d{3}-
    \d{4},? *)+$/) {
10    print "You entered the phone
      number(S) <B>$phone</B>";
11  } else {
12    print "Please enter the phone
      number(s) in the form <P>(123)
      456-7899<P>(The area code is
      optional.)";
13  }
```

8:   The number within curly brackets indicates
     exactly how many of the preceding element
     (in this case the \d) are required for a match.

Figure 11.31 *The regular expression in line 9 above is equivalent to the one in Figure 11.29 on page 154. But it's shorter, easier to type, more legible, and nicer looking.*

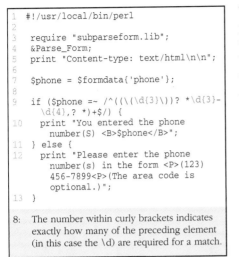

Figure 11.32 *The script works exactly as before. But it's neater.*

There's one shortcut we can add to our phone number regex. Instead of repeating \d over and over again, you can use a number to denote how many should be required for a match.

To match at least *m* and at most *n* elements:

1. Type the elements to match.

2. Type **{m,n}** where *m* is the minimum number of instances necessary for the element to appear in the search string and *n* is the maximum.

✔ Tips

- If you leave off the second number completely (as in the example), both *m* and *n* are set by the first number. So, {3} requires exactly three repetitions of the element to match successfully. No more, no less.

- If you leave off the second number, but keep the comma, the *n* is set to infinity. Therefore, {3,} requires at least three instances of the element to be successful but will also be successful with four or five or however many more.

- If you like, you can think of the ? as {0,1}, the + as {1,}, the * as {0,} and anything without a quantifier as having {1} by default.

- It's not particularly obvious at first, but **\d{3}** is successful at matching *1234*. Why? Because it can match exactly three digits *(123)* at the beginning of the string. Remember not to think about word or numbers as units. Perl doesn't either. To match only three digit numbers, you need to anchor the expression *(see page 152)*.

Choosing how many to match

Curbing a quantifier's greediness

A quantifier's greediness has nothing to do with manners. Instead, it means that a quantifier will match as much of the string as it can, as long as that doesn't mean that the entire regular expression will fail. This is especially important in less specific expressions where it's easier for a quantifier to grab more than its due.

For example, suppose you want to cull either the area code or the telephone exchange (the first three digits of the number) out of the phone number. You might think something like /.*(\d{3}).*/ would do just fine. You've got an unlimited number of characters, than 3 digits and then some more characters. The problem is that first .* is *greedy*. It not only takes up to the first three numbers, but it keeps going until it risks failing to match—which in this case is just before the last three numbers in the string. Since the last .* can match something or nothing, the first .* leaves it nothing with little compunction.

One way to get around greediness is to enclose an unlimited quantifier in specific elements that must match. For example, the * quantifier in /\(\d*\)/ is greedy but since the expression has to match a closing parentheses, the quantifier is limited to the area code—as long as there are no additional closing parentheses in the search string.

You can make quantifiers non-greedy by adding a ? to them (*?, +?, ??). Non-greedy quantifiers will match as little of the search string as possible while still attempting to match the entire regular expression.

```
1   #!/usr/local/bin/perl
2
3   require "subparseform.lib";
4   &Parse_Form;
5   print "Content-type: text/html\n\n";
6
7   $phone = $formdata{'phone'};
8
9   if ($phone =~ /^((\(\(\d{3}\))?
    *\d{3}(-| )\d{4},? *)+$/) {
10      print "You entered the phone
    number(S) <B>$phone</B>";
11  } else {
12      print "Please enter the phone
    number(s) in the form <P>(123) 456-
    7899<P>(The area code is
    optional.)";
13  }
```

8: The highlighted section allows the visitor to
    separate the three digit exchange from the
    last four digits of the number with *either* a
    dash *or* a space.

Figure 11.33 *You must enclose the dash, vertical
bar, and space within parentheses. Otherwise, the
alternation would look for either the first half of the
entire expression (the area code and exchange) or the
second half (the last four digits of the phone number), which wouldn't make much sense.*

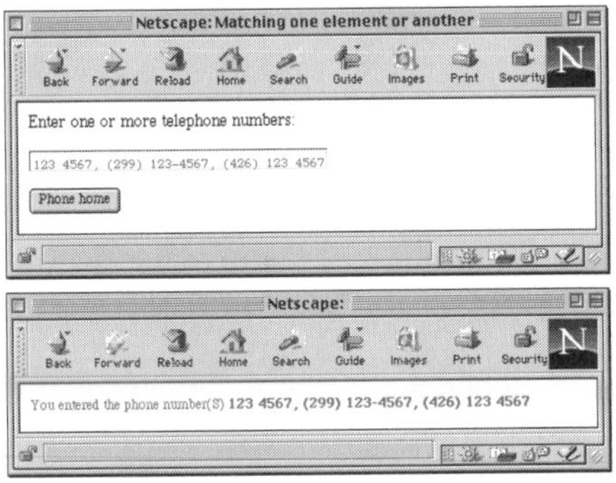

Figure 11.34 *Now the visitor can type the telephone
number with a dash or with a space. While it's
important to check incoming data for proper formatting, the more flexibility you can allow, the happier
your visitors will be.*

Matching one element or another

One final tool in Perl's regex arsenal is alternation, a fancy word that means "or". It is
often useful to be able to match one of two
patterns, or one of two elements within a
larger pattern. Alternation makes this
possible.

To match one element or another:

1. Type the first element that you want to
search for.

2. Type | (the vertical bar).

3. Type the next element that you want to
search for.

4. Repeat steps 2–3, as desired.

✔ Tips

■ In contrast with the quantifiers that affect
only the single preceding element,
alternation affects as much of the
regular expression as it can. Therefore,
/ice tea|coffee/ matches *ice tea* or *cof-
fee*. Use parentheses to limit alternation:
/ice (tea|coffee)/ matches either *ice tea*
or *ice coffee*.

■ For a simple choice between individual
characters, you could use a character
class. For example, **/[nr]ice tea/** would
match either *nice tea* or *rice tea*. Using
alternation lets you choose between two
or more complete regular expressions.

■ Elements in an alternation are matched
in the order in which they appear. So,
/ice tea|coffee/ will match the *ice tea* in
"Would you like ice tea or some hot
coffee?" and then simply stop, never
checking to see if the second choice was
present.

157

More on using what you already matched

You've already seen how parentheses can extend the power of quantifiers (see page 151) and limit the reach of alternation (see page 157), but parentheses serve one more useful function. Perl will automatically remember what was matched by the contents of each set of parentheses. This information is stored in special numbered variables, where the number reflects the order of the parentheses starting from the left.

To mark what you want to remember:

1. Enclose the part of your search pattern in parentheses that you want to reference.

2. In your mind (or on scratch paper), number the opening parentheses from left to right, starting with 1. Note the number of the parentheses whose match you're interested in.

To use what was matched in your pattern:

After the referenced parentheses in the search pattern, type **\n**, where *n* corresponds to the number of the parentheses (that you noted in step 2 above).

To use what was matched in the replacement text:

In the replacement text, type **$n**, where *n* corresponds to the number of the parentheses (that you noted in step 2 above).

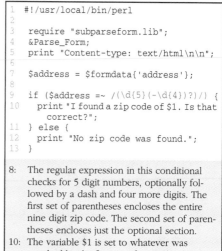

```
1   #!/usr/local/bin/perl
2
3   require "subparseform.lib";
4   &Parse_Form;
5   print "Content-type: text/html\n\n";
6
7   $address = $formdata{'address'};
8
9   if ($address =~ /(\d{5}(-\d{4})?)/) {
10    print "I found a zip code of $1. Is that
         correct?";
11  } else {
12    print "No zip code was found.";
13  }
```

8: The regular expression in this conditional checks for 5 digit numbers, optionally followed by a dash and four more digits. The first set of parentheses encloses the entire nine digit zip code. The second set of parentheses encloses just the optional section.

10: The variable $1 is set to whatever was matched by the first set of parentheses.

Figure 11.35 *Even though the second set of parentheses is mostly for applying the optional ? quantifier to the dash and four digits, it also serves to save that information into the $2 variable (which is not used in this script).*

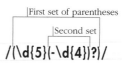
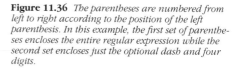

Figure 11.36 *The parentheses are numbered from left to right according to the position of the left parenthesis. In this example, the first set of parentheses encloses the entire regular expression while the second set encloses just the optional dash and four digits.*

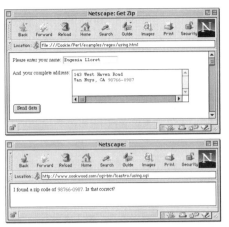

Figure 11.37 *The data that was matched by the first parenthesized section of the regular expression is saved in the $1 variable and then printed out.*

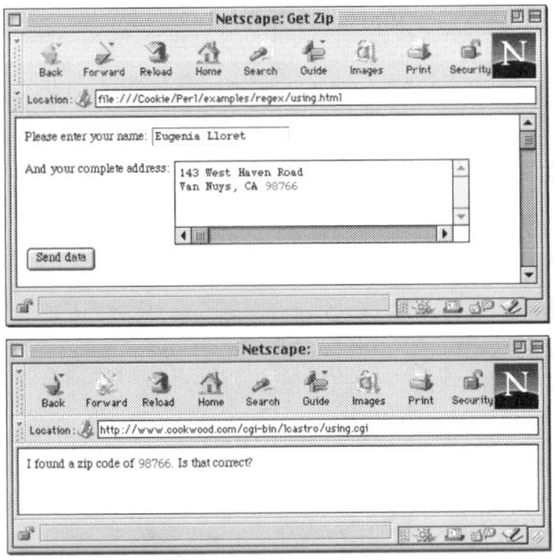

Figure 11.38 *If the visitor only types a five digit number (with no optional dash and extra four digits), that will be the data that is matched by the parenthesized section of the regular expression and saved in the $1 variable.*

To store what was matched in one or more variables:

1. Type **($scalar1, $scalar2)**, where *$scalar1* and *$scalar2* (and any others) are the variables in which you want to store the matched pieces of the search string.

2. Type **=**.

3. Type **$base**, where *base* is the name of the variable that contains the string to be searched.

4. Type **=~**.

5. Type **/pattern/**, where *pattern* is the regular expression that describes what you're looking for. Be sure to enclose in parentheses the parts of the pattern that you want to store.

6. Type **;** to finish the line.

✔ Tips

- If you have more scalar variables in step 1 than parenthesized elements, the rightmost scalar variables will be undefined. If you have more parenthesized elements than scalar variables, the rightmost elements will not be stored.

- You could just as easily store the parenthesized elements in an array (or a hash, if that makes sense). Type **@array** for step 1 where *array* is the name of the array.

- If you append a *g* to the end of the matching operator as in **m/pattern/g**, all of the matches throughout the search string will be saved to the specified variables (and not just the first match that Perl comes across).

- In this example, a five-digit house number would give unexpected results.

More on using what you already matched

159

Remembering What Your Visitors Tell You

Each time your visitor activates a CGI script by pressing a submit button, the browser treats that person as a new, separate individual, even if it's the same exact person that submitted a CGI script a second earlier.

Nevertheless, it's often useful to remember information about a visitor from one page to the next. For example, if you ask a visitor to fill out his name, address, and phone number, and then direct him to another page where he can order your handcrafted maple furniture, you don't want to bother him again later for the same personal information. Or, if you allow your visitors to set particular preferences for viewing your pages—like background color, language, or anything else—being able to remember the visitor's settings each time she visits your site will make your visitor feel special and well taken care of.

There are two simple ways of remembering things about your visitors: cookies and hidden fields. This chapter will explain the basic concepts behind each one and tell you how to put them to use.

About hidden fields

HTML forms allow for a special kind of field that doesn't appear in the browser, and yet is part of the form. These hidden fields seem counterproductive at first glance: if your visitors can't see them, how will they fill them in? The answer is they won't. Instead, you will use hidden fields to store information gathered from an earlier form so that it can be combined with the present form's data.

Imagine, for example, that on the first page, you ask for a visitor's name, address, and telephone number. You then want to send them to your catalog page where they can choose which piece of furniture they wish to order. Instead of asking them for their personal data a second time, you can use a CGI script to collect the data from the first form and then generate the hidden fields that will contain this data in the second form. Then, when you go to process the data from the second form, all of the fields, including both the items ordered and the personal data, will be analyzed.

Don't get carried away by the word *hidden*. While hidden fields are not shown by the browser, they still form part of the HTML code that makes up the page (so the CGI script can get at them), and thus are not at all invisible if someone should look at the source code for your page *(see Figure 12.4 on page 165).*

```
                code.html
<FORM METHYOD=POST ACTION="whatever.cgi">

<INPUT TYPE=hidden NAME=name VALUE=value>

<INPUT TYPE=submit VALUE="Submit Data">
```

Figure 12.1 *An excerpt from the HTML file used to create the form shows the syntax for hidden elements. It doesn't make much sense to write such code yourself and thus I'm reluctant to create such an example. On the following page you'll see how to use a CGI script to generate this HTML code.*

Adding hidden fields to a form

Although you hardly ever add hidden fields to an HTML document yourself, you'll have to know how to do it so you can make your Perl script create them.

To add hidden fields to a form:

1. Within the form on your HTML page, type **<INPUT TYPE=hidden**.

2. Type **NAME="name"** where name is a short description of the information to be stored.

3. Type **VALUE="value"** where value is the information itself that is to be stored.

4. Type **>**.

✔ Tips

- It doesn't matter where the hidden fields appear in your form since they won't appear in the browser anyway. As long as they are within the opening and closing FORM tags, you're OK.

- You don't have to use the quotation marks around the name and value if the name and value are comprised of only alphanumeric characters—that is, no spaces and no funny symbols. Since quotation marks have a special meaning in a Perl script and will thus need to be backslashed to get rid of that special meaning, it's often simpler to leave them out altogether where possible.

Adding hidden fields to a form

Storing collected data in a hidden field

Hidden fields are best generated by the same CGI script that processes the initial form—that is, the one that contains the data to be stored. Then you'll create a second script to process the final form—the one that contains both the new data and the stored data.

To store collected data in a hidden field:

1. Parse the information from the initial form as usual, with the &Parse_Form subroutine *(see page 66)*.

2. Generate the HTML code for the page that should appear when the initial form has been submitted. This page may contain some kind of confirmation that the first bit of information has been received and processed, together with a new form to collect the new data. For more information on printing HTML tags, consult *Formatting output with HTML* on page 178.

3. At some point after generating the opening HTML FORM tag, type **foreach $key (keys %formdata) {**, where *%formdata* is the name of the hash that contains the data from the first form. (It will be called *%formdata* if you use the &Parse_Form subroutine described on page 66.)

4. Type **print "<INPUT TYPE=hidden NAME=$key VALUE=$formdata {$key}>\n";**

5. Type **}** to complete the foreach loop that creates the hidden fields for each key-value pair that was collected from the initial form.

Figure 12.2 *Here is the form that gathers the information that we want to store in the hidden fields.*

```
1  #!/usr/local/bin/perl
2
3  require "subparseform.lib";
4  &Parse_Form;
5
6  print "Content-type:text/html\n\n";
7  print "<HTML><HEAD><TITLE>Using Hidden
      Fields</TITLE></HEAD><BODY>\n";
8  print "Thanks, $formdata{'name'}, for
      entering your personal data. Now you
      can choose which items you'd like to
      purchase.\n";
9
10 print "<FORM METHOD=POST
      ACTION=\"hidden2.cgi\">\n";
11 print "Item <INPUT TYPE=text
      NAME=item>\n";
12
13 foreach $key (keys %formdata) {
14   print "<INPUT TYPE=hidden NAME=$key
        VALUE=$formdata{$key}>\n";
15   }
16
17 print "<INPUT TYPE=submit
      VALUE=\"Send order\">\n";
18 print "</FORM></BODY></HTML>\n";
```

3: Lines 3–4 analyze the incoming data as usual.

6: Lines 6–11 generate the beginning of the HTML page, including the form and its new fields. Notice how it was necessary to backslash the quotes in line 10 to keep from confusing Perl.

13: Lines 13–15 generate a hidden field for each key-value pair collected by the subroutine in line 4.

17: Lines 17–18 complete the form and the HTML page itself. Notice how it was necessary to backslash the quotes in line 17 to keep from confusing Perl.

Figure 12.3 *This script has two jobs. First, it parses the data from the form (shown in Figure 12.2 above) and second, it generates a new form into which it stores the collected data in hidden fields.*

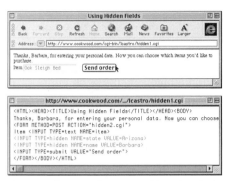

Figure 12.4 *Here is the generated form (in which the visitor has entered new data). Notice that the hidden fields are invisible in the browser (top) but are definitely present in the source code.*

```
1   #!/usr/local/bin/perl
2
3   require "subparseform.lib";
4   &Parse_Form;
5
6   print "Content-type:text/html\n\n";
7   print "<HTML><HEAD><TITLE>Using Hidden
       Fields</TITLE></HEAD><BODY>";
8
9   print "The item ordered by
       $formdata{'name'} from
       $formdata{'state'} is";
10  print "<P>$formdata{'item'}";
11  print "<P>Thanks. It's on its way.";
12  print "</BODY></HTML>";
```

3: Lines 3 and 4 analyze the incoming data—both the new and hidden fields.
9: Line 9 prints the data from the hidden fields.
10: Line 10 prints the new data.

Figure 12.5 *The CGI script called by the generated form is different from the one that actually generated the form. To keep things simple, this script just parses the incoming data and prints it out. You'll probably want to do more than that. (Thankfully, you won't have space restraints.)*

Figure 12.6 *The data from the new field (Item) is analyzed and processed together with the data from the hidden fields (Name and State). All of the data is displayed in this final result.*

✔ **Tips**

■ Processing the hidden fields is just like processing any form data—use the &Parse_Form subroutine.

■ I've used the simplest possible example so that you can understand the underlying technique. Once you get the idea, you can embellish in lots of ways—including reading in the HTML tags from a template *(see page 195)*, creating more complicated scripts that complete more serious processing of the information gathered, and whatever else you can think up. Just remember the basic premise: the script that processes the data to be stored should generate the hidden fields in the next form.

■ Hidden fields are useful but transitory. Once your visitor leaves your site or even jumps to a page that's outside the realm of the interconnected scripts that store and generate the hidden fields, the connection between that visitor and the information you're currently collecting is lost.

Storing collected data in a hidden field

165

About cookies

If you want to respond to each visitor personally, it would be ideal if they would simply identify themselves in some way each time they visit the pages on your site. Of course, it's unlikely that folks will take the time to do that. Instead, Netscape Communications created a way to *mark* visitors when they come to your site and then look at that mark when they return. The mark is called a *cookie* ("for no compelling reason" according to Netscape's documentation, although the image of Hansel and Gretel marking the way home with bits of cookie would be a good excuse).

For example, imagine that a visitor comes to your site and tells you, via a form, that they would prefer to read the information from your site in French. You could send a cookie to their browser that says "language=French". The browser will save the cookie (until it expires) and offer it to you in an environment variable the next time the visitor comes to your site. You can then read the cookie, find out that this particular visitor prefers French, and even though you know nothing more about them, you can provide the content in that language to a satisfied, and now duly impressed, visitor.

Cookies are almost completely safe (although crackers are terribly resourceful) since they are text files and not executable and thus cannot harbor nasty viruses. Nevertheless, visitors sometimes don't like them because they don't want to be tracked. Most browsers allow the visitor to reject all or some of the cookies that get sent their way *(see page 176)*. You'll want to keep that in mind.

Figure 12.7 *If you open the cookies.txt file in your Netscape directory on your Windows machine, you'll see something like this. The first column gives the domain, the third column shows the path, the fourth column denotes whether the cookie must travel on secure connections, the fifth gives the expiration date, and the sixth and seventh give the name and value of the information stored in the cookie.*

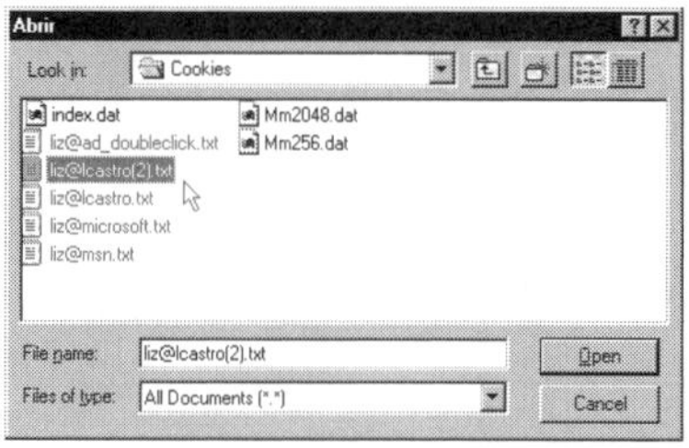

Figure 12.8 *Internet Explorer for Windows stores each cookie in its own individual file in the Cookies folder, inside the Windows folder.*

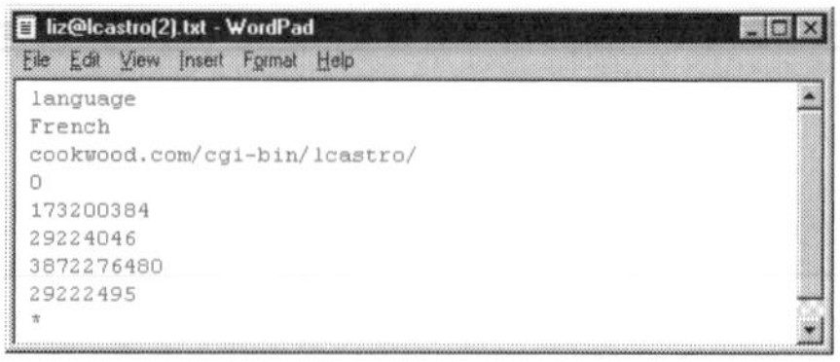

Figure 12.9 *When you open a cookie stored with Internet Explorer for Windows, you'll see the name and value on the first and second lines, respectively, followed by the domain name.*

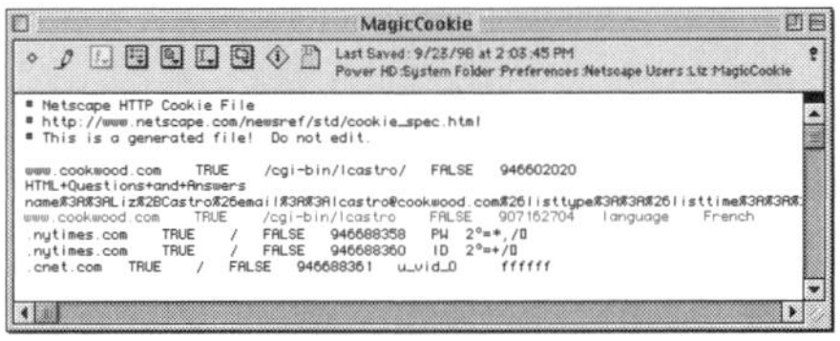

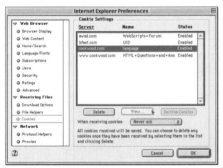

Figure 12.10 *When you open Netscape for Macintosh's MagicCookie file (that is stored in the Netscape folder, in the Preferences folder, in the System Folder), you'll see something like this. The first column is for the domain, the third for the path, the fourth for security, the fifth for the expiration date, and the sixth and seventh for the name and value of the information stored in the cookie.*

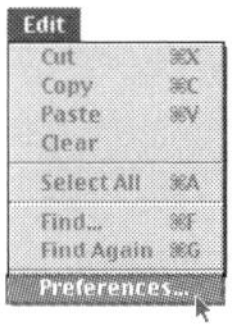

Figure 12.11 *To view the cookies that Internet Explorer for Mac saves, open that browser and choose Edit > Preferences.*

Figure 12.12 *Click Cookies in the left-hand column (under Receiving Files) and then, in the list at right, choose the cookie you want to view and click the View button.*

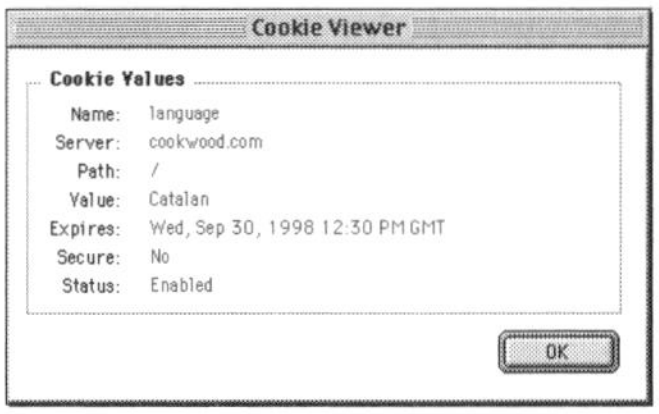

Figure 12.13 *Explorer labels each bit of information stored in the cookie.*

Looking at your browser's cookies

Perhaps the best way to understand cookies is to take a look at them. If you've been traveling around the Web, and allow other sites to send you cookies *(see page 176)*, your browser will have saved a text file that contains those cookies. You can open the cookie file in any text editor.

To look at (and edit) your browser's cookies:

1. Open your text editor.

2. If you use Netscape for Windows, there will be a file called *cookies.txt* in the directory that contains Netscape **(Figure 12.7)**.

   For Explorer for Windows, look in the Cookies folder in your Windows folder. Explorer creates individual files for each cookie **(Figures 12.8 and 12.9)**.

   For Netscape Mac, open the MagicCookie file inside the Netscape folder in the Preferences folder inside your System Folder **(Figure 12.10)**.

   For Explorer for Macintosh, choose Edit > Preferences **(Figure 12.11)**. Then click Cookies in the left-hand column (under Receiving Files). Then, select the desired cookie and click View **(Figure 12.12)**. Explorer displays the stored data **(Figure 12.13)**.

3. Delete unwanted cookies stored by Netscape by selecting the entire cookie and pressing Delete. In the case of Explorer for Windows, delete the whole unwanted cookie file. In Explorer for Mac, select the cookie and press the Delete button in the Internet Explorer Preferences box.

Sending a cookie

To save information on your visitor's browser you'll have to do two things. You'll first collect some information to save and give it a name and then you'll create and send that information to the visitor's browser.

To send a cookie:

1. Collect the data that you want to send to the visitor and decide on the name that will identify that data.

2. In your Perl script, before printing anything to the browser—that is, before the MIME content line *(see page 34)*—type **print "Set-Cookie:** .

3. Type **name**, where *name* is either a variable or a constant that identifies the data to be stored in the cookie. Don't type a space between steps 2 and 3.

4. Type **=** to separate the name and value with an equals sign.

5. Type **value**, where *value* is either a variable or a constant that represents the actual data that you want to store.

6. Type **\n"** to add a newline at the end of the Set-Cookie header.

7. Type **;** to complete the sentence.

✓ Tips

■ The data can come from processing a form, opening an external file, analyzing an earlier cookie, or it may just be a constant. It's up to you.

■ The name and the value cannot contain semicolons, commas, or white space. If you need to include such characters you must first convert them to their hexadecimal equivalents.

```
1   #!/usr/local/bin/perl
2
3   require "subparseform.lib";
4   &Parse_Form;
5
6   print "Set-Cookie:language=$formdata
        {'language'}\n";
7
8   print "Content-type: text/html\n\n";
9   print "<HTML><HEAD><TITLE>Thanks for
        choosing!</TITLE></HEAD><BODY>";
10  print "You chose $formdata{'language'}.
        Next time you visit, I'll greet you
        accordingly.";
```

3: Lines 3 and 4 analyze the incoming data.
6: This line sends a cookie to the server with a name of *language*, and a value that corresponds to whatever the visitor typed in the language field on the form. Notice the single newline (\n) at the end of the print statement.
8: Lines 8-10 give feedback to the visitor as usual. Remember that the browser doesn't like having nothing to do.

Figure 12.14 *You have to print the Set-Cookie header (line 6) before printing the Mime content line for the HTML page with the feedback (line 8).*

Figure 12.15 *The visitor doesn't see anything different about the form. They simply make their selection and submit the form as usual.*

Figure 12.16 *Depending on the preferences that the visitor has set for the browser (see page 176), an alert may appear advising the visitor that a cookie is about to be sent and allowing them to refuse it. The alert will contain the name and value of the information contained in the cookie as well as the expiration date (see page 170), domain (see page 171), and path (see page 172).*

Figure 12.17 *There is no outward evidence for the visitor (except the alert shown in Figure 12.16, which only appears in certain circumstances) that a cookie has been sent. It's up to you to tell your visitors what's going on.*

- You can send several cookies with the same script. Simply repeat steps 1–7 as necessary.

- Cookies can include additional data. For more details, see pages 170–173.

- *You* decide exactly what information you want to store. You can save a visitor's name (which you'll have to ask them for), or note if they've visited you before, and if so, how many times. It's up to you. You can store any information at your disposal in a cookie, including data you cull from environment variables *(see page 59)*.

- You don't have to store juicy data in the cookie itself—you can store an identification code for the visitor and then use that code to access data stored in another file. If you create codes for your visitors that link them to sensitive information, you'll want to encrypt them in some way so that sneaky visitors cannot change their own cookies *(see page 167)* in an attempt to get to other folks' data.

- Devise an alternate system (or error message) for visitors who don't accept cookies. Pages that don't work for no apparent reason are annoying.

- You can send up to 20 cookies, with a maximum size of 4Kb—which is approximately 4000 characters, a sizable amount—per cookie. Each visitor can store up to 300 cookies from all the sites they've visited. Matt Wright offers a clever CGI script that combines (he says *compresses*, but I find that term misleading) several cookies into one in order to keep the count down. It's called HTTP Cookie Library and you can find it at *http://worldwidemart.com/scripts/*.

Setting a cookie's expiration date

By default, cookies are temporarily stored in the browser's RAM and disappear when the visitor quits out of the browser. If you want to be able to access the information at a later date, you have to add an expiration date to the cookie. The expiration date simply determines how long the cookie will remain in the cookie file—assuming the visitor doesn't manually erase it first *(see page 167)*.

To set a cookie's expiration date:

1. Follow steps 1–5 on page 168 to begin the Set-Cookie header.
2. Type **;** to separate the name-value pair from the expiration date.
3. Type **expires=Wdy, DD-Mon-YYYY HH:MM:SS GMT**, where *Wdy* is the three letter abbreviation for the day of the week, *DD* is the two digit number of the day of the month, *Mon* is the three letter abbreviation for the name of the month, *YYYY* is the four digit representation of the year, *HH* is the two digit number for the hour, in 24-hour format and corresponding to Greenwich Mean Time, *MM* is the two digit number for the minutes, and *SS* is the two digit number for the seconds. Type *GMT* as is—it means *Greenwich Mean Time*.
4. Complete the Set-Cookie line by following steps 6–7 on page 168.

✔ Tip

- 24-hour format (often referred to as *military time*) means that 12am is 00, 1am is 01, and so on, and that 1pm is represented as 13, 2pm is 14, and so on up to 23 for 11pm.

```
1  #!/usr/local/bin/perl
2
3  require "subparseform.lib";
4  &Parse_Form;
5
6  print "Set-Cookie:language=$formdata
     {'language'}; expires=Thu,
     31-Dec-1998 00:00:00 GMT\n";
7
8  print "Content-type: text/html\n\n";
9  print "<HTML><HEAD><TITLE>Thanks for
     choosing!</TITLE></HEAD><BODY>";
10 print "You chose $formdata{'language'}.
     Next time you visit, I'll greet you
     accordingly.";
```

6: This line now contains an expiration date for the cookie. Notice the format for the date and the semi-colon that separates it from the cookie's data.

Figure 12.18 *Setting an expiration date for a cookie is the only way you can get rid of it. (The visitor can manually edit it from their cookie file, but few know how—see page 167.)*

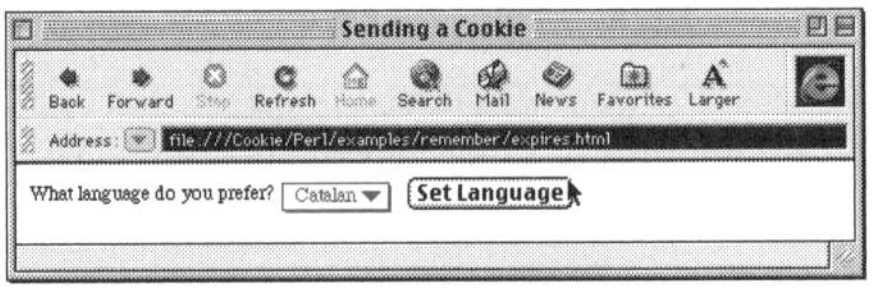

Figure 12.19 *The cookie will be sent when the visitor activates the form.*

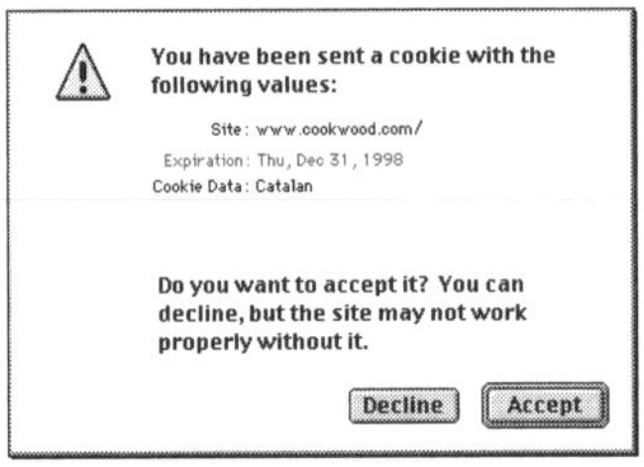

Figure 12.20 *Depending on the preferences the visitor has set for the browser, an alert may appear with information—including the expiration date—about the cookie.*

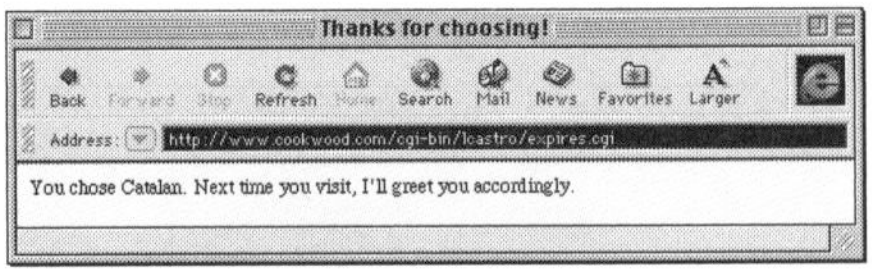

Figure 12.21 *You should always give your visitor some output.*

```
1   #!/usr/local/bin/perl
2
3   require "subparseform.lib";
4   &Parse_Form;
5
6   print "Set-Cookie:language=$formdata
       {'language'}; expires=Thu,
       31-Dec-1998 00:00:00 GMT;
       domain=help.cookwood.com\n";
7
8   print "Content-type: text/html\n\n";
9   print "<HTML><HEAD><TITLE>Thanks for
       choosing!</TITLE></HEAD><BODY>";
10  print "You chose $formdata{'language'}.
       Next time you visit, I'll greet you
       accordingly.";
```

6:   This line now contains a limited domain for
     the cookie. Don't forget to separate it from
     the rest of the Set-Cookie line with a semi-
     colon.

Figure 12.22 *Only requests for cookies that come from the help.cookwood.com domain will be honored.*

Figure 12.23 *The cookie will be sent when the visitor activates the form.*

Figure 12.24 *Depending on the preferences the visitor has set for the browser, an alert may appear with information—including the domain—about the cookie.*

Figure 12.25 *You should always give your visitor some output.*

Limiting a cookie to a domain

While a visitor's browser may store up to 300 cookies from a variety of different Web sites, the browser will only let *you* read cookies that came from *your* domain. In order to determine which cookies came from you, the browser looks at the domain attribute— which is set by default to the same domain that sent the cookie. If your domain is divided into smaller subdomains (home.domain.com, help.domain.com, etc.), you can set the cookie's domain to any of the more limited domains so that only those domains have access to the cookie.

To limit a cookie to a domain:

1. Follow steps 1–5 on page 168 to begin the Set-Cookie header.

2. If desired, set the expiration date as explained on page 170.

3. Type **;** to separate the rest of the Set-Cookie header from the domain.

4. Type **domain=www.domain.com**, where *www.domain.com* is the name of the domain that will be able to read the cookie once it is has been sent.

5. Complete the Set-Cookie line by following steps 6–7 on page 168.

✔ Tips

■ The domain you use must have at least two periods if it belongs to one of the seven special top-level domains (com, edu, net, org, gov, mil, or int), or three periods if it ends some other way.

■ You can't set cookies for domains other than the one you're sending the cookie from.

Limiting a cookie to a domain

Limiting a cookie to a part of your server

If you don't have to save CGI scripts in the cgi-bin directory, and thus are setting cookies from different locations, you may want to limit a part of your server's access to cookies. You can do this by specifying the path (or a part of the path) from which a cookie can be read.

To limit a cookie to a particular area of your server:

1. Follow steps 1–5 on page 168 to begin the Set-Cookie header.

2. If desired, set the expiration date and domain *(see pages 170–171).*

3. Type **;** to separate the rest of the Set-Cookie header from the domain.

4. Type **path=/directory**, where *directory* is the path that will be authorized to read the cookie once it is has been sent.

5. Complete the Set-Cookie line by following steps 6–7 on page 168.

✔ Tips

■ The domain *(see page 171)* is checked before the path. If the domain doesn't match, the path is not even looked at.

■ As you might expect, **/** is the most general path possible, and thus refers to the largest area on the server.

■ If you don't specify a path, it is automatically set as the same path as the file that sent the cookie.

■ If all your scripts are in the cgi-bin directory then it doesn't make much sense to alter the path.

```
1   #!/usr/local/bin/perl
2
3   require "subparseform.lib";
4   &Parse_Form;
5
6   print "Set-Cookie:language=$formdata
       {'language'}; expires=Thu,
       31-Dec-1998 00:00:00 GMT;
       domain=help.cookwood.com;
       path=/help\n";
7
8   print "Content-type: text/html\n\n";
9   print "<HTML><HEAD><TITLE>Thanks for
       choosing!</TITLE></HEAD><BODY>";
10  print "You chose
       $formdata{'language'}. Next time
       you visit, I'll greet you
       accordingly.";
```

6: This line now sets a limited path for the cookie. Don't forget to separate it from the rest of the Set-Cookie line with a semi-colon.

Figure 12.26 *Now, only requests for cookies that come from the paths that match /help (including / helpers and /help/files on the help.cookwood.com domain will be honored.*

Figure 12.27 *The cookie will be sent when the visitor activates the form.*

Figure 12.28 *Depending on the preferences the visitor has set for the browser, an alert may appear with information—including the path—about the cookie.*

Figure 12.29 *You should always give your visitor some output.*

```
1   #!/usr/local/bin/perl
2
3   require "subparseform.lib";
4   &Parse_Form;
5
6   print "Set-Cookie:language=$formdata
       {'language'}; expires=Thu,
       31-Dec-1998 00:00:00 GMT;
       domain=help.cookwood.com;
       path=/help; secure\n";
7
8   print "Content-type: text/html\n\n";
9   print "<HTML><HEAD><TITLE>Thanks for
       choosing!</TITLE></HEAD><BODY>";
10  print "You chose
       $formdata{'language'}. Next time
       you visit, I'll greet you
       accordingly.";
```

6: This line now limits the cookie to secure connections. Don't forget to separate it from the
   rest of the Set-Cookie line with a semi-colon.

Figure 12.30 *Only requests for cookies that come
from secure servers will be honored.*

Figure 12.31 *The cookie will be sent when the visitor activates the form.*

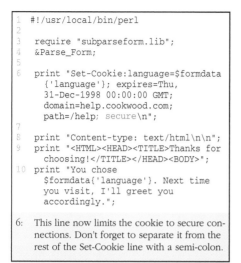

Figure 12.32 *Depending on the preferences the visitor has set for the browser, an alert may appear with information—including the path—about the cookie.*

Figure 12.33 *You should always give your visitor some output.*

Limiting cookies to secure connections

If you are saving particularly sensitive information—or an identification code that leads to sensitive information—via a cookie, you might want to limit sending the cookie to secure connections. This means that the cookie will only be sent to secure servers.

To limit cookies to secure connections:

1. Follow steps 1–5 on page 168 to begin the Set-Cookie header.

2. If desired, set the additional attributes as explained on pages 170–172.

3. Type ; to separate the rest of the Set-Cookie header from the domain.

4. Type **secure**.

5. Complete the Set-Cookie line by following steps 6–7 on page 168.

Reading and using a cookie

OK, you've stored a bit of information on your visitor's computer. Now how do you read it and use it? In fact, the server sends you all the information in all of the cookies available to you (given the domain and the path) each time you send a script to the server. That information is stored in the HTTP_COOKIE environment variable. Your job then is to analyze that variable to see what it contains.

To read and use a cookie:

1. Type **if ($ENV{'HTTP_COOKIE'}) {** to check to see if any cookies are available.

2. Type **@cookies = split (/;/, $ENV{'HTTP_COOKIE'});** to store each individual cookie (separated by semi-colons in the HTTP_COOKIE environment variable) in the @cookies array.

3. Type **foreach $cookie (@cookies) {** to begin a loop that looks at each individual cookie received.

4. Type **($name, $value) = split (/=/, $cookie);** to divide each cookie into its name and value components.

5. Type **$crumbs{$name} = $value;** to generate the %crumbs hash which will contain each cookie's name and value.

6. Type **}** to complete the foreach loop.

7. Create the part of the script that uses the information read from the cookie.

8. Type **}** to complete the if conditional.

9. If desired, create an else clause that prints an error if no cookies are set in the HTTP_COOKIE variable.

```
1   #!/usr/local/bin/perl
2
3   print "Content-type: text/html\n\n";
4
5   if ($ENV{'HTTP_COOKIE'}) {
6     @cookies = split (/;/,
        $ENV{'HTTP_COOKIE'});
7     foreach $cookie (@cookies) {
8       ($name, $value) = split (/=/,
          $cookie);
9       $crumbs{$name} = $value;
10    }
11
12    $language = $crumbs{'language'};
13    %greeting = (Catalan, "Bon dia.
        <P>Benvingut a la nostra
        p&agrave;gina Web.", Spanish,
        "Buenos d&iacute;as. <P>Bienvenidos
        a nuestra p&aacute;gina Web.",
        French, "Bon jour. Bienvenue!",
        English, "Hello. <P>Welcome to our
        Web page.");
14  print "<HTML><HEAD><TITLE>Greeting
        </TITLE></HEAD><BODY>";
15  print "<CENTER><H1>$greeting
        {$language}</H1></CENTER>";
16  print "</BODY></HTML>";
17
18  } else {
19    print "Couldn't find any cookies.
        Perhaps you've got your browser
        set to refuse all cookies? ";
20  }
```

5: The server sends the name and value of each available cookie to the HTTP_COOKIE environment variable. Line 5 checks if there are any cookies available.

6: Since multiple cookies are separated with a semi-colon, this line divides the incoming data into individual cookies and store them in the @cookies array.

7: The name and value (other cookie information, like the expiration date, is neither sent nor stored in the environment variable) are connected with an equals sign. Lines 7 and 8 separate each cookie into its name and value.

9: Line 9 generates the %crumbs hash out of the names and values of each cookie received in HTTP_COOKIE.

12: Lines 12–16 use the information gleaned from the cookie named "language" to decide which greeting to display.

18: If the HTTP_COOKIE environment variable is empty, lines 18–20 print out an error message.

Figure 12.34 *Since you can store up to 20 individual cookies on the visitor's browser, you'll have to specify the cookie you want to use by name (line 12).*

Figure 12.35 *So, the visitor fills out the form and activates the script that sends the cookie.*

Figure 12.36 *You give them confirmation that you've received the information.*

Figure 12.37 *In this example, I used the cookie to save information about the visitor's preferred language. Then I used that information to actually print out a greeting in that language—Catalan in this case—the next time they visit.*

Figure 12.38 *If there are no cookies to read (in the HTTP_COOKIE environment variable), the visitor will see this error.*

✔ Tips

- You can create a subroutine to read in cookies so that you can access it from the scripts that use the information gleaned from those cookies.

- For more information on using environment variables, consult Chapter 4, *Environment Variables*.

- You can use different names for the @cookies array and %crumbs hash. Just be consistent.

- Although you may have set the expiration date, domain, and other cookie information, only the name and value are available in the HTTP_COOKIE environment variable.

How (and why) your visitors refuse cookies

Some folks are not interested in anyone keeping tabs on them. They may have unfounded worries of you copying personal data from their computers or infecting them with a virus (neither is possible—you can only store non-executable files with data they have given you, along with environment variables). And they may know that some sites compile information about which pages folks visit and then use it for marketing purposes. Therefore, some visitors may either refuse all or some of the cookies that are sent their way.

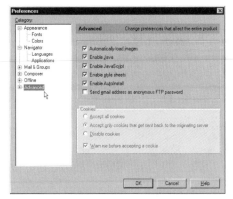

Figure 12.39 *In Netscape for Windows or Mac (they're virtually identical in this respect), choose Edit > Preferences, click the Advanced tab at the left and then choose the cookie option at right.*

To control cookies:

1. Choose Edit > Preferences in your browser. The Preferences dialog box appears.

2. In Netscape (Mac and Windows), click Advanced under Category in the left list.

   In Explorer for Mac, click Cookies under Receiving Files in the left list. (For Explorer for Windows, see Figure 12.41.)

   Either way, the Cookies preferences appear at the right side of the window **(Figures 12.39 and 12.40)**.

3. Choose whether to accept all cookies, whether you want the browser to ask you about each cookie, or if you want to refuse all cookies.

4. Click OK to save the preferences.

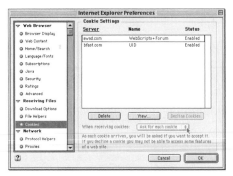

Figure 12.40 *In Explorer for Mac, click Cookies at left and then choose the desired option from the pop-up menu.*

✔ Tip

■ Tell your visitors what you're doing to put them at ease. Remind them that you can't access, save, or share their personal data unless they give it to you first. Stating your privacy policy is also an easy way to assure your visitors.

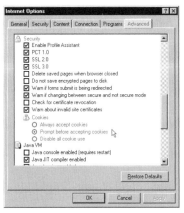

Figure 12.41 *With Internet Explorer for Windows, you choose View > Internet Options and then click the Advanced tab. Scroll down a ways until you get to the Security section. The available cookie options are at the bottom of the section.*

Printing and HTML

The print function is so essential to creating Perl CGI scripts that I included it in Chapter 2, *Creating Perl CGI Scripts*. Since then, you'll have seen it used in absolutely every single script in this book. The print function is the key to displaying the information gathered or processed by your script.

This book assumes that most of your output is printed to a browser like Netscape Communicator or Internet Explorer in HTML format. Thankfully, most major browsers will not complain a bit if you leave out the header tags, specifically HTML, HEAD and BODY—and, in fact, I've done just that throughout this book in order to save space. Just the same, it's a good idea to create standard HTML pages, complete with headers—you'll run into less compatibility snags and get less complaints from persnickety browsers.

Of course, you can do a lot more with HTML than just format the headers and footers. HTML formatting is instrumental in highlighting the information that you want your visitors to pay attention to. While it's not technically required, it makes all the difference in the world.

There is some formatting, especially of numerical output, that is easier to do in Perl than in HTML. I'll discuss the printf and sprintf functions on pages 186–188.

Formatting output with HTML

You can print HTML tags with your script as you would any other constant.

To add HTML formatting to output:

1. Type **print**.

2. Type ".

3. Type **<TAG>**, where *TAG* is the name of the HTML tag and includes any desired attributes.

4. If desired, type **data**, where data is the output from the Perl script that you wish to output.

5. If necessary, type **</TAG>**, where */TAG* is the closing tag that corresponds to the tag used in step 3.

6. Type ".

7. Type **;** to complete the sentence.

✔ Tips

- There are several symbols used in HTML tags—including double and single quotation marks, semicolons, and the ampersand. If any of these symbols appear in the HTML formatting you'll have to precede them with a backslash so that Perl doesn't confuse them with the corresponding elements in the Perl statement.

- Since HTML does not require using quotation marks except when enclosing two word phrases or words with non-alphanumeric symbols, I would recommend leaving them out wherever possible.

- To create legible source code, add a newline character (\n) where you would like a return in the HTML code **(Figures 13.5, 13.6, and 13.7)**.

```
1   #!/usr/local/bin/perl
2
3   ($sec,$min,$hour,$mday,$mon,$year,
     $wday,$yday,$isdst)=localtime(time);
4
5   @days = (Sunday,Monday,Tuesday,
     Wednesday,Thursday,Friday,Saturday);
6   @months =(January,February,March,
     April, May,June,July,August,
     September,October,November,
     December);
7
8   print "Content-type: text/html\n\n";
9   print "Today is <B>$days[$wday],
     $months[$mon] $mday</B>.";
```

3: The Perl aspects of this script are explained in detail on page 85.
9: I've added the HTML bold tags <B> around the date so that the results are more obvious in the browser.

Figure 13.1 *Adding HTML to your results is just like adding HTML anywhere else. Just insert the proper tags (and attributes) before and after the text you want to format.*

Figure 13.2 *The visitor clicks the link to the script...*

Figure 13.3 *...and the result is shown in the browser. Notice how the bold formatting helps highlight the important part of the result of the script.*

```
1   #!/usr/local/bin/perl
2
3   ($sec,$min,$hour,$mday,$mon,$year,
      $wday,$yday,$isdst)=localtime(time);
4
5   @days = (Sunday,Monday,Tuesday,
      Wednesday,Thursday,Friday,Saturday);
6   @months =(January,February,March,
      April, May,June,July,August,
      September,October,November,
      December);
7
8   print "Content-type: text/html\n\n";
9   print "<HTML>\n<HEAD>\n<TITLE>Get the
      date</TITLE>\n</HEAD>\n<BODY>\n";
10  print "<P>Today is <B>$days[$wday],
      $months[$mon] $mday</B>.\n";
11  print "</BODY>\n</HTML>";
```

9: Line 9 creates the standard opening for an HTML document, including a title for the page. The newlines (\n) will make the HTML source code more legible.

10: Officially, all new paragraphs in HTML should begin with a <P> tag.

11: This line prints the closing tags for the HTML document.

Figure 13.4 *While including standard opening and closing HTML tags is a good idea, most browsers will cut you some slack if you omit them.*

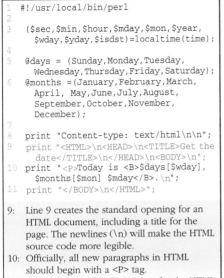

Figure 13.5 *The only difference here (besides the new date) is the title in the title bar.*

Figure 13.6 *If you or your visitors choose View > Page Source in Netscape (shown), or View > Source in Internet Explorer, the HTML code (but not the CGI script) used to generate the page will be shown.*

Figure 13.7 *The source code for the generated document is easy to read, thanks to the newlines. The browser doesn't care either way, but if you want to be able to decipher the generated code, newlines make it a lot easier.*

- Remember that HTML and Perl treat newlines differently. A browser will not recognize any newlines inserted in the HTML code: to insert returns or line breaks between lines of text, you must use <P> or <BR>, respectively. On the other hand, Perl doesn't recognize HTML tags, so if you want the output to look recognizable when you're testing locally without a browser, you might want to add some newlines as well.

- You can use one print statement for each HTML tag, or print several tags at once, as you prefer. Or use special here documents as described on page 180.

- You can add foreign characters and special symbols to your HTML formatting. Just be sure to escape (precede with a backslash) the semicolons.

- Since the beginning and end of an HTML document are always the same, you can create a subroutine to generate these parts *(see page 182)*.

- The popular CGI.pm module, available at *http://www.wiley.com/compbooks/stein/*, written by Lincoln Stein, lets you use a whole system of variables to add HTML formatting to Perl output. Personally, I prefer creating my HTML tags the way I already know how without having to learn a whole new set of variable names. Nevertheless, many folks use the CGI.pm module and are very happy with it and claim it saves them lots of time and typing. Just know it's completely optional.

- Last plug. If you want to learn more about HTML's formatting possibilities, check out my other book, *HTML 4 for the World Wide Web: Visual QuickStart Guide*, also published by Peachpit Press.

Formatting output with HTML

Printing several lines at a time

It can get downright tedious typing a lot of quotation marks and a million print statements to type out all the HTML code that you may want to use. Perl has a nifty shortcut, cryptically called a "here" document, that can save you a lot of typing (and tedium).

To print several lines at a time:

1. Type **print <<"label";**, where *label* is the word or phrase that you will type to signal the end of the print statement.

2. Type all of the HTML codes and Perl content you want to print.

3. Begin a new line and type **label**, where *label* matches the label you chose in step 1. No semicolon is necessary at then end of this line. In fact, the line should contain nothing except the label itself.

✔ Tips

- By default, the text is considered enclosed in double quotation marks and any variables therein will be interpolated as such *(see page 28)*. You can enclose the label text in single quotation marks in step 1 if you prefer the text not to be interpolated.

- As long as you're happy with interpolation—and your label text doesn't contain any spaces—you can omit the double quotation marks from step 1.

- You don't have to backslash special symbols within a here document.

- A here document is something similar to the <PRE> tag in HTML. Everything contained within will be printed just as it is.

```
1   #!/usr/local/bin/perl
2
3   ($sec,$min,$hour,$mday,$mon,$year,
       $wday,$yday,$isdst)=localtime(time);
4
5   @days = (Sunday,Monday,Tuesday,
       Wednesday,Thursday,Friday,Saturday);
6   @months =(January,February,March,
       April, May,June,July,August,
       September,October,November,
       December);
7
8   print "Content-type: text/html\n\n";
9
10  print <<"HTML code";
11
12  <HTML>
13  <HEAD>
14  <TITLE>Get the date</TITLE>
15  </HEAD>
16  <BODY>
17
18  <P>Today is <B>$days[$wday],
       $months[$mon]  $mday</B>
19
20  </BODY></HTML>
21
22  HTML code
```

10: This line begins the here document. The label I've chosen, "HTML code" contains a space so I've enclosed the whole thing in quotation marks. If the space weren't there, the quotation marks wouldn't be necessary.

12 Lines 12–20 are equivalent to lines 9–11 in Figure 13.4 on page 179, but are a good deal easier to type without all of the quotation marks, and newlines (\n).

12: This line contains the label from the opening print statement and nothing else—not even a leading or trailing space.

Figure 13.8 *This script is equivalent to the one shown in Figure 13.4 on page 179 but it was much easier to write.*

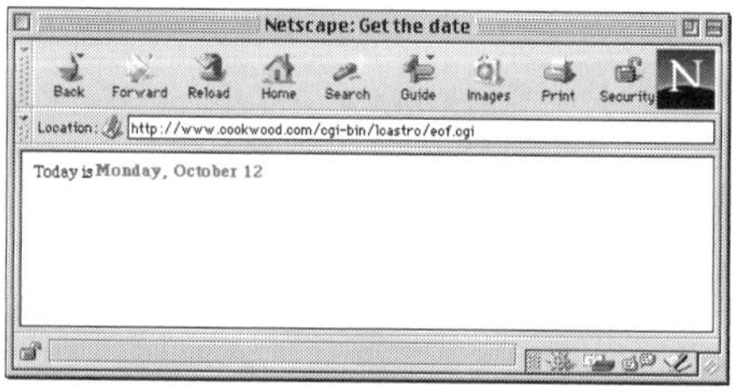

Figure 13.9 *The result is identical to that shown in Figure 13.5 on page 179.*

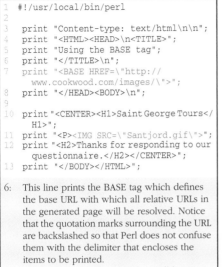

```
1   #!/usr/local/bin/perl
2
3   print "Content-type: text/html\n\n";
4   print "<HTML><HEAD>\n<TITLE>";
5   print "Using the BASE tag";
6   print "</TITLE>\n";
7   print "<BASE HREF=\"http://
       www.cookwood.com/images/\">";
8   print "</HEAD><BODY>\n";
9
10  print "<CENTER><H1>Saint George Tours</
       H1>";
11  print "<P><IMG SRC=\"Santjord.gif\">";
12  print "<H2>Thanks for responding to our
       questionnaire.</H2></CENTER>";
13  print "</BODY></HTML>";
```

6: This line prints the BASE tag which defines the base URL with which all relative URLs in the generated page will be resolved. Notice that the quotation marks surrounding the URL are backslashed so that Perl does not confuse them with the delimiter that encloses the items to be printed.

11: The relative URL for the image will be resolved as *http://www.cookwood.com/images/Santjord.gif*. Again, notice the backslashed quotation marks!

Figure 13.10 *The BASE tag lets you define the URL for the generated document with which all the relative URLs for images, links, applets, and other referenced files will be resolved.*

Figure 13.11 *The actual location of this image is* http://www.cookwood.com/images/Santjord.gif. *Without the BASE tag, I would either have to use this absolute URL or figure out the relative location of the generated document (in the cgi-bin directory or somewhere else?) with respect to the image.*

Simplifying paths to images and links

It's sometimes a little tricky to figure out what path to use to images and links that you want to reference from an HTML document that you've generated with a script. Unless you use absolute paths, you'll need to know what the relationship is between the location of the images and the location of the HTML page. But, where is the generated document located? Depending on how your server is set up, your answer may vary. The easiest way to get around this problem is to avoid it altogether. You can use HTML's BASE tag to override the page's physical location and make the HTML document act as if it were in a particular directory of your choosing on the server. Then you can use that information to set up the links to images (and other files).

To simplify paths to images and links:

1. Decide which directory you want the generated page to act as if it were located in.

2. In the script, after printing the opening HEAD tag but before printing the closing HEAD tag, type **print "<BASE HREF=\"pretend. location.url\">"**, where *pretend.location.url* is the directory that you've chosen in step 1. Notice that the quotation marks around the URL are backslashed so that Perl doesn't think they mark the end of the print statement.

✔ **Thanks!**

■ Special thanks to Christian (Dimmy) Tan for opening my eyes to the BASE tag's incredible usefulness.

Simplifying paths to images and links

Creating header and footer subroutines

Since the header and footer sections of an HTML document are always the same, you can create a subroutine to generate them automatically.

To create a header subroutine:

1. Create a text document.

2. Type **sub Header {**.

3. Type **print "Content-type: text/ html\n\n";**. Including the Mime content line in the subroutine is a good way to make sure you don't forget it.

4. Type **print "<HTML><HEAD><TITLE>";**.

5. Type **print $_[0];** in order to print out the argument that was passed to the subroutine (the title of the page).

6. Type **print "</TITLE></HEAD> <BODY>\n";**. The newline will separate the header from the rest of the source code, but it's optional.

7. Type **}** to complete the definition of the header subroutine.

8. Type **sub Footer {**.

9. Type **print "\n</BODY></HTML>";**. Again, the optional newline (\n) separates the closing HTML tags from the rest of the generated page.

10. Type **}** to complete the definition of the Footer subroutine.

11. Type **1;** to complete the subroutine file.

12. Save the file as text-only. Give it a name like *header_footer.lib*. Make sure the permissions are 644. (As a subroutine it doesn't need to be executable).

```
1   sub Header {
2      print "Content-type:text/html\n\n";
3      print "<HTML><HEAD><TITLE>";
4      print "$_[0]";
5      print "</TITLE></HEAD><BODY>\n";
6   }
7
8   sub Footer {
9      print "\n</BODY></HTML>";
10  }
11  1;
```

1: This lines begins the definition of the Header subroutine. Notice that the shebang line *(see page 32)* is not required.

2: Line 2 prints the Mime content line *(see page 34)*.

3: Line 3 prints the standard opening tags for an HTML document.

4: Line 4 takes the argument passed to the subroutine *(step 3 on page 183)* and prints it as the title of the HTML page.

5: This line prints the closing TITLE and HEAD tags, starts the BODY section of the HTML document, and uses a newline to separate all the header HTML tags from the body of the generated page.

6: The closing curly bracket completes the definition of the Header subroutine.

8: The sub function begins the definition of the Footer subroutine.

9: This line prints the standard closing HTML tags. The newline visually separates the closing HTML tags from the rest of the generated page and is optional.

10: The curly bracket completes the definition of the Footer subroutine.

11: This line gives a true value (1) when the subroutine file is required by another Perl script. Otherwise, the require function *(see line 3 in Figure 13.13 on page 183)* will fail.

Figure 13.12 *Creating a subroutine file for common operations like printing out the header or footer of an HTML page makes it easy to create HTML pages that conform to the current standards requested by major browsers.*

```
1   #!/usr/local/bin/perl
2
3   require "header_footer.lib";
4
5   ($sec,$min,$hour,$mday,$mon,$year,
       $wday,$yday,$isdst)=localtime(time);
6
7   @days = (Sunday,Monday,Tuesday,
       Wednesday,Thursday,Friday,Saturday);
8   @months =(January,February,March,
       April, May,June,July,August,
       September,October,November,
       December);
9
10  &Header("Get the Date");
11  print "<P>Today is <B>$days[$wday],
       $months[$mon] $mday</B>.\n";
12  &Footer;
```

3: This line opens the file that contains the sub-
    routines (header_footer.lib) and makes those
    subroutines available to this script.
10 This line calls the Header subroutine and
    passes to it the argument "Get the Date"
    (which will be the title of the page).
12: This line calls the Footer subroutine.

Figure 13.13 *You must access the subroutine file with the require function before calling the subroutines.*

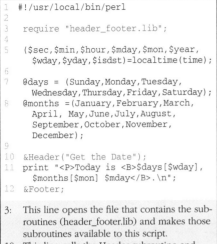

Figure 13.14 *As usual, the visitor clicks the link to the script.*

Figure 13.15 *And the result looks pretty much the same. Only you know that the script was much simpler.*

Figure 13.16 *The source code shows the standard opening and closing HTML tags.*

To call the header subroutine:

1. At the top of your script, after the first line, type **require "header_footer.lib";** where *header_footer.lib* is the name (and path if necessary) of the file containing the header and footer subroutines.

2. Later in your Perl script, but before printing anything else (except cookie headers), type **&Header(**, where *Header* is the name of the subroutine, as defined in step 2 on page 182.

3. Type **"Page Title"**, where *Page Title* is the desired title for the HTML document, or a variable containing that name.

4. Type **);** to close the argument to the subroutine and complete the sentence.

To call the footer subroutine:

1. At the beginning of your Perl script, if you haven't done so already, type **require "header_footer.lib";** where *header_footer.lib* is the name (and path if necessary) of the file that contains the Footer subroutine.

2. Later in your Perl script after printing all of the rest of the output that will go to the browser, type **&Footer,** where *Footer* is the name of the subroutine, as defined in step 8 on page 182.

✔ Tips

■ You can combine print statements, use individual ones, or use here documents *(see page 180)*, as you prefer. Perl doesn't care one way or the other.

■ For more information about creating subroutines, consult Chapter 9, *Subroutines* starting on page 117.

Creating header and footer subroutines

Outputting a hash as a table

One of the nice things about outputting Perl data using HTML tags is that you can add formatting that makes your data really stand out and get noticed. One great way to view data from a hash is to format it as a table.

To output a hash as a table:

1. Start your Perl script the regular way—using the Header subroutine explained on page 182, if desired.

2. Create the part of the script that generates the data that will be contained in the table.

3. Type **print "<TABLE>\n";** to begin the HTML table. Add any TABLE attributes as desired.

4. If desired, **print "<TR><TH>Key <TH>Value";** where *Key* and *Value* are the headers for the key and value columns of the table.

5. Type **foreach $key (keys %hash) {**, where *%hash* is the name of the hash that you want to output to the browser in the form of a table.

6. Type **print "<TD>$key";** to print the keys in the first column of the table.

7. Type **print "<TD>$hash{$key}";** to print the values in the second column of the table.

8. Type **}** to complete the foreach loop.

9. Type **print "</TABLE>";** to complete the table definition.

10. Print the closing HTML tags, using the &Footer subroutine *(see page 182)*, if desired.

```
1   #!/usr/local/bin/perl
2
3   require "subparseform.lib";
4   &Parse_Form;
5
6   print "Content-type: text/html\n\n";
7   print "<HTML><HEAD>\n<TITLE>";
8   print "Showing off with HTML";
9   print "</TITLE>\n</HEAD><BODY>\n";
10
11  print "<H2>Thanks for responding. Here's
      what you told us:</H2>";
12  print "<TABLE BORDER=3 WIDTH=60%>\n";
13  print "<TR><TH>Key<TH>Value\n";
14  foreach $key (keys %formdata){
15    print "<TR><TD>$key
        <TD>$formdata{$key}\n";
16    }
17  print "</TABLE>";
18  print "</BODY></HTML>";
```

12: This line begins the table.

13: This line prints the header cells.

14: After you've begun the table and printed the header cells, if any, the foreach loop prints creates a new row for each key and value in the hash.

17: If you forget this all important closing TABLE tag, the table will simply not appear.

Figure 13.17 *The only part of the table that should be within the foreach loop is the actual contents of each of the cells.*

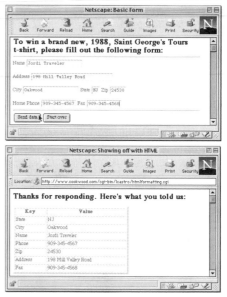

Figure 13.18 *The information entered by the visitor is displayed neatly in a table.*

```
1  #!/usr/local/bin/perl
2
3  require "subparseform.lib";
4  &Parse_Form;
5
6  $building = $formdata{'building'};
7  @buildings = split(/,/, $building);
8
9  print "Content-type: text/html\n\n";
10 print "<UL>You chose:";
11
12 foreach $item (@buildings) {
13     print "<LI>$item\n";
14 }
15
16 print "</UL>";
```

6: Lines 6 and 7 get the information from the visitor and split it into an array.
10: This line begins the unordered list and prints a header.
12: The foreach loop prints each element in the array as a list item (LI).
13: Don't forget the closing list tag.

Figure 13.19 *Lists are particularly useful for formatting multiple choices.*

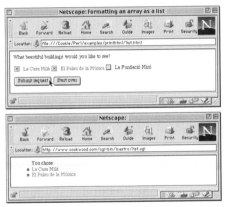

Figure 13.20 *The options chosen by the visitor are displayed neatly in a list.*

Outputting an array as a list

Arrays, or lists of elements, can be outputted effectively using HTML's list formatting tags.

To output an array as a list:

1. Start your Perl script the regular way—using the &Header subroutine as discussed on page 182, if desired.

2. Create the part of the script that generates the data that will be contained in the list.

3. Type **print "<OL>\n";** to begin an ordered list.

   Or type **print "<UL>\n";** to begin an unordered list.

4. If desired, **print "list header";** where *list header* explains what the list contains.

5. Type **foreach $item (@array) {**, where *@array* is the name of the array that you want to output to the browser in the form of a list.

6. Type **print "<LI>$item\n";** to print each element of the array as a list item. The newline (\n) makes the source code easier to read, but is optional.

7. Type **}** to complete the foreach loop.

8. Type **print "</OL>";** to complete the ordered list definition.

   Or type **print "</UL>";** to complete the unordered list definition.

9. Print the closing HTML tags for the document, using the &Footer subroutine *(see page 182)*, if desired.

Formatting numbers and strings

Perl has a couple of important functions for formatting data. The first, printf, lets you format output as you print. The second, sprintf, uses exactly the same parameters, but instead of printing out the result, saves the result into another variable that you can then continue to process as necessary.

To print or save formatted data:

1. Type **printf(** to simply print out the formatted data.

   Or type **$formatted = sprintf(**, where *$formatted* is the name of the scalar variable in which you wish to store the newly formatted data.

2. Type **"format"**,, where *format* is the code you've created in the steps on these pages. Don't forget the comma.

3. Type **$data**, where *$data* is the scalar variable that contains what you want to format.

4. Type **)**.

5. Type **;** to complete the print statement.

✔ Tip

■ The two most common formats are discussed on pages 187–188.

```
1   #!/usr/local/bin/perl
2
3   require 'subparseform.lib';
4   &Parse_Form;
5   print "Content-type:text/html\n\n";
6
7   $price = $formdata{'price'};
8   $tax = $formdata{'tax'}/100;
9
10  $salestax = $price * $tax;
11
12  $formattax = sprintf("\$%.2f",
      $salestax);
13
14  print "You'll have to pay $formattax in
      sales tax, unformatted it would look
      like $salestax";
```

7: In the real world I'd want to make sure that the visitor had typed numbers (and no extraneous symbols or text) in the price and tax fields.

12: This line formats the contents of the $salestax variable and stores the results in the $formattax variable.

Figure 13.21 *The sprintf function makes it easy to format your data properly as dollars and cents.*

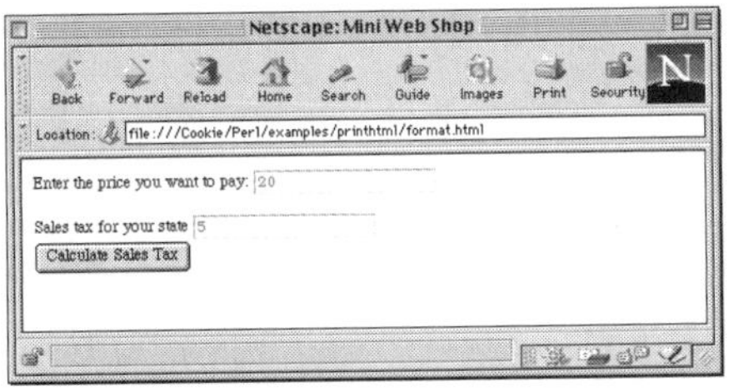

Figure 13.22 *The visitor enters the price and the tax.*

Figure 13.23 *The sales tax is calculated and then printed out first in dollars and cents and then as a regular integer (for comparison).*

Formatting numbers as dollars and cents

Perhaps the most common formatting issue is trying to format numbers as dollars and cents. Perl makes this easy.

To format numbers as dollars and cents:

1. Follow step 1 on page 186 to set up either the **printf** or **sprintf** function.

2. To begin the format definition, type **"\$**. The backslash is necessary to remove the special meaning from the dollar sign.

3. Type **%.2f** to format the number with two decimal points (cents). The *f* stands for fixed point format floating-point number, and shouldn't be changed.

4. Type **"**.

5. Type **,** (a comma) to separate the format from the data you're formatting.

6. Continue with step 3 on page 186.

Padding numbers

To pad numbers with leading zeros and/or spaces:

1. Follow step 1 on page 186 to set up either the **printf** or **sprintf** function.

2. Type "**%**.

3. If desired, type **-** in order to pad the extra spaces to the right of the number. (The default is for padding to go to the left of the number.)

4. If desired, type **m**, where *m* is the total number of digits and spaces that should be in the final formatted result.

5. Type **.nd**, where *n* is the total number of digits (not counting spaces) that should be in the final result. Leading zeros will be added as necessary. The *d* stands for decimal integer, and should not be changed.

6. Type **"**.

7. Type **,** (a comma) to separate the format from the data you're formatting.

8. Continue with step 3 on page 186.

✔ Tip

■ You can pad *strings* by using **"%ms"**, where *m* is the total number of characters and spaces that should be in the final formatted result. Add the hyphen as in step 3 to pad the spaces to the right.

```
1   #!/usr/local/bin/perl
2
3   ($sec,$min,$hour,$mday,$mon,$year,$wday,$
    yday,$isdst)=localtime(time);
4   $min=sprintf("%02d", $min);
5   $sec=sprintf("%02d", $sec);
6
7   print "Content-type: text/html\n\n";
8   print "According to my server, right now
    the time is: $hour:$min:$sec";
9
```

3: The localtime and time functions get the local time from the server. The rest of this line stores the resulting data into nine scalar variables.

4: The initial format for the contents of the $min and $sec variables are integers, which due to the way we usually give the time, will look downright strange for numbers less than 10 (imagine a time of 12:5:9). So, lines 4 and 5 pad an extra zero to the left of the number where necessary.

Figure 13.24 *The sprintf function is essential for properly formatting hours and minutes.*

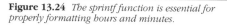

Figure 13.25 *The script is activated by a link.*

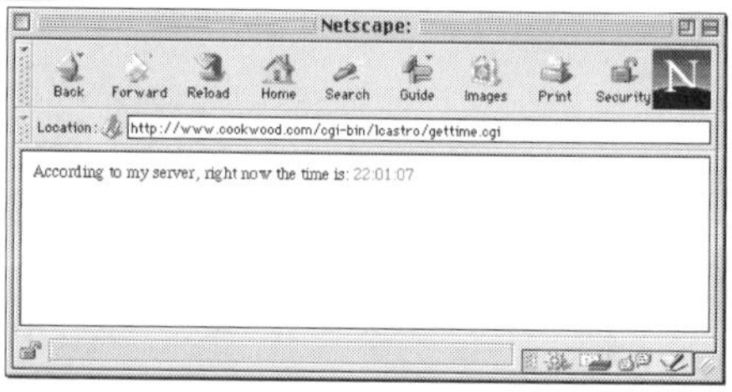

Figure 13.26 *The time is formatted properly. Without sprintf, the time would look like 22:1:7.*

Files and Directories

We've already talked about how to input data from a form and how to output data to the browser. You can also input and output data to and from a file on the server. This is handy when you want to store information for longer periods of time, or when you want to access that stored data. In Perl, you create a label for the file, called a *filehandle*, and then refer to the label when opening, closing, writing, or otherwise working with the files.

Working with external files raises additional security concerns. You don't want just anybody to be able to remove directories or overwrite your log files. Be sure and read Appendix C, *Security*.

Chapter 14

Opening a file

Before you can read or write to a file, you have to open a connection to it.

To open a file:

1. Type **open(**.

2. Type **LABEL,**, where *LABEL* is the filehandle. You'll use this label from this point on when referring to the file. Don't forget the comma.

3. Type **"**.

4. If you want to be able to write to the file, type **>**. Any existing contents in the file will be lost.

   Or, to append data to the file, type **>>**. Existing data is left unchanged with new data following directly thereafter (with no spaces or returns separating them).

   Or, to simply read or input data from the file, no extra symbol is required. (If you like being explicit, type **<**.)

5. Type **filename,** (directly after the symbol in step 4, if any) where *filename* is the actual name, including the path if necessary, of the file that you wish to open. You can also use a scalar variable or expression for the filename.

6. Type **"**.

7. Type **)** to complete the function.

8. Type **;** to complete the line.

```
1   #!/usr/local/bin/perl
2
3   require "subparseform.lib";
4   &Parse_Form;
5
6   $comments = $formdata{'comments'};
7
8   open(LOG, ">>../../logs/logfile.txt")
9   printLOG "$comments\n";
10  close(LOG);
11
12  print "Content-type: text/html\n\n";
13  print "<P>You commented thusly:
        <BLOCKQUOTE><P><I>$comments</I>
        </BLOCKQUOTE>\n";
14  print "<HR>Would you like to see all the
        messages? <A HREF=\"http://
        www.cookwood.com/cgi-bin/lcastro/
        readfromlog.cgi\">Yes</A>";
15
```

8: This lines assigns the filehandle LOG to the *logfile.txt* file and opens it for appending data (with the >>). Notice the quotation marks that enclose the greater-than signs, the path, *and* the filename.

Figure 14.1 *Before reading from or writing to a file, you must open it and assign it a label or* filehandle. *You can't really see the effect of the open function— it is a precursor to reading from or writing to an external file.*

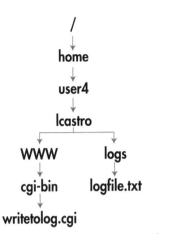

Figure 14.2 *Probably the hardest part about the open function is getting the path names right. Here is a partial map of my directories. The script is called* writetolog.cgi *and is located in the* cgi-bin *directory. I want to open the* logfile.txt *file. To reference that file, I could either use an absolute file name like "/home/user4/lcastro/logs/logfile.txt" or a relative name like "../../logs/logfile.txt". I chose the latter because it's shorter. For more about paths on Unix servers, consult* Dealing with paths in Unix *on page 243. Also note that by putting the* logfile.txt *file outside my WWW directory, I make it impossible for folks to access it by typing its URL in their browser. It has no URL.*

✔ Tips

- It's considered good style and Perl convention to use all uppercase letters for the filehandle.

- Since Perl won't alert you or your visitors to any problems, it's a good idea to create a subroutine that quits out of the script if a problem opening the file should occur. For more information, consult *Verifying file and directory operations* on page 192.

- If the script writes to an external file, you'll want to make sure it has exclusive access, so that several visitors don't use the script at once and leave you with a garbled file. For more information, consult *Getting exclusive access to a file* on page 194.

- It's important to close the file as soon as possible after opening it so that other visitors can use it. For details, consult *Closing a file* on page 196.

- If you try to open a file for writing or appending (that is with > or >>) that doesn't exist, Perl will create it for you—*as long as* the permissions of the directory in which the file is being created are amenable.

- If you try to open a file for reading that doesn't exist (with < or nothing), Perl will ignore you. (Hey, it's hard to read nothing.) This is a good time to use an error subroutine *(see page 192).*

Opening a file

Verifying file and directory operations

Unfortunately, Perl will continue running a script even if it hasn't been able to open the external file. Therefore, it's a good idea to create a manual alert system in case something goes wrong. You can create a subroutine that prints out an error message and then exits the script.

To verify file and directory operations:

1. Type the desired function (for example, the **open** function as described on page 190).

2. On the same line, type **||**. This is a logical or operator. It requires that one of its two arguments be true. Therefore, if the open function fails, what follows the **||** will run (and therefore be true).

3. Continuing on the same line, type **&Error**, where *Error* is the name of the subroutine that prints out an error message and then exits the script.

4. Type **;** to finish the line.

5. Create the subroutine elsewhere in the script (or in an external file).

✔ Tips

■ For more information on the **exit** function and creating an error subroutine, see page 214. You might also consult Chapter 9, *Subroutines*.

■ The most common problems that trip up the open function are incorrectly set permissions (of either the file or the directory that contains the file) and erroneous path names. Check both carefully.

```
1   #!/usr/local/bin/perl
2
3   require "subparseform.lib";
4   &Parse_Form;
5
6   $comments = $formdata{'comments'};
7
8   open(LOG, ">>../../logs/logfile.txt")
       || &ErrorMessage;
9   print LOG "$comments\n";
10  close(LOG);
11
12  print "Content-type: text/html\n\n";
13  print "<P>You commented thusly:
       <BLOCKQUOTE><P><I>$comments</I>
       </BLOCKQUOTE>\n";
14  print "<HR>Would you like to see all
       the messages? <A HREF=\"http://
       www.cookwood.com/cgi-bin/lcastro/
       readfromlog.cgi\">Yes</A>";
15
16  sub ErrorMessage {
17    print "Content-type: text/
       html\n\n";
18    print "The server can't open the
       file. It either doesn't exist or
       the permissions are wrong. \n";
19    exit;
20  }
```

8:   The || operator requires that either the open function return true (that is, be successful) or the &ErrorMessage subroutine be executed.

16   I've included the &ErrorMessage subroutine in the same script but you could easily move it to another file *(see page 124)*.

18:   This message will be output to the browser if Perl can't open the file referenced in line 8.

19:   In addition, the exit function aborts the entire script—if you can't open the log file, there's not much point in continuing.

Figure 14.3 *An error subroutine for the open function should include two parts: an error message that will advise the visitor of the problem and an exit line that will abort the script.*

Figure 14.4 *If the open function fails, instead of continuing merrily along, Perl will output this error message and abort the rest of the script.*

```
1   #!/usr/local/bin/perl
2   require "subparseform.lib";
3   &Parse_Form;
4   $comments = $formdata{'comments'};
5
6   open(LOG,">>../../logs/logfile.txt")||
       &ErrorMessage;
7   print LOG "$comments\n";
8   close(LOG);
9
10  print "Content-type: text/html\n\n";
11  print "<P>You commented thusly:
       <BLOCKQUOTE><P><I>$comments</I>
       </BLOCKQUOTE>\n";
12  print "<HR>Would you like to see all the
       messages? <A HREF=\"http://
       www.cookwood.com/cgi-bin/lcastro/
       readfromlog.cgi\">Yes</A>";
```

6:   The >> before the filename indicates that
     print statements will be *appended* to the file.
7:   This line prints the contents of the variable
     $comments and a newline (\n) to the file
     referenced by the filehandle LOG (that is,
     logfile.txt).
10: Lines 10–12 create output for the browser.
     Without them, line 7 is still executed prop-
     erly, but the visitor will get an error from the
     browser. (Browsers can't show "nothing").

Figure 14.5 *The newline in line 7 ensures that each
visitor's comments will be on their own line and will
thus be easier to read later.*

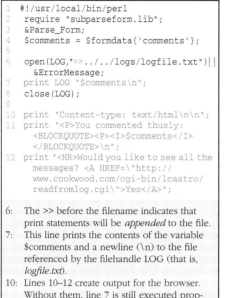

Figure 14.6 *The visitor enters comments and then
clicks Submit Form to start the script.*

Figure 14.7 *The visitor's comments are written to
the external file,* logfile.txt...

Figure 14.8 *...and the browser displays the output
you've sent its way (lines 10–12).*

Writing to an external file

You may want to save some output from a
script in an external file.

To write to an external file:

1. Open the file as described on page 190,
paying special attention to step 4.

2. Type **print LABEL**, where LABEL is the
same filehandle as you used in step 2 on
page 190.

3. Type **$scalar** to write the contents of
scalar to the open file. Or type **"string"**,
(and don't forget the quotes) where
string is a constant you wish to write to
the open file.

4. Type **;** to finish the line.

5. Close the file *(see page 196)*.

6. Create some output for the browser. Otherwise, the visitor will get an error.

✔ Tips

■ If you do print a string constant to a file,
you should enclose the string in quotation marks. It's not necessary to enclose
a variable within quotes.

■ If you use the **print** function without a
filehandle while the file is open, it simply
goes to the browser (*standard output* in
Perlspeak) as usual.

■ Nothing extra is written or appended to
the external file. If you want to separate
a series of comments from each other,
add a newline (\n) to the external file
after each set of comments.

■ You can only write to an external file if
you've opened it with the > or >> symbols. See step 4 on page 190 for more
details.

Getting exclusive access to a file

If several visitors simultaneously try to use a CGI script that writes to an external file, you'll have a problem—and perhaps a damaged file. The solution is Perl's flock function, which lets a script hold on to the file for the time necessary to write to it without any interruption.

To get exclusive access to a file:

1. After opening the file, type **flock(LABEL**, where *LABEL* is the filehandle for the file.

2. Type **, 2)**. The 2 indicates that you want exclusive access to the file.

3. Type **;** to end the line.

To release exclusive access to a file:

1. Type **flock(LABEL**, where *LABEL* is the filehandle for the file.

2. Type **, 8)**. The 8 indicates you wish to release the file.

3. Type **;** to end the line.

✔ Tip

■ Since no other visitor can access the file while the file is flocked, you want to keep flock time to an absolute minimum. Make sure you prepare any necessary data before flocking the file, and then unflock it as soon as you're done with it.

```
1   #!/usr/local/bin/perl
2
3   require "subparseform.lib";
4   &Parse_Form;
5
6
7   $comments = $formdata{'comments'};
8
9   open(LOG,">>../../logs/logfile.txt")||
        &ErrorMessage;
10  flock(LOG, 2);
11  print LOG "$comments\n";
12  flock(LOG, 8);
13  close(LOG);
14
15  print "Content-type: text/html\n\n";
16  print "<P>You commented thusly:
        <BLOCKQUOTE><P><I>$comments</I></
        BLOCKQUOTE>\n";
17  print "<HR>Would you like to see all the
        messages? <A HREF=\"http://
        www.cookwood.com/cgi-bin/lcastro/
        readfromlog.cgi\">Yes</A>";
```

10: Directly after opening the logfile in line 9, the flock function locks the file referenced by the LOG filehandle so that only this invocation of this script can access it.

16 After the printing is finished, use flock on the LOG filehandle again, but this time with a value of 8, in order to unlock the file so that other scripts can access it.

Figure 14.9 *It's a good idea to flock a file before writing to it. This ensures that two visitors won't try to write on the script simultaneously, possibly damaging or garbling the file's contents.*

Getting exclusive access to a file

```
1   #!/usr/local/bin/perl
2
3   open(LOG,"<../../logs/logfile.txt")||
      &ErrorMessage;
4   @logmessages = <LOG>;
5   close(LOG);
6
7   print "Content-type: text/html\n\n";
8   $n=1;
9   print "<UL>Messages</UL>";
10  foreach $message (@logmessages) {
11      print "<LI>Message # $n was
      $message\n";
12      $n++;
13  }
```

3: The < before the filename indicates that it is being opened for reading.

4: Line 4 stores each line of the file referenced by the LOG filehandle as individual elements in the @logmessages array.

7: Lines 7–13 print out the contents of the array (which contains the contents of the external file).

Figure 14.10 *Notice that it was not necessary to call the subparseform.lib subroutine for this script since all the input comes from the external file and none comes directly from the visitor.*

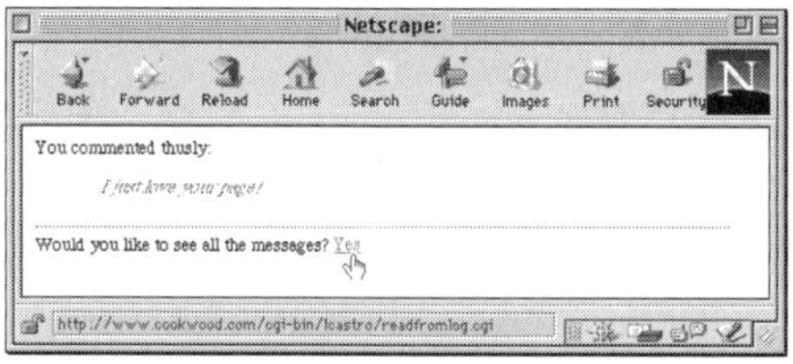

Figure 14.11 *The visitor clicks a link to activate the script that reads the logfile.txt file.*

Figure 14.12 *Here is the current contents of the log-file.txt file that will be read by the script and stored in the @logmessages array.*

Figure 14.13 *The contents of the @logmessages array are printed using a foreach loop.*

Reading data from an external file

You can use external files to hold accumulated data (like a log file for guestbook entries) or for templates for your Web pages, among many other possibilities. You can read in one or more lines from the external file as necessary.

To read all the data from an external file:

1. Open the file as described on page 190, paying special attention to step 4.

2. Type **@array**, where *array* is the name of the array that will contain each of the lines from the external file.

3. Type **=**.

4. Type **<LABEL>**, where *LABEL* corresponds to the filehandle for the file as used in step 2 on page 190.

5. Type **;** to finish the line.

6. Remember to close the external file *(see page 196)*.

✔ Tips

■ Once the array contains the external file's contents (each line will be an individual element in the array), you can process the data as usual. For more information about arrays, consult Chapter 7, *Working with Arrays*.

■ To read and process one line at a time, use **while <FILE> { processes; }** using $_ to refer to each line of the external file.

Closing a file

Although a file will be closed automatically when you exit a program, it's good practice to close it manually when you are finished with it.

To close a file:

Type **close(LABEL);**, where *LABEL* is the file-handle for the file.

```
1    #!/usr/local/bin/perl
2
3    open(LOG,"<../../logs/logfile.txt")||
         &ErrorMessage;
4    @logmessages = <LOG>;
5    close(LOG);
6
7    print "Content-type: text/html\n\n";
8    $n=1;
9    print "<UL>Messages</UL>";
10   foreach $message (@logmessages) {
11       print "<LI>Message # $n was
         $message\n";
12       $n++;
13   }

5:   This line closes the file referenced by the
     LOG filehandle (which is logfile.txt).
```

Figure 14.14 *It's good practice to close a filehandle as quickly as possible after using the file's contents.*

```
1   #!/usr/local/bin/perl
2
3   ($sec,$min,$hour,$mday,$mon,$year,$wday,
        $yday,$isdst)=localtime(time);
4   $mon = $mon + 1;
5   $mon = sprintf("%02d", $mon) if $mon
        <= 9;
6   $mday = sprintf("%02d", $mday) if
        $mday <= 9;
7
8   $date=$year . $mon . $mday;
9   $filename="logfile" . $date .
        "\.txt";
10
11  rename("../../logs/logfile.txt", "../
        ../logs/" . $filename) ||
        &ErrorMessage;
12
13  print "Content-type: text/html\n\n";
14  print "The new name of the file is
        $filename";
```

3: Lines 3–9 get the date, format it, insert it
    between "logfile" and ".txt" and store the
    resulting name in $filename.

11: This line renames the *logfile.txt* file with the
    name stored in $filename. Notice I've
    appended the path name to the new file-
    name. Otherwise, Perl would try to create the
    new file in the current working directory
    (usually cgi-bin) and may give an error.

Figure 14.15 *Be especially careful with paths and
filenames. They are often the culprit when something
isn't working. For more help, consult* Dealing with
paths in Unix *on page 243.*

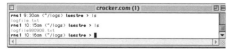

Figure 14.16 *The first* ls *command shows the original filename. After running the script, the second* ls
shows the new name.

Figure 14.17 *Since the visitor can't access or see the
contents of the logs directory, the output to the
browser shows the new name that has been given to
the log file. However, although it's nice to tell your
visitor what's going on, it's essential to give the
browser some output—otherwise, it will give you an
error.*

Renaming a file

Sometimes it becomes necessary to change
the name of a file. For example, you might
want to periodically change the name of a log
file with your guestbook entries so that it is
not replaced with the new log file.

To rename a file:

1. Type **rename(name,**, where *name* is the
    current filename for the file, or a scalar
    variable that refers to the filename.

2. Type **newname**, where *newname* is the
    desired new name that you want the file
    to have. You may also use a scalar vari-
    able that contains the new name.

3. Type **)** to complete the function.

4. Type **;** to complete the sentence.

✔ Tips

■   Either the file must be located in the
    working directory *(see page 203)* or you
    must provide the full path to the file.

■   You can use the rename function to
    move a file to a new location. Just make
    sure that the new name that you use in
    step 2 contains the correct new path. The
    file will no longer exist in the old
    location.

■   As always, literal filenames (but not vari-
    ables) should be enclosed in quotation
    marks.

■   If a file already exists with the filename
    (and path) given in step 2, it will be over-
    written by the file you're renaming.

Renaming a file

Removing a file

You can eliminate a file from within your Perl script. This is handy if you've created temporary files that you're now ready to get rid of.

To remove a file:

1. Type **unlink(**.

2. Type **filename**, where *filename* is the filename (and path, if necessary) of the file that you want to delete. Separate multiple filenames with commas.

   Or type **$scalar**, where *scalar* is the name of a scalar variable that contains the filename.

   Or type **@array**, where *array* is the name of the array that contains the filenames of the multiple files that you wish to eliminate.

3. Type **)**.

4. Type **;** to complete the sentence.

✔ Tips

- You could also use an expression for the filename. Something like **$path . $filename** is not uncommon.

- Literal filenames (that is, not variables) should always be enclosed in quotation marks.

- The path is necessary if you're eliminating a file that is not in the working directory *(see page 203)*. In this example, I've changed the working directory so I wouldn't have to worry about adding all the paths.

- It's a good idea to check if the file has really been eliminated. For more details, consult *Verifying file and directory operations* on page 192.

```
1   #!/usr/local/bin/perl
2
3   require "subparseform.lib";
4   &Parse_Form;
5   $year = $formdata{'year'};
6
7   print "Content-type: text/html\n\n";
8
9   opendir(LOGFILES, "../../logs");
10  @logfiles = readdir(LOGFILES);
11  closedir(LOGFILES);
12  chdir("../../logs") || &ErrorMessage;
13
14  foreach $file (@logfiles) {
15    if ($file =~ /^logfile$year.*/) {
16      unlink($file) || &ErrorMessage ;
17      print "<P>$file was deleted";
18    } else {
19      print "<P>$file will not be
            deleted";
20    }
21  }
```

9: The functions in lines 9–12 are explained on pages 200–203.

16: The filename contained in $file is eliminated. If it cannot be eliminated (perhaps because it doesn't exist, the permissions are wrong, or the path is incorrect), the &ErrorMessage subroutine (not shown) is called.

Figure 14.18 *The chdir function (see page 203) allows me to refer to the filename without its path in line 16. Without it, Perl would try to delete the file from the current directory (usually cgi-bin) and not finding the file, would give an error.*

```
crocker.com (1)
rme1 9:28am (~/logs) leastre > ls
logfile971120.txt  logfile980112.txt  logfile980607.txt
logfile971212.txt  logfile980403.txt
rme1 9:28am (~/logs) leastre > ls
logfile971120.txt  logfile971212.txt
```

Figure 14.19 *The first ls command shows the original contents of the logs directory. The visitor chose to eliminate all the scripts from 1998.*

Netscape: Delete Results

Location: http://www.cookwood.com/cgi-bin/lcastro/delete.cgi

```
...will not be deleted
... will not be deleted
logfile971212.txt will not be deleted
logfile980112.txt was deleted
logfile980403.txt was deleted
logfile980607.txt was deleted
logfile971120.txt will not be deleted
```

Figure 14.20 *The output to the browser shows the visitor exactly what's happened since they can't access or see the contents of the logs directory.*

```
1   #!/usr/local/bin/perl
2
3   print "Content-type: text/html\n\n";
4   require "subparseform.lib";
5   &Parse_Form;
6   $year = $formdata{'year'};
7   $month = sprintf("%02d",
        $formdata{'month'});
8   $day = sprintf("%02d",
        $formdata{'day'});
9
10  $desired_file = "logfile" . $year .
        $month . $day . ".txt";
11
12  chdir("../../logs");
13
14  if (-e $desired_file) {
15      open(LOG, $desired_file) ||
            &ErrorMessage;
16      @messages = <LOG>;
17      close(LOG);
18      $n=1;
19      foreach $message (@messages) {
20          print "<LI>Message # $n is
                <I>$message</I>";
21          $n++;
22      }
23  } else {
24      print "Log doesn't exist.";
25  }
```

4: Lines 4–10 create a filename based on the input from the visitor.
12: This line changes the working directory to the one that contains the log files *(see page 203)*.
14: The condition checks to see if the file the visitor requested exists. If so, it is displayed in the browser (lines 15–22). If not, the visitor is told that the log file doesn't exist (line 24).

Figure 14.21 *The -e operator is often used in conditionals.*

Figure 14.22 *The visitor enters the year, month, and day of the desired log file.*

Figure 14.23 *If the file exists, the script prints out its contents. If not, the visitor gets an error message.*

Checking a file's status

It's often useful to know whether a file already exists, if it's readable, writable, or executable, and so on. You can combine the use of a conditional with a special set of codes that test for certain file states.

To check a file's status:

1. Type **-e** to check if the file exists.

    Or type **-r** to check if its permissions are set such that it can be read.

    Or type **-x** to check if its permissions are set such that it can be executed.

    Or type **-w** to check if its permissions are set such that it can be written to.

    Or type **-d** to check if it's a directory.

2. Type the filename that you're interested in checking. You can use either a scalar variable or a constant. If you use a constant, enclose it in quotation marks.

✔ Tips

■ There is a difference between a file being *able to be* read (it exists, has the proper permissions, and so on) and it being opened properly for reading or for writing *(see step 4 on page 190)*.

■ If you prefer, you can use a filehandle LABEL instead of the filename in step 2.

■ There are several other ways to check a file or directory. The full table can be found on the Web site *(see page 22)*.

■ In Unix, directories are considered nothing more than special kinds of files. Therefore, you can also check a directory's status using the steps outlined above.

Checking a file's status

Accessing a directory

Imagine saving each message in a guestbook in an individual file within the Messages directory. It would be very useful to be able to look at the directory's contents from within the script to see the files it contains. The opendir function lets you do just that.

To access a directory:

1. Type **opendir(LABEL,**, where LABEL is the label you'll use to reference the directory throughout the script. Don't forget the comma after the label.

2. Type **"path/directory"**, where *path/directory* (with no trailing forward slash) is the path to the desired directory on your Unix server.

3. Type **)**.

4. Type **;** to finish the statement.

✔ **Tips**

■ Once you've accessed a directory with opendir, you can view its contents *(see page 200)*. Don't forget to close the directory when you're done *(see page 202)*.

■ You can use **"."** to refer to the working directory and **".."** to refer to the parent directory, that is, the directory that contains the working directory. For more information on constructing relative paths, consult *Absolute and relative paths* on page 244.

```
23  } else {
24    print "Log doesn't exist.";
25    opendir(LOGDIR, ".") ||
        &ErrorMessage;
26    @logfiles = readdir (LOGDIR);
27    closedir(LOGDIR);
28      if (@logfiles) {
29        print "<P>You can choose from
          the following logs:";
30        foreach $filename (@logfiles) {
31          print "<LI>$filename" unless
          ($filename =~ /^\.+$/);
32        }
33      }
34  }
```

4: Lines 1–22 are the same as in Figure 14.21.
25: This line opens the working directory (as represented by a single dot) and assigns it the directory handle LOGDIR. Note that if the script is unable to open the directory (perhaps the permissions don't allow it), it will return false. The || operator requires that one of the two halves of the statement return true, and thus will run the &ErrorMessage subroutine (not shown).
26: The functions in lines 26–27 are explained on pages pages 201–202.
28: Lines 28–33 print the contents of the directory opened in line 25.

Figure 14.24 *You must open a directory before you can look at or access its contents.*

Accessing a directory

```
23  } else {
24    print "Log doesn't exist.";
25    opendir(LOGDIR, ".") ||
        &ErrorMessage;
26    @logfiles = readdir (LOGDIR);
27    closedir(LOGDIR);
28      if (@logfiles) {
29        print "<P>You can choose from
          the following logs:";
30        foreach $filename (@logfiles) {
31          print "<LI>$filename" unless
          ($filename =~ /^\.+$/);
32        }
33      }
34  }
```

4: Lines 1–22 are the same as in Figure 14.21.
25: This line opens the working directory *(see page 200)*.
26: Line 26 stores the name of each file and directory contained in the directory referenced by the filehandle, LOGDIR, (which in this case is the working directory—*logs*) in the @logfiles array.
27: See page 202.
28: Lines 28–33 print the contents of the @logfiles array. Notice the use of the regular expression in line 31 to avoid printing the . and .. filenames.

Figure 14.25 *The readdir function is handy for looking inside a directory and working with the files and directories that it contains.*

Figure 14.26 *In this example, the visitor has entered a date for which there is no log.*

Figure 14.27 *This script looks inside the logs directory and lists its contents so that the visitor can see which log files exist.*

Reading the contents of a directory

Once you've opened a directory, you can see which files it contains.

To see what's in the directory:

1. Open the directory as explained on page 200.

2. Type **@array**, where *array* is the name of the array that will contain the names of all the files (and directories) in the open directory.

Or type **$scalar**, where *scalar* is the variable that will contain only the next single item in the directory.

3. Type **=**.

4. Type **readdir(LABEL)**, where *LABEL* corresponds to the label you gave the opened directory *(see step 1 on page 200)*.

5. Type **;** to finish the statement.

✔ Tips

■ It's a good idea to close the directory after reading its contents *(see page 202)*.

■ Each time you use **$scalar_variable = readdir(LABEL);**, you will get the *next* filename contained in the opened directory.

Reading the contents of a directory

Closing a directory

Once you've finished looking at a directory's contents, you should close the directory.

To close a directory:

1. Type **closedir(LABEL)**, where *LABEL* corresponds to the directory handle you used when opening the directory in step 1 on page 200.

2. Type **;** to finish the sentence.

```
35  } else {
36    print "Log doesn't exist.";
37    opendir(LOGDIR, ".") ||
        &ErrorMessage;
38    @logfiles = readdir(LOGDIR);
39    closedir(LOGDIR);
40      if (@logfiles) {
41        print "<P>You can choose from
          the following logs:";
42        foreach $filename (@logfiles) {
43          print "<LI>$filename" unless
            ($filename =~ /^\.+$/);
44        }
45      }
46  }
```

27: This line closes the directory referenced by the directory handle, LOGDIR (which was opened in line 25 and read in line 26).

Figure 14.28 *If you don't use the closedir function, the directory is automatically closed when the script is completed or just before the directory is reopened.*

Closing a directory

```
1    #!/usr/local/bin/perl
2
3    print "Content-type: text/html\n\n";
4    require "subparseform.lib";
5    &Parse_Form;
6    $year = $formdata{'year'};
7    $month = sprintf("%02d",
        $formdata{'month'});
8    $day = sprintf("%02d",
        $formdata{'day'});
9
10   $desired_file = "logfile" . $year .
        $month . $day . ".txt";
11
12   chdir("../../logs");
13
14   if (-e $desired_file) {
15     open(LOG, $desired_file) ||
          &ErrorMessage;
16     @messages = <LOG>;
17     close(LOG);
18     $n=1;
19     foreach $message (@messages) {
20       print "<LI>Message # $n is
            <I>$message</I>";
21       $n++;
22     }
23   } else {
24     print "Log doesn't exist.";
25   }
```

12: This line changes the working directory to
the one that contains the log files. This means
that in line 15, you don't have to specify the
path to the $desired_file—as long as it
resides in the current directory specified with
chdir.

Figure 14.29 *The chdir function is useful when you
want to access several files or directories that are
contained in one given directory. However, you can
always spell out each path name in full, if you like
typing a lot.*

Changing the working directory

The default working directory is the one that
contains the script itself. If you want to work
with another file (or directory) in that same
directory, you don't need to specify any path
information. However, if you want to work
with a file in some other directory, you either
have to specify the absolute or relative path
that indicates the file's location, or you have
to change the working directory to the directory that contains the file, and then just use
the filename. If you'll be using several files
within a directory, the second option is often
quicker.

To change the working directory:

1. Type **chdir(**.

2. Type **directory**, where *directory* is the
   path that leads to the new working
   directory.

3. Type **)** to complete the function.

4. Type **;** to finish the sentence.

✔ Tips

- You can use a scalar variable (or even an
  expression) that references the directory,
  if desired.

- You can use an absolute or a relative path
  name to indicate the location of the new
  working directory. For more details, consult *Absolute and relative paths* on
  page 244.

203

Creating a directory

You can use a script to create a new directory that will accommodate new files.

To create a new directory:

1. Type **mkdir(**.

2. Type **directory**, where *directory* is the name (and path, if necessary) of the new directory.

3. Type **0oge**, where *0* is a zero, and *oge* indicates the directory's initial permissions, before the umask takes effect. Generally, you'll want to use **0777**, which, with the standard umask of 22, will result in a directory with 755 permissions *(see page 234)*.

4. Type **)** to complete the function.

5. Type **;** to finish the sentence.

✔ Tips

■ The directory will be created within the working directory *(see page 203)* unless you specify its full path. For more information on absolute and relative paths in Unix, consult *Absolute and relative paths* on page 244.

■ When you create a directory with a script, the script is considered the directory's owner, with respect to permissions. This may make it difficult for you to change permissions manually from within Unix. For details, consult *Who's the owner?* on page 232.

■ For more information on umask, consult *Default permissions* on page 233.

■ You can create a script that changes the permissions of a directory *(see page 205)*.

```perl
1   #!/usr/local/bin/perl
2
3   print "Content-type: text/html\n\n";
4   ($sec,$min,$hour,$mday,$mon,$year,$wday,
        $yday,$isdst)=localtime(time);
5   $mon = $mon + 1;
6   $mon = sprintf("%02d", $mon) if $mon
        <= 9;
7   $mday = sprintf("%02d", $mday) if
        $mday <= 9;
8
9   $date=$year . $mon . $mday;
10  $filename="logfile" . $date .
        "\.txt";
11
12  if (-e "../tmp/archives") {
13    print "<P>The archives directory
        does exist.";
14    } else {
15    print "<P>The archives directory
        does not exist.";
16    mkdir("../tmp/archives", 0777) ||
        &ErrorMessage;
17    print "<P>The archives directory has
        been created.";
18  }
19
20  rename("../../logs/logfile.txt",
        "../tmp/archives/" . $filename) ||
        &ErrorMessage;
21
22    print "The new name of the file is
        $filename";
```

12: First, the script checks to see if the directory already exists. If so, it won't be necessary to create it.

16: As long as the condition in line 12 is false, that is, the directory does not exist, this line creates the directory with 777 permissions. Note that with a standard umask of 755, the directory will have 755 permissions, with the script as owner.

Figure 14.30 *This script differs from the one shown in Figure 14.15 only with respect to the new directory. Instead of renaming the file in the same directory, in this script, the renamed file is placed in the new directory.*

Figure 14.31 *It's always a good idea to tell your visitor what's happening, especially since they cannot see inside your directories themselves.*

Figure 14.32 *Since I'm not the owner, I can't delete the archives directory nor change any of its files—even though they're in my space on the server.*

```
1  #!/usr/local/bin/perl
2  print "Content-type: text/html\n\n";
3
4  if (-e "../tmp/archives") {
5    chmod(0777, "../tmp/archives") ||
       &ErrorMessage;
6    print "<P>The permissions have been
       changed";
7  }
```

5: This line gives everyone (including me!) full permissions to the archives directory. If for some reason the chmod function cannot change the permissions, the &ErrorMessage subroutine (not shown) will run.

6: This line is not fluff! Without it, the browser would have nothing to do and would complain.

Figure 14.33 *You might want to keep a script like this handy in case you need to change the permissions of a directory created by a script.*

Figure 14.34 *When the script runs, the browser confirms the permission change—and is happy because it's outputting something.*

Figure 14.35 *After the script runs, you can go back to the server and delete the directory and its contents (or rename them or whatever) at will.*

Changing permissions from within a script

Whether a file can be accessed—by you, your script, or your visitors—depends on the file's permissions *(see page 231)*. You can change a file or directory's permissions either from the Unix prompt *(see page 39)* or from within your script, as described here.

To change a file or directory's permissions:

1. Type **chmod(**.

2. Type **0oge,**, where *0* is a zero, *o* is the number that indicates the owner permissions, *g* is the number that indicates the owner's group's permissions, and *e* is the number that indicates everyone else's permissions *(see page 234)*.

3. Type the name of the file or directory whose permissions you want to change.

4. Repeat step 3 as desired, separating each element with a comma.

5. Type **)** to complete the function.

6. Type **;** to complete the sentence.

✔ Tips

■ Since you are not the owner of files and directories created with a script, it is sometimes essential to use a script like this one to get the permissions you need.

■ For more information about permissions, consult *Figuring out the new permissions code* on page 234.

■ Filenames should always be enclosed in quotation marks.

■ You may use scalar variables or an array in the **chmod** function.

Changing permissions from within a script

Removing a directory

You can eliminate any directory—as long as it is empty—from within the Perl script.

To remove a directory:

1. Type **rmdir(**.

2. Type **directory**, where *directory* is the name (and path, if necessary) of the directory that you wish to eliminate.

3. Type **)** to complete the function.

4. Type **;** to finish the sentence.

✔ Tip

- If the directory is not empty, you'll have to remove its contents before deleting it. For more information on deleting files, consult *Removing a file* on page 198.

```
1   #!/usr/local/bin/perl
2   print "Content-type: text/html\n\n";
3
4   if (-e "../tmp/archives") {
5     chdir("../tmp/archives") ||
        &ErrorMessage("chdir");
6     opendir(ARCHIVES, ".") ||
        &ErrorMessage("opendir");
7     @archives = readdir (ARCHIVES);
8     closedir(ARCHIVES);
9     shift(@archives);
10    shift(@archives);
11
12    if (@archives) {
13      foreach $file (@archives) {
14        print "<P>looking at file
          $file";
15        unlink($file) ||
          &ErrorMessage("unlink");
16        print "<P>$file was deleted";
17      }
18    } else {
19      print "<P>the archives directory
          was empty";
20    }
21    rmdir("/home/user4/lcastro/WWW/tmp/
        archives") ||
        &ErrorMessage("rmdir");
22    print "<P>The directory has been
        removed";
23  } else {
24    print "<P>The directory could not be
        found";
25  }
```

4: This line checks to see if the directory exists.
5: Lines 5–20 open the directory and delete its contents, if any *(see page 198)*.
21: This line removes the directory. If the rmdir function has a problem, the &ErrorMessage subroutine is run (with a parameter—see page 214).
22: Confirmation is printed for the visitor's benefit and so the browser won't complain about having nothing to output.

Figure 14.36 *The series of conditional statements makes this script more flexible. It is able to deal with several different situations (Does the directory exist? Is it empty? and so on) without sending out a server error.*

Figure 14.37 *Once the directory is empty, it can be deleted.*

```
1  #!/usr/local/bin/perl
2
3  require "subparseform.lib";
4  &Parse_Form;
5  print "Content-type:text/html\n\n";
6
7  $to = $formdata{'to'};
8  $from = $formdata{'from'};
9
10 $subject = $formdata{'subject'};
11 $contents = $formdata{'contents'};
12
13 open(MAIL, "|/usr/sbin/sendmail -t") ||
      &ErrorMessage;
14
15 print MAIL "To: $to \nFrom: $from\n";
16 print MAIL "Subject: $subject\n";
17 print MAIL "$contents\n";
18
19 close(MAIL);
20
21 print "Thanks for your comments.";
22
23 sub ErrorMessage {
24     print "<P>The server has a problem.
      Aborting script. \n";
25     exit;
26 }
```

13: Here I've opened a connection to the send-
    mail program on the server, and called it
    MAIL for future reference. The -t flag ensures
    that the sendmail program will check the
    incoming data for the mail headers like To:,
    From: and Subject:. Notice that both the verti-
    cal line (which means the connection is to a
    program) and the path to that program are
    enclosed in quotation marks. Finally, if there
    is a problem opening the connection, the
    &ErrorMessage subroutine will run.

15: Lines 15–17 are explained on page 208.

21: Don't forget to send some output to the
    browser. Otherwise it will complain.

Figure 14.38 *Opening a connection to a program
like sendmail is similar to opening a file or directory.
The main syntactical difference is the vertical line
preceding the path to the program.*

Getting ready to e-mail output

Most Unix systems include an e-mail program
called *sendmail* that you can use to send the
output from a form via e-mail.

To prepare sendmail to receive output:

1. Type **open(MAIL**, where *MAIL* is the label
    you'll use to reference your mail
    program.

2. Type **"**.

3. Type **|**. This is called the pipe symbol
    and is necessary when you want to
    send data to a separate program (like
    sendmail).

4. Type **/path/sendmail**, where */path/send-
    mail* is the path to the sendmail program
    on your Unix server. You can also use a
    variable that contains such a path.

5. Type a space and then **-t**. The *-t* tells
    sendmail to check the incoming data for
    the To:, From: and Subject: lines.

6. Type **"** to complete the piped in
    information.

7. Type **)** to complete the open function.

8. Type **;** to finish the line.

✔ Tips

■ If you don't know where the sendmail
   program is on your Unix server, try typing **whereis sendmail**. In the response
   that appears, choose the path that *ends* in
   sendmail. Or just ask your ISP!

■ You can open connections this way to
   other Unix programs, like grep or cat.

Sending output via e-mail

Once you've set up sendmail to receive the output, you're ready to actually send it.

To send output via e-mail:

1. Complete steps 1–8 on page 207.

2. Type **print MAIL "To:**, where MAIL is the same label that you used in step 1 on page 207.

3. Type the address (or scalar variable that contains the address) to which the message should be sent.

4. Type **\n** to create a newline between the To: and From: lines.

5. Type **From:** .

6. Type the address (or scalar variable that contains the address) that should appear in the message's From line.

7. Type **\n** to create a newline between the From: and Subject: lines.

8. Type **Subject:** .

9. Type the text (or the scalar variable that contains the text) that should appear in the Subject line of the e-mail message.

10. Type **\n** to separate the Subject line from the contents.

11. Type the contents (or the scalar variable that contains the contents) of the e-mail message.

12. Type **";**.

13. Close the connection to the mail program by typing **close(MAIL);** where MAIL is the same label that you used in step 1 on page 207.

Sending output via e-mail

```
1   #!/usr/local/bin/perl
2
3   require "subparseform.lib";
4   &Parse_Form;
5   print "Content-type:text/html\n\n";
6
7   $to = $formdata{'to'};
8   $from = $formdata{'from'};
9
10  $subject = $formdata{'subject'};
11  $contents = $formdata{'contents'};
12
13  open(MAIL, "|/usr/sbin/sendmail -t") ||
       &ErrorMessage;
14
15  print MAIL "To: $to \nFrom: $from\n";
16  print MAIL "Subject: $subject\n";
17  print MAIL "$contents\n";
18
19  close(MAIL);
20
21  print "Thanks for your comments.";
22
23  sub ErrorMessage {
24      print "<P>The server has a problem.
       Aborting script. \n";
25      exit;
26  }
```

3: Lines 3–11 get the data for the message from the Web page.

13: See page 207.

15: Once the connection to the sendmail program is opened, you can send data there with the print function and the filehandle (MAIL), Notice there is no comma or parentheses.

Figure 14.39 *Opening a connection to a program like sendmail is similar to opening a file or directory. The main syntactical difference is the vertical line preceding the path to the program.*

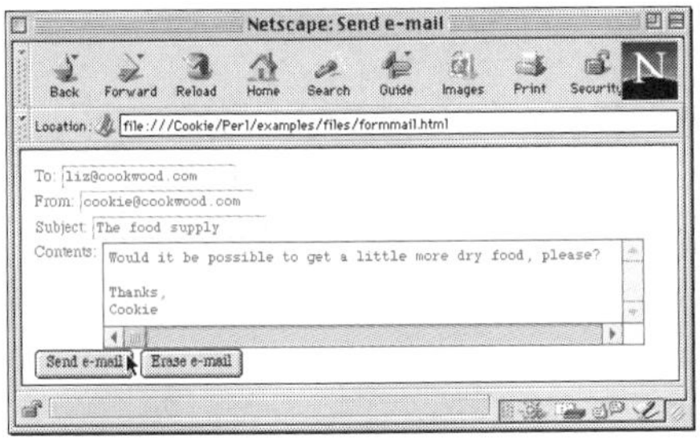

Figure 14.40 *The visitor enters the data on the Web form. The contents of each field will be used to send the e-mail message.*

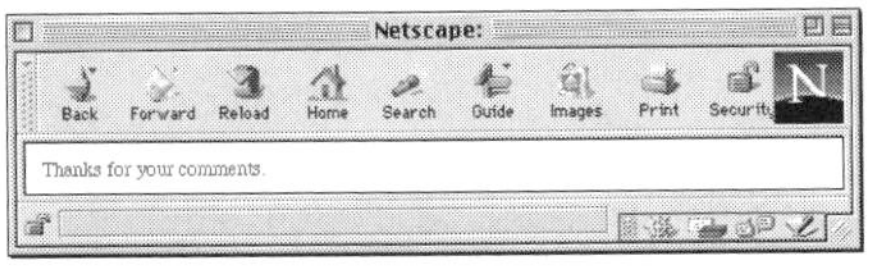

Figure 14.41 *Once again, it's not only helpful for your visitor to get confirmation that everything's going ok, it's also important that the browser have something to output. Otherwise, it'll will output an error.*

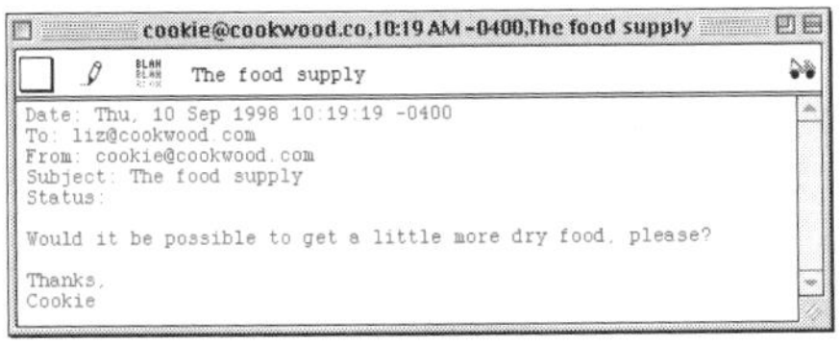

Figure 14.42 *Here's the message once it's been received in Eudora. (Eudora is my e-mail program, but any e-mail program would work just fine.)*

✔ Tips

■ You may specify any part of the message with a variable. For example, you might use **print MAIL "To: $recipient\nFrom: $sender\nSubject:New Web Site\n$body";**.

■ If you prefer, you can split up the contents of the message into various lines. You can use an individual print statement for each header, or combine all the headers into one print statement. The most important thing is that you separate each header from the next with newlines (\n).

■ If you type the addresses as constants (that is, not with a scalar variable), you must precede each @ in the address with a backslash so that Perl doesn't think it's an array. For example, you might use **print MAIL "To: liz\@cookwood.com";**

■ If you create a subroutine that opens the mail program, sends the message, and then closes the mail program, you could use return close(MAIL); as the last line of the subroutine. That way, you'll only be able to successfully access the subroutine if it can successfully close the mail program.

■ You can use this syntax of the open function to send output to other Unix programs besides sendmail, like grep or cat.

Eliminating extra returns

When you input directly from visitors or from an external file, it's possible that the data will have extra spaces or returns tacked to the end of it (because visitors often type Enter or Return to have the program accept the input). You can use the chop and chomp functions to clean up the incoming data.

To get rid of any character at the end of a string:

1. Type **chop**.

2. Type **($data)**, where *$data* is the variable that contains the data that possibly ends in a newline.

3. Type **;** to finish the statement.

To get rid of a newline at the end of a string:

1. Type **chomp**.

2. Type **($data)**, where *$data* is the variable that contains the data that possibly ends in a newline.

3. Type **;** to finish the statement.

✔ Tips

- The chomp function returns the number of characters deleted (1, if it's just a newline). The chop function returns the actual character deleted. This is the main reason why **$input = chop($input);** gives possibly unexpected results; *$input* is set to the character that has been eliminated, not to the newly cleaned up input.

- Text areas *(see page 49)* are really the only place you can get extra returns from a Web page. External files, on the other hand, often have extra returns.

Figure 14.43 *With the script shown on page 193, the extra returns that a visitor enters in the text area box are saved in the external file and look like blank comments.*

```
1   #!/usr/local/bin/perl
2
3   require "subparseform.lib";
4   &Parse_Form;
5   print "Content-type: text/html\n\n";
6
7   $comments = $formdata{'comments'};
8   print "<P>Before cleaning the data, the
        comments are <PRE>--$comments--</
        PRE>";
9   while ($comments =~ /\s$/) {
10      chop($comments);
11  }
12  print "<P>After cleaning the data, the
        comments are <PRE>--$comments--
        </PRE>";
```

8: Line 8 is just to show you, the reader, the original comments, with extra returns. Without the <PRE> tags, the extra returns won't be visible in the HTML page.

9: Line 9 looks at the comments to see if there is any space character at the very end.

10: If so, that character is removed with the chop function. Then the condition in step 9 is tested again. For more information about while loops, consult *Repeating a block while a condition is true* on page 110.

13: For the rest of the script, see *page 193*.

Figure 14.44 *Getting rid of the extra lines will make the final log file look much neater.*

Figure 14.45 *The while conditional executes the chop function until there are no more returns (or other spaces) at the end of the visitor's comments.*

Debugging

Debugging is one of those scary programming words with a simple meaning: reviewing your script and getting out all the kinks (or *bugs*, as programmers call them). Strangely enough, the most common bugs have nothing to do with Perl and all to do with typing. If you type *pirnt* instead of *print*, Perl will spit out an error. On the next two pages, I point you in the direction of many of these simpler bugs.

You can also create an error subroutine, and then use it in your main script to output specific information (detailed by you) when something happens that shouldn't. Notice, I didn't say "unexpected". Part of your job is to anticipate what might go wrong, or at least test that things go right, and then provide alternatives for when they don't.

A good way to debug your programs is to get rid of all the fluff. If you've got a lot of HTML formatting, get rid of it. If you've got a whole branch of the program that only runs in extreme cases, lose it. You can test bits and pieces of your program by commenting out the parts you don't want to look at momentarily. For more details, consult *Narrowing it down by commenting it out* on page 215.

Checking the easy stuff

Perhaps the biggest mistake that folks make when debugging a script is to look at the most complicated parts first, thinking that that's where an error would be most likely to crop up. The problem is that the complicated parts are complicated to fix but no more likely to contain errors than the simple sections. My advice is to start with the simple stuff and work your way up.

To check the easy stuff:

- If you're creating and editing scripts on a local computer (say, a Mac or PC), did you actually upload the new version to the server or just save the changes locally? (I've done this a million times!) For more details on uploading files, consult *Uploading your script to the server* on page 36.

- Does the ACTION attribute in the FORM tag of the HTML page that calls the script actually point to the right place—including the file name and path?

- Did you use the Perl interpreter to check your script's syntax? It'll give you clues about where the problem lies *(see page 40)*.

- Does your script have a shebang line? Does that shebang line correctly point to the Perl interpreter on your server? For more details, consult *Starting a Perl CGI script* on page 32.

- Did you set the proper permissions for the script and any other external files and directories that it uses, creates, reads from, or writes to? For more details, consult *Changing permissions* on page 39 and Appendix B, *Permissions*.

- Does your script produce output for the browser? Just processing input is not enough. Something, no matter how small, must go to the browser or else your visitor will get a "Document contains no data" error.

- Did you insert the Mime content line before any output that goes to the browser? For more details, consult *Creating output for a browser* on page 34.

- Does every line in your script end with a semicolon? (OK, except the first and last lines of conditional blocks and the she-bang line.)

- Have you preceded quotation marks in HTML coding with backslashes so that Perl doesn't think the quotation marks are meant for it? Have you backslashed other special characters that you want Perl to ignore?

- Have you spelled everything right, including function names, names and values that must match their counterparts on the HTML form, subroutine names, and others. Watch out for extra spaces, upper and lowercase letters, and special symbols.

- Are you using the right variable symbol: $ for scalars, @ for arrays and % for hashes? Are you using parenthcses instead of curly brackets or vice versa?

- Do your external files that contain subroutines contain a last line of **1;**? If they don't you won't be able to require them successfully *(see page 124)*.

- Are you mixed up about a function's return value versus its immediate result? Consult *Result vs. Return value* on page 27 for more details.

Checking the easy stuff

Creating an error subroutine

If you're sick of the plain vanilla errors produced by your browser in conjunction with the server, you can create a special error subroutine that may be able to give you more information during testing.

To create an error subroutine:

1. Type **sub ErrorMessage {**, where *ErrorMessage* is the name of the subroutine that will output the information about the error.

2. Type **print "Content-type: text/ html\n\n";**. This line will only be necessary if the error is called before the Mime content line in your main script.

3. Type **print "An error has occurred. <P>$_[0]";** where *An error has occurred.* is the default error message. The $_[0] variable will contain the argument passed to the subroutine (which you can personalize as desired in the main script).

4. If desired, type **exit;**. The exit function immediately stops the script. You'll want to abort the script if, for example, you haven't been able to open a required external file.

5. Type **}** to complete the subroutine definition.

6. Type **1;** so that when you require the external file that contains the subroutine, the require function will return true (that is, be successful).

✔ Tip

■ This subroutine will be particularly helpful if you pass detailed information as the argument to the subroutine in the main script.

```
1  sub ErrorMessage {
2    print "Content-type: text/
     html\n\n";
3    print "An error occurrd. <P>$_[0]
     \n";
4    exit;
5  }
6  1;
```

1: This line defines the name of the subroutine. Notice that the shebang line is not required in external files that contain subroutines.
2: This line prints the Mime content line for the error output.
3: This line prints a default error message and the contents of the variable passed to the subroutine.
4: This line aborts the entire script.
5: The curly bracket completes the definition of the subroutine.
6: This line ensures that the require function that calls this file will return true.

Figure 15.1 *You can add this subroutine within the main script itself, or as in this example, create a separate file in which to store it.*

```
1  #!/usr/local/bin/perl
2  require "sub_error.lib";
3
4  open (FILE, "nofile.txt") ||
     &ErrorMessage("Can't open file");
```

1: In the main script, the shebang line is required.
2: This line calls the external file that contains the error subroutine.
4: On this line, I attempt to open a non-existent file (for demonstration purposes). If it fails (and I know it will), the &ErrorMessage subroutine is called with the argument "Can't open file".
5: If I hadn't written this script specifically to fail, I would presumably want to do something with the file I just opened.

Figure 15.2 *If you used the ErrorMessage to test other file operations (or anything else), you would want to pass specific arguments that spelled out where the error had occurred.*

Figure 15.3 *If the error message is for your visitors, you might want to add some HTML formatting to jazz it up (see page 178).*

```
1   #!/usr/local/bin/perl
2
3   print "Content-type: text/html\n\n";
4   print "<HTML><HEAD><TITLE>Showing off
       in either browser</TITLE></
       HEAD><BODY>";
5
6   $browser = $ENV{'HTTP_USER_AGENT'};
7
8   if ($browser =~ /Mozilla/) {
9     print "You're using Netscape";
10    print "You can show off in Netscape
         with the <BLINK>Blink</BLINK> tag";
11  }
12  #else {
13    #print "You're not using Netscape,
         which means you're probably using
         Explorer";
14    #print "In Internet Explorer, a cool
         tag is the <MARQUEE BEHAVIOR=
         "scroll"> Marquee tag</MARQUEE>";
15  #}
```

12: After getting an Internal Server Error, I
    decided to comment out lines 12 through 15
    by preceding them with a #. Now, when I
    check the script, there is no error and I know
    the error must be in lines 12–15. Can you see
    it? (You could also catch this error by using
    the -c flag on your server—see page 40.)

14: Those quotation marks around *scroll* are
    messing Perl up. Since *scroll* contains no
    spaces or symbols, the quotation marks are
    unnecessary and I can delete them. Other-
    wise, I'd have to backslash them to take away
    their special meaning for Perl *(see page 178)*.

Figure 15.4 *There are actually two problems with
this script. By isolating part of the script, we can find
the problem with the quotation marks. The second
problem is solved on page 216.*

Narrowing it down by commenting it out

If you've written a long or complicated script,
it's sometimes hard to figure out where the
problem is. One solution is to create specific
error messages, using the subroutine
described on page 214. Another solution is to
comment out parts of the script so you can
test one section at a time. Commenting out is
a quick and easy way to temporarily hide
troublesome parts of the script without having to remove them from the file completely.

To narrow it down by commenting it out:

Type a **#** in front of each line in the Perl script
that you want to hide. When you run the
script, Perl will act as if those lines did not
exist.

✔ Tips

- For more information on commenting,
  consult *Documenting your script* on
  page 35.

- To make the lines active again, simply
  remove the # symbol.

- Be careful that you don't comment out
  parts of the script that you need in the
  uncommented sections.

Following a variable's progress

Another way to test what's going in your script is to use the print statement exhaustively for watching each variable's progress. Once you figure out where the problem is, you can get rid of the extra printing.

To follow a variable's progress:

Add a print statement after each change to the variable. When you run the script, you'll be able to see what the variable is doing and compare it with what you expected.

✔ Tip

■ For testing arrays and hashes, you might want to add a foreach loop before the print statement in order to print out each element in the array or hash.

Figure 15.5 *The script "works", but clearly doesn't work very well. This is Explorer, and yet the script is telling me it's Netscape. What's the deal?*

```
1   #!/usr/local/bin/perl
1
2   print "Content-type: text/html\n\n";
3   print"<HTML><HEAD><TITLE>Showingoffin
        either browser</TITLE>
        </HEAD><BODY>";
4
5   $browser = $ENV{'HTTP_USER_AGENT'};
6   print "browser is $browser";
7
8   if ($browser =~ /Mozilla/) {
9     print "You're using Netscape";
10    print "<P>You can show off in Netscape
        with the <BLINK>Blink
        </BLINK> tag";
11
12  } else {
13    print"You'renotusingNetscape,which
        means you're probably using
        Explorer";
14    print "<P>In Internet Explorer, a cool
        tag is the <MARQUEE
        BEHAVIOR=scroll>Marquee tag</
        MARQUEE>";
15  }
```

6:   This line prints the contents of the $browser variable so I can see where the problem is.

Figure 15.6 *Printing variables as you operate on them can help you pinpoint where things start to go wrong.*

Figure 15.7 *By printing out the $browser variable, I can see that for some strange reason, Internet Explorer identifies itself as* Mozilla, *Netscape's code name. I'll have to think of another way to distinguish between the two—perhaps searching on* MSIE.

Using Other Folks' Scripts

One of the nice things about Perl and CGI is that they've been around for a while and most of the things that you'll want to do on your Web site have already been done. Instead of reinventing the wheel, many people will let you copy their wheel and use it on your own site.

The most common kinds of Perl scripts are access counters, guestbooks, Web based bulletin boards, randomizers, and, of course, shopping carts. Nevertheless, you can find other kinds of programs available, including an Engineering Units Conversion Calculator, games like chess, hangman, and concentration, and a program called WebHints that lets you create a Joke (or Hint) of the Day page for your visitors, among many others.

Where to find scripts?

While you can do a search at AltaVista or Yahoo, I've listed a couple of my favorite sites in Appendix E, *Perl and CGI Resources.*

Using other folks' scripts

Using other folks' scripts

As you might expect, installing someone else's script is not so different from installing your own. You simply save the step of writing the script itself. Since I've already explained how to install your own scripts in Chapter 2, *Creating Perl CGI Scripts*, I will simply reference the pertinent sections here instead of repeating them. The rest of this chapter is devoted to the specific steps that deal with borrowed scripts.

To use other people's scripts:

1. Find the script you want to use and download it *(see page 219)*.

2. Expand the script if it's compressed *(see page 220)*.

3. Configure the script for your server and needs *(see page 221)*. It may be necessary to adjust the shebang line and any paths.

4. Customize the script, if desired *(see page 222)*.

5. Upload the script to the server *(see page 36)* paying attention to any special instructions in the documentation.

6. Adjust the permissions as necessary *(see page 39)*.

7. Check the syntax *(see page 40)* to make sure the script still works after your changes to it.

✔ Tip

■ You could conceivably upload the script (step 5) and *then* configure and customize it on the Unix server itself (steps 3–4), but I'm assuming you'd prefer to edit the script in the comfort of your own desktop computer.

Using other folks' scripts

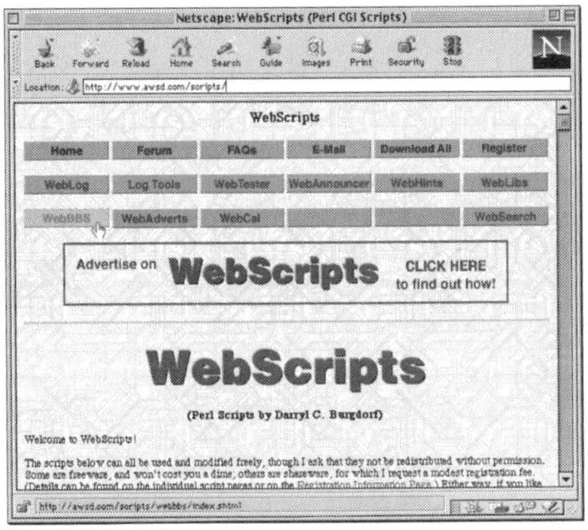

Figure 16.1 *This is the home page for The Web-Scripts Archive, by Darryl Burgdorf. I've clicked on WebBBS to show you the download page for his excellent bulletin board system.*

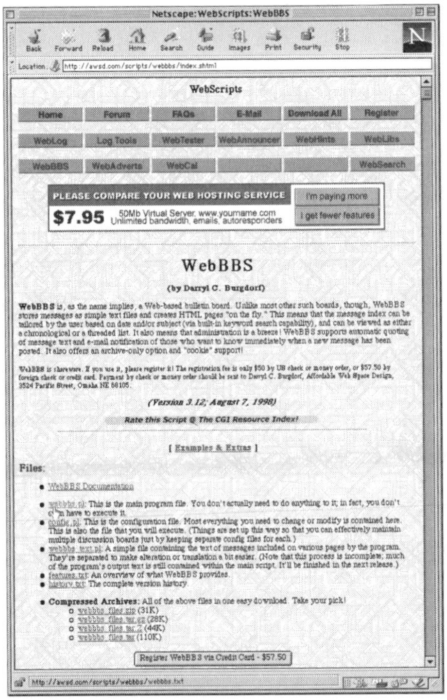

Figure 16.2 *Click on the download links to copy the script to your computer. If you download the uncompressed form (as shown here), be aware that you may need to change the extension once the file is downloaded.*

Getting other people's scripts

In your search for already-written scripts, you should keep in mind that some programmers offer scripts—and very decent scripts at that—for free, while others charge. Some offer documentation, limited technical support, and other services, and others don't. And some let you make changes to their scripts, while some ask that you refrain from doing so.

To get other people's scripts:

1. Use your browser to jump to a site that lists or offers scripts. (For my list of favorites, consult *Other folks' scripts* on page 256.)

2. Browse around the site until you find the script you need.

3. Click the Download link.

✔ **Tips**

■ You can (of course) do a search at AltaVista *(http://altavista.digital.com)*, Yahoo *(http://www.yahoo.com)*, or wherever for your own sources of CGI scripts.

■ Make sure the script you're interested in is compatible with Unix servers (assuming your server is a Unix machine, since that what this book focuses on).

■ Don't forget to download the documentation and configuration files. You'll need them to figure out how to install, configure, and customize the script. If there is no documentation, don't despair. You may find information in the form of commented lines within the script itself. If even that is not available, I'd recommend finding a different script.

Getting other people's scripts

219

Expanding compressed scripts

Scripts are text files and can therefore be opened and looked at on practically any kind of platform, including Macs, PCs, and Unix machines. However, scripts are often compressed in order to save downloading time, and the particular compression format is often platform-specific.

Figure 16.3 *Aladdin Systems offers a range of decompression products for Macs and Windows machines.*

Aladdin Systems *(http://www.aladdinsys.com)* offers a range of excellent freeware and shareware programs for both Macs and PCs that can decompress the most common compression schemes used on all platforms. For Macintosh, StuffIt Expander plus the Expander Enhancement plug-ins can expand .zip, .tar, .tar.gz files and others, as well as the Macintosh .sit, .sea, .hqx., and .bin files. Aladdin Expander for Windows is a freeware program that expands all the above formats for Windows users. To use these programs, simply drag the compressed file over the icon of the expander program.

If you download files compressed in a Unix format, you can upload them to your server and then decompress them with the programs available on your Unix server. For more details, consult *Decompressing tar and zipped files* on page 251.

Finally, you can simply download the uncompressed version. This might take slightly longer in the short run, but save you time overall by avoiding the need for compression software. In this case, be aware that sometimes the extension of the file will be changed from .cgi or .pl to .txt so that you can download the file instead of executing it. You'll have to change the extension back once you've uploaded it to your server.

Figure 16.4 *Open the configuration file, or the script if applicable, and select the setting that you need to change.*

Figure 16.5 *Replace the example text with the actual path or data that you will need to make the script work. Consult the script's documentation as necessary.*

Configuring borrowed scripts

Depending on its complexity, there are several elements in the script which may need to be configured for your system. For example, if the script generates a log, you'll have to tell the script where on your server it should create and write the log file. Or, if it sends you the data collected from forms via e-mail, you'll want to give it your e-mail address.

Some Perl programmers create a separate configuration file that contains all the data that needs to be personalized **(Figures 16.4 and 16.5)** while others sprinkle the configurable elements throughout their scripts, making it a bit harder to find what needs to be changed.

To configure a borrowed script:

1. Read the documentation that hopefully explains what needs to be configured.

2. Open the script in your text editor.

3. Make sure the shebang line reflects the location of the Perl interpreter on your server.

4. Make sure the paths are correct and point to directories and files on your server.

5. Change the variables that need to reflect the circumstances of your particular server.

6. Save the file as text-only with Unix line endings. (This option is often available through the Save As box.)

✔ Tip

■ If you edit a script locally on a Mac or PC be sure to save it in text-only format and then upload it with Text or ASCII (and not binary). Or, you can use one of the special text editors that save in Unix format *(see page 254)*.

Configuring borrowed scripts

221

Customizing borrowed scripts

If you're not crazy about the way a borrowed script outputs data, you can often change the script so that it better suits your taste. For example, if the programmer doesn't know much about HTML, or is more interested in processing data than making it look pretty, you might want to add some extra formatting touches to wow your visitors' eyes as well as their brains.

Figure 16.6 *I love Darryl Burgdorf's WebBBS script (see page 256), but I wanted to make it fit in with the look of the rest of my site.*

To customize borrowed scripts:

1. Open the script and analyze what it does. Figure out where you would like to make changes.

2. Edit away. Now that you know how to program in Perl, you can use the script as a base and go from there.

3. Save the file as text-only with Unix line endings.

Figure 16.7 *One of the purely cosmetic changes I made was to comment out (with a #) the two lines that print the name of the bulletin board (so that these lines would be ignored—see page 35). That way, I could use my own titling system, without it looking strangely repeated.*

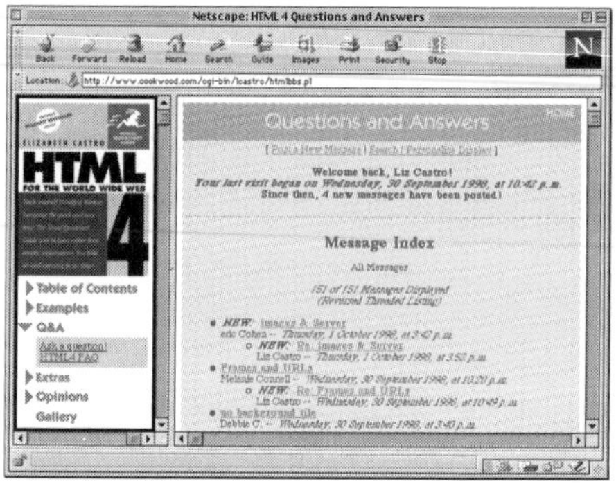

✔ Tips

■ Make sure the script's author permits you to make changes to the script. You'll often find a copyright and warning at the beginning of the script. Just because a script is offered free of charge does not always give you permission to make changes to it.

■ Keep a copy of the unedited file, just in case you somehow corrupt the script and need to go back.

■ Some programmers are interested in the changes you make to their scripts. If you feel so inclined, drop them a note—certainly a thank you is *always* in order.

■ For more details on adding HTML formatting to output, see page 178.

Figure 16.8 *While the guts of the script are virtually identical, the outward appearance is quite different, all due to three or four minor edits to the HTML coding within the script. I've also shoehorned the whole thing into one of my framesets.*

Parsing Form Input

```
1   sub Parse_Form {
2
3   if ($ENV{'REQUEST_METHOD'} eq 'GET') {
4       @pairs = split(/&/,
            $ENV{'QUERY_STRING'});
5   } elsif ($ENV{'REQUEST_METHOD'} eq
        'POST') {
6       read (STDIN, $buffer,
            $ENV{'CONTENT_LENGTH'});
7       @pairs = split(/&/, $buffer);
8
9           if ($ENV{'QUERY_STRING'}) {
10              @getpairs =split(/&/,
                    $ENV{'QUERY_STRING'});
11              push(@pairs,@getpairs);
12          }
13
14  } else {
15      print "Content-type: text/
            html\n\n";
16      print "<P>Use Post or Get";
17      }
18
19  foreach $pair (@pairs) {
20      ($key, $value) = split (/=/, $pair);
21      $key =~ tr/+/ /;
22      $key =~ s/%([a-fA-F0-9][a-fA-F0-9])
            /pack("C", hex($1))/eg;
23      $value =~ tr/+/ /;
24      $value =~ s/%([a-fA-F0-9][a-fA-F0-9])
            /pack("C", hex($1))/eg;
25
26      $value =~s/<!--(.|\n)*-->//g;
27
28  if ($formdata{$key}) {
29      $formdata{$key} .= ", $value";
30  } else {
31      $formdata{$key} = $value;
32  }
33  }
34  }
35  1;
```

Figure A.1 *Here is the parsing form subroutine that is used throughout this book. I'll explain it in detail in this chapter.*

The keystone to many Perl scripts is being able to interpret or parse the information that comes from the Web. The script at left is just one example of many approaches to this problem, and is described in detail in this chapter.

Creating a subroutine

I've made the form-parsing script into a subroutine so that you can access it from any other script, as needed.

To create a subroutine:

1. Type **sub Parse_Form {**, where *Parse_Form* is the name of the subroutine (line 1).

2. Write the code for the subroutine.

3. Type **}** to complete the definition of the subroutine (line 34).

4. Type **1;** to ensure that the subroutine will return a true value when it is required by the main script, and thus be called successfully (line 35).

✔ Tips

- Notice that you don't need to begin a subroutine file with the shebang line *(see page 32)*. It's also not necessary to change a subroutine's permissions to make it executable *(see page 39)*.

- For more information about subroutines, see Chapter 9, *Subroutines*, starting on page 117.

Determining which method was used

Data is sent from the browser to the server by one of two methods, *GET* or *POST.* Since the method used determines how the data is stored, you must first figure out what method was used—by looking at the value of the REQUEST_METHOD environment variable—before parsing the data.

To determine which method was used:

1. Type **if ($ENV{'REQUEST_METHOD'} eq 'GET') {** to check if the environment variable REQUEST_METHOD has been set to GET (line 3).

2. Process the data sent with GET *(see page 226).*

3. Type **}** to complete the if block (line 5).

4. Type **elsif ($ENV{'REQUEST_METHOD'} eq 'POST') {** to check if the environment variable REQUEST_METHOD has been set to POST (line 5).

5. Process the data sent with POST *(see page 227).*

6. Type **if ($ENV{'QUERY_STRING'}) {** to check if any data has been appended to the URL—in addition to the data sent with the POST method (line 9).

7. Process the data in the QUERY_STRING variable *(see page 226).*

8. Type **}** to finish the if block from step 6 (line 12).

9. Type **}** to finish the elsif block in step 4 (line 14).

10. Type **else {** to take care of the possibility that the data was not sent either by GET or POST (line 14).

```
1   sub Parse_Form {
2
3   if ($ENV{'REQUEST_METHOD'} eq 'GET') {
4     @pairs = split(/&/,
        $ENV{'QUERY_STRING'});
5   } elsif ($ENV{'REQUEST_METHOD'} eq
      'POST') {
6     read(STDIN, $buffer,
        $ENV{'CONTENT_LENGTH'});
7     @pairs = split(/&/, $buffer);
8
9       if ($ENV{'QUERY_STRING'}) {
10        @getpairs =split(/&/,
            $ENV{'QUERY_STRING'});
11        push(@pairs,@getpairs);
12      }
13
14  } else {
15    print "Content-type: text/
      html\n\n";
16    print "<P>Use Post or Get";
17    }
18
19  foreach $pair (@pairs) {
20    ($key, $value) = split (/=/, $pair);
21    $key =~ tr/+/ /;
22    $key =~ s/%([a-fA-F0-9][a-fA-F0-9])
      /pack("C", hex($1))/eg;
23    $value =~ tr/+/ /;
24    $value =~ s/%([a-fA-F0-9][a-fA-F0-9])
      /pack("C", hex($1))/eg;
25
26    $value =~s/<!--(.|\n)*-->//g;
27
28  if ($formdata{$key}) {
29    $formdata{$key} .= ", $value";
30  } else {
31    $formdata{$key} = $value;
32  }
33  }
34  }
35  1;
```

Figure A.2 *Before parsing data, you have to know how it was sent from the browser to the server. The method used is stored in the REQUEST_METHOD environment variable.*

11. Type **print "Content-type: text/html \n\n";** so that the error message in the following line will be output properly to the browser (line 15).

12. Type **print "<P>Use Post or Get";** (line 16).

13. Type **}** to complete the else clause begun in step 10 (line 17).

✔ Tips

■ While *you* could figure out how the data was sent by looking at the value of the METHOD attribute in the HTML FORM tag, you still want your form-parsing subroutine to determine this information on its own so that it can properly handle input, no matter where it comes from. Then you'll be able to use the parsing subroutine in a variety of situations without having to worry about which method was used.

■ Usually data is sent either with the GET or with the POST method. However, if you submit the form data with the POST method and also append data to the URL (either in the ACTION attribute or in the link that calls the script) the appended data is actually stored in the QUERY_STRING environment variable as if it were sent via the GET method. For more details, consult *Adding default data to a form* on page 58. In this case, you'll need steps 6–8 to parse the additional data.

Determining which method was used

Getting name-value pairs from GET

All of the name-value pairs sent from a form with the GET method or appended to a URL in a link (or in the ACTION attribute of a form) are stored in the QUERY_STRING environment variable in one long stream of data **(Figure A.4)**. Each name-value pair is separated from the next by an ampersand (&). It's easier to use this information if you separate out each name-value pair and then store the pairs as individual elements in an array **(Figure A.5)**.

To get name-value pairs from GET:

1. Type **@pairs=**, where *pairs* is the name of the array that will contain the name-value pairs (lines 4 and 10).

2. Type **split (/&/, $ENV{'QUERY_STRING'})**. The split function will go through the stream of data contained in the QUERY STRING environment variable and divide it into chunks every time it finds an ampersand.

3. Type **;** to complete the sentence.

✔ Tip

■ You can name the array created in step 1 however you like, as long as you're consistent throughout the script.

```
3   if ($ENV{'REQUEST_METHOD'} eq 'GET') {
4     @pairs = split(/&/,
        $ENV{'QUERY_STRING'});
5   } elsif ($ENV{'REQUEST_METHOD'} eq
      'POST') {
6     read(STDIN, $buffer,
        $ENV{'CONTENT_LENGTH'});
7     @pairs = split(/&/, $buffer);
8
9       if ($ENV{'QUERY_STRING'}) {
10        @getpairs =split(/&/,
            $ENV{'QUERY_STRING'});
11        push(@pairs,@getpairs);
12      }
```

Figure A.3 *To split the incoming data string sent with GET into name-value pairs, use the split function to divide the QUERY_STRING.*

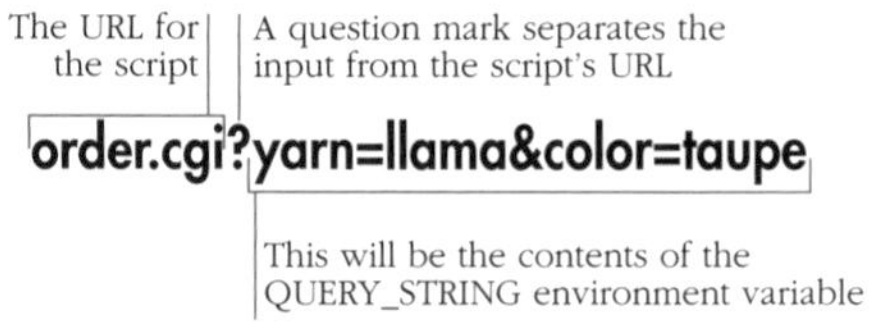

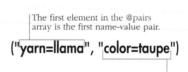

The URL for the script | A question mark separates the input from the script's URL

order.cgi?yarn=llama&color=taupe

This will be the contents of the QUERY_STRING environment variable

Figure A.4 *While you can send form data with the GET method, it's more common to tack on data to the end of the script's URL, either in a link or in the ACTION attribute of a form.*

The first element in the @pairs array is the first name-value pair.

("yarn=llama", "color=taupe")

The second element in the array is the second name-value pair.

Figure A.5 *After the split function, the @pairs array contains two elements: the two name-value pairs that were contained in the QUERY_STRING environment variable.*

```
5   } elsif ($ENV{'REQUEST_METHOD'} eq
      'POST') {
6   read(STDIN, $buffer,
      $ENV{'CONTENT_LENGTH'});
7   @pairs = split(/&/, $buffer);
```

Figure A.6 *There are two steps to parsing data sent with the POST method—first read it in from standard input, and then use the split function to divide it into pieces as we did with the "gotten" data.*

The name-value pairs are temporarily stored in standard input (STDIN).

`yarn=llama&color=taupe`

Figure A.7 *The names (*yarn *and* color*) come from the NAME attribute in the HTML form tag. The values (*llama *and* taupe*) come from the visitor input. When the form is submitted with the POST method, the stream of data is sent to standard input (STDIN). The length of the stream (22) is stored in the CONTENT_LENGTH environment variable.*

The first element in the @pairs array is the first name-value pair.

`("yarn=llama", "color=taupe")`

The second element in the array is the second name-value pair.

Figure A.8 *The stream of data is temporarily stored in the $buffer variable before it is split and its individual elements (name-value pairs) are stored in the @pairs array. Notice that this is precisely the same result we got from parsing the data that was sent with the GET method (cf. Figure A.5).*

Getting name-value pairs from POST

Data sent via the POST method is stored in a place called *standard input*. To get accurate data from standard input, you have to know how much data you're getting: that number, in bytes, is stored in the CONTENT_LENGTH environment variable.

To input data from a form:

1. Type **read (STDIN, $buffer,**, where *$buffer* is the name of the variable that will temporarily contain the entire stream of unparsed data (line 6).

2. Type **$ENV{'CONTENT_LENGTH'}**. This element of the environment variables hash contains the length of the data posted from the form. The read function needs this number to know how much data to input.

3. Type **)** to complete the function.

4. Type **;** to complete the line.

5. Type **@pairs=**, where *@pairs* is the name of the array that will contain the name-value pairs (line 7).

6. Type **split(/&/, $buffer);**. The split function will go through the stream of data contained in the *$buffer* variable and divide it into chunks every time it finds an ampersand.

✔ Tips

■ For more information on the environment variables hash, consult Chapter 4, *Environment Variables*.

■ For more details on the split function, consult *Splitting a value into pieces* on page 141.

Getting name-value pairs from POST

Storing name-value pairs in a hash

Once you have an array with a set of name-value pairs, you can separate these out into individual elements and store them in pairs in a hash. The name and value in each pair is separated by an equals sign (=). Spaces are substituted with plus signs (+). Any other non-alphanumeric symbols will be in hexadecimal format.

To store name-value pairs in a hash:

1. To process each name-value pair collected, type **foreach $pair (@pairs) {**, where *@pairs* is the name of the array that you used in step 1 on page 226 and in step 5 on page 227 (line 19).

2. Type **($key, $value) = split (/=/, $pair);** where *$key* and *$value* are the names of the variables that will temporarily hold the name and value, respectively, and *$pair* is the variable used to pass through the foreach loop begun in step 1 (line 20).

3. Type **$key =~ tr/+/ /;** to replace the plus signs in $key with spaces (line 21).

4. Type **$key =~ s/%([a-fA-F0-9][a-fA-F0-9]) /pack("C", hex($1))/eg;** to convert the symbols in $key from hexadecimals to their more common representations (line 22).

5. Type **$value =~ tr/+/ /;** to replace the plus signs in $value with spaces (line 23).

6. Type **$value =~ s/%([a-fA-F0-9][a-fA-F0-9])/pack("C", hex($1))/eg;** to convert the symbols in $value from hexadecimals to their more common representations (line 24).

```
19  foreach $pair (@pairs) {
20    ($key, $value) = split (/=/, $pair);
21    $key =~ tr/+/ /;
22    $key =~ s/%([a-fA-F0-9][a-fA-F0-9]) /
        pack("C", hex($1))/eg;
23    $value =~ tr/+/ /;
24    $value =~ s/%([a-fA-F0-9][a-fA-F0-9]) /
        pack("C", hex($1))/eg;
25
26    $value =~ s/<!--(.|\n)*-->//g;
27
28    if ($formdata{$key}) {
29      $formdata{$key} .= ", $value";
30    } else {
31      $formdata{$key} = $value;
32    }
33  }
34  }
35  1;
```

Figure A.9 *The end result of the Parse_Form subroutine is to create a hash with the name-value pairs that were input from the form or link.*

Storing name-value pairs in a hash

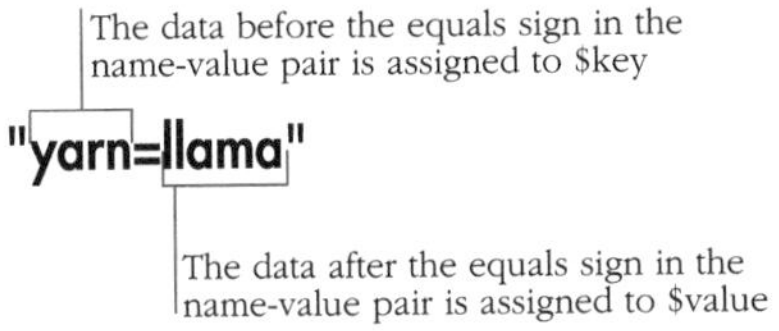

The data before the equals sign in the name-value pair is assigned to $key

"yarn=llama"

The data after the equals sign in the name-value pair is assigned to $value

Figure A.10 *The first step to creating a hash with the incoming data is to separate each name-value pair into its name ($key) and value ($value).*

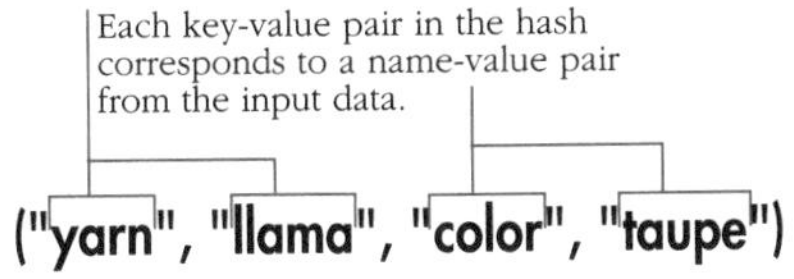

Each key-value pair in the hash corresponds to a name-value pair from the input data.

("yarn", "llama", "color", "taupe")

Figure A.11 *The completed hash contains each name and value as separate but related elements. This makes them easy to access and use later in your script.*

7. Type **$value =~s/<!--(.|\n)*-->//g;**, to eliminate any possible server side includes (SSI) from incoming data as a security precaution (line 26).

8. Type **if ($formdata{$key}) {** where *formdata* is the name of the hash that you are creating from the name-value pairs. The if conditional checks to see if the name has already been assigned to the hash—perhaps because it has multiple values, like a menu or set of checkboxes (line 28).

9. Type **$formdata{$key} .= ", $value";** so that if the name has already been assigned to the hash, the value will be added to any existing values that correspond with that name, separated by a comma (line 29).

10. Type **}** to complete the if conditional from step 8 (line 30).

11. Type **else {** to set up the processes that will occur if the name has not yet been stored in the formdata hash (line 30).

12. Type **$formdata{$key} = $value;** to store the name and the value as corresponding elements in the formdata hash (line 31).

13. Type **}** to complete the else clause from step 11 (line 32).

14. Type **}** to complete the foreach loop begun in step 1 (line 33).

Storing name-value pairs in a hash

Using the parsed data

Once you've converted the incoming stream of data into an organized hash, accessing and using the data is as easy as using any member of a hash.

To use the parsed data:

1. Type **$formdata{**, where *formdata* is the name of the hash that you created in step 12 (and step 9) on page 229.

2. Type **'name'**, where name is the value of the NAME attribute in the HTML form of the desired piece of input data (or the word that identifies the data coming from a link).

3. Type **}**.

✔ Tips

■ You can use a variable that references the name in step 2. if you prefer. In that case, you won't need to enclose it in quotation marks.

■ For more information on using hashes, consult Chapter 10, *Working with Hashes.*

```
1  #!/usr/local/bin/perl
2
3  require "subparseform.lib";
4  &Parse_Form;
5
6  print "Content-type:text/html\n\n";
7  print "<P>You chose $formdata{'yarn'}
     yarn ";
8  print "and seem to prefer the
     $formdata{'color'} color";
9  print "<P>Thanks for your order."
```

1: This is not a subroutine and so you definitely do have to put the shebang line.
3: This line opens the file that contains the subroutine that we've been discussing throughout this chapter.
4: This line actually calls the subroutine to create a hash out of the incoming data.
7: This line prints out the value that corresponds to the name "yarn".
8: This line prints out the value that corresponds to the name "color".

Figure A.12 *This simplest of scripts reveals how to get to and use the incoming data that has been processed and stored in the formdata hash.*

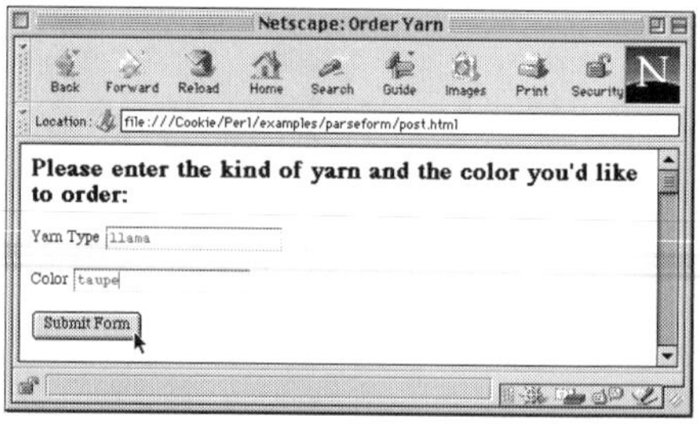

Figure A.13 *The visitor enters the data and then submits the form.*

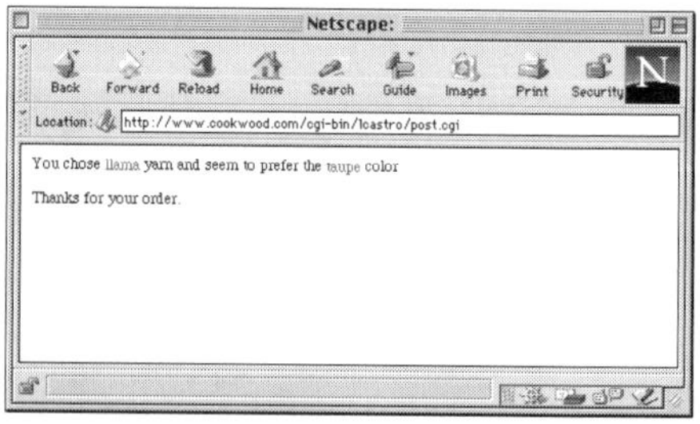

Figure A.14 *The script (shown in Figure A.12) calls the Parse_Form subroutine to create a hash from the incoming data. It then prints out the collected values (along with some explanatory filler).*

Using the parsed data

Permissions

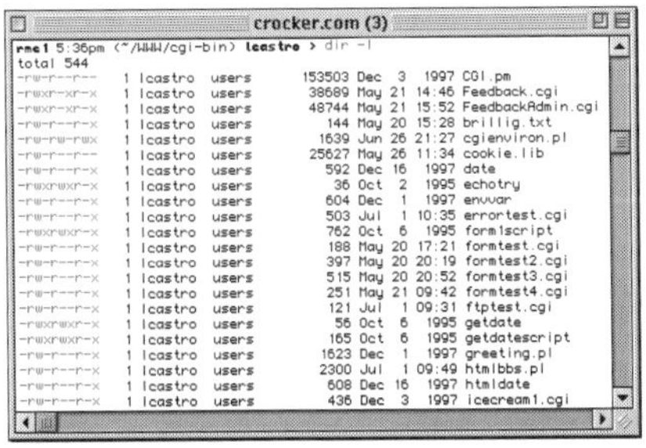

Figure B.1 *If you type* **ls -l** *at the prompt from within the desired directory, you'll get a list of the directory's contents, together with the permissions of each file.*

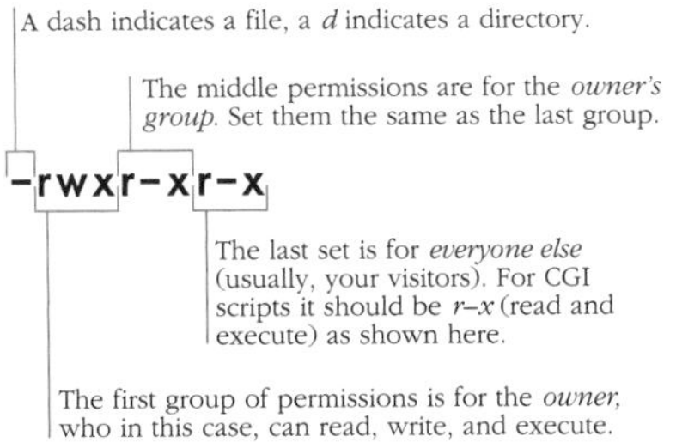

A dash indicates a file, a *d* indicates a directory.

The middle permissions are for the *owner's group.* Set them the same as the last group.

-rwxr-xr-x

The last set is for *everyone else* (usually, your visitors). For CGI scripts it should be *r–x* (read and execute) as shown here.

The first group of permissions is for the *owner,* who in this case, can read, write, and execute.

Figure B.2 *You can tell what permissions a file or directory has by looking at the weird string of characters to the left of its name when you type* **ls -l** *(Figure B.1).*

Every file and directory on a Unix server has a set of permissions that determine who can use that file or directory and just what they can do with it. It's essential to set enough permissions so that your scripts will work properly while at the same time restricting permissions enough to secure your scripts from invaders.

There are three kinds of permission: read, write, and execute. The creator or *owner* of the file or directory can bestow any or all of these privileges on each of three groups: the owner, the owner's group (a Unix thing that you probably don't need to worry about), and everyone else.

The meaning of permissions varies slightly for files and directories. A file that is read protected cannot be read or opened. For a directory, read protection means its contents cannot be listed. A file that is write protected cannot be written to (that is, changed). Similarly, you cannot create, move, rename, copy, or delete the contents of a write-protected directory. A file—particularly a CGI script—without execute permissions cannot be run. A directory without execute permissions will not let you read, write, or execute the files that it contains.

To view a file or directory's permissions:

Type **ls -l** at the Unix prompt. Permissions are displayed in a Unix server with a series of letters: *r* for read, *w* for write, and *x* for executable, in each of three columns which represent the owner, the owner's group, and everyone else (**Figures B.1 and B.2**).

Who's the owner?

Before you can analyze a particular file or directory's permissions, you have to know who owns it.

When you upload or create a file or directory on your Unix server, *you* are set as its owner. That means that the first number in the permissions code refers to you while the third number refers to everyone else, including your visitors.

If one of your scripts creates a file or directory, on most servers, you are *not* the owner. On my ISP for example, the owner is set to "nobody" since the script was run from an external site. That means you will only have the permissions granted by the third number, as part of "everyone else" while your scripts, executed by your visitors, will have the owner's permissions.

To see who the owner is:

1. Telnet to the directory that contains the file or directory in question.

2. Type **ls -l**. (Those are letter *l's.*) The contents of the directory is displayed with expanded information. The third column shows the owner of the file or directory **(Figure B.3)**. On some servers, the fourth column will show the owner's group.

✔ Tip

■ The second number in the permissions code refers to the user's group, which has more meaning if you work together with a group of people on a Unix system. The easiest way to deal with the user group is to assign it the same privileges as everyone else—that is, set the second and third numbers the same.

Figure B.3 *When you type* **ls -l** *at the Unix prompt, the contents of the current directory are displayed. Notice that the first entry (for the* archives *directory) is owned by "nobody". It was created by a script. Even though it's in my space on the server, I can't open it or delete it. The second entry (for the* logfile.txt *file) was created by "lcastro"—that's me— which means that I created or uploaded it myself and that the owner's permissions apply to me.*

Why does it matter?

In order to create, delete, or rename files in a directory, a script has to have full permissions for that directory (7).

If *you* create a directory in Unix, the 7 in the default 755 permissions applies to *you* and you can do whatever you want with the file or directory. Meanwhile, your scripts will be restricted from creating, renaming, or deleting the directory's contents.

If you create a directory through a script, your *script* is the owner of the directory and the 7 in the default 755 permissions applies to your scripts (and now *you* are restricted from adding or deleting the directory's contents—bizarre but true).

Who's the owner?

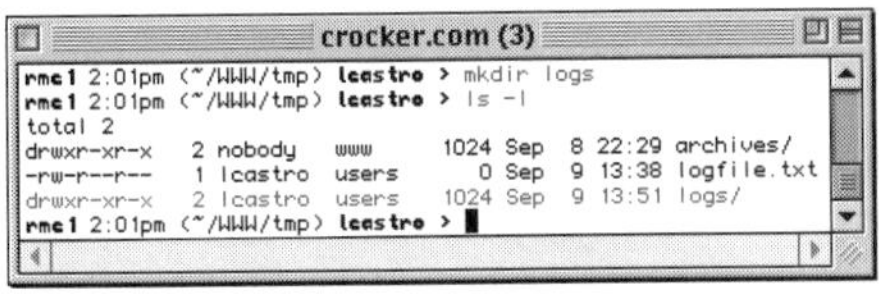

Figure B.4 *When you create a directory in Unix, it automatically is assigned 777 permissions, restricted by the value of umask. On my system, umask is 22, which leaves me with a directory with 755 permissions. If I wanted to let scripts create, rename, or delete files in this directory I'd have to change the permissions to 777 with chmod (see page 39).*

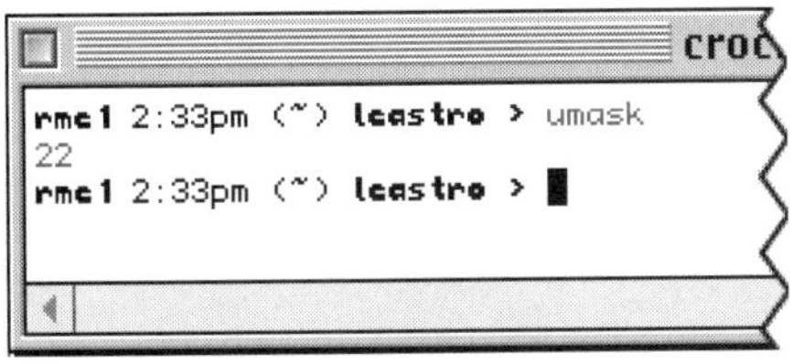

Figure B.5 *To view the umask settings on your system, type* **umask** *at the Unix prompt.*

Default permissions

When you create a file or directory on a Unix server, its permissions are set and restricted automatically. Files start with 666 while directories start with 777. The restrictions are determined by the value of the *umask*, which is usually set at 022, although you can change it if you like.

For example, if you create a file on a Unix system with a umask of 022, the file's permissions are set at 644—anyone can read the file, only the owner can write to it, and nobody can execute it. If the file is a script, you'll have to change the permissions to at least 755, so that the owner can read, write, and execute, and everyone else can read and execute. On the other hand, if the file is just a logfile or other non-executable file, 644 will be fine.

If you create a directory on a Unix system with a umask of 022, the directory's permissions are set at 755. In order to let scripts (which are considered "everyone else") create, rename, and delete files, among other things, in that directory, you'll have to change its permissions to 777.

To see the value of the umask:

Type **umask** at the Unix prompt. Its current setting will be displayed **(Figure B.5)**.

To change the value of the umask:

Type **umask oge**, where the *oge* corresponds to the new restrictions you want to apply automatically.

✔ Tip

Although it looks like the umask value is simply subtracted from the original permissions, it's a bit more complicated than that. See the Web page *(see page 22)* for more details.

Default permissions

Figuring out the new permissions code

There are two ways to change the permissions of a file or directory—either by telnetting to the Unix server *(see page 39)* or by using a script that contains the Perl commands for changing permissions *(see page 205)*. In either case, you'll use a four digit numerical code that determines the new permissions.

To figure out the new permissions code:

1. Determine which permissions you want to bestow on which groups.

2. Assign a value of 4 for read permission, 2 for write permission, and 1 for execute permission.

3. Add the values of the permissions together for each individual group.

4. Type **0oge**, where *0* is just zero, *o* is the sum of the values for the owner's permissions, *g* is the sum of the values for the group's permissions, and *e* is the sum of the values for everyone else's permissions.

✔ Tip

■ You can usually omit the initial 0 when changing the permissions on the Unix server itself. Perl, on the other hand, requires it.

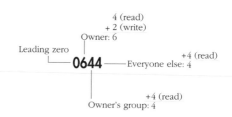

Figure B.6 *Use the 0644 permissions code for any non-executable file, including configuration files, preferences files, log files, and others.*

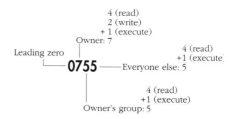

Figure B.7 *Use the 0755 permissions code for any executable files (including CGI scripts). Directories created by a script that contain files that will need to be changed, renamed, or deleted should also have 0755 permissions.*

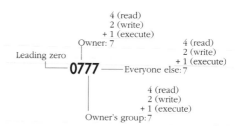

Figure B.8 *Use the 0777 permissions code for any directory that you yourself create on the Unix server directly in which you'll want a script to be able to create, rename, delete, or otherwise change files.*

Figure B.9 *Here I've changed the permissions of the logs directory to 777. The new permissions (777=rwxrwxrwx) are displayed in the listing.*

Security

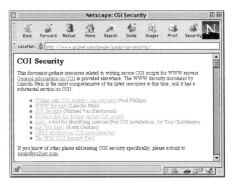

Figure C.1 *Paul Phillips' list of pages with information about CGI Security can be found at http://www.go2net.com/people/paulp/cgi-security/*

Figure C.2 *Lincoln Stein's World Wide Web Security FAQ should be required reading for all CGI Perl programmers.*

In the introduction to this book, I raised the question of whether programming is dangerous. In fact, while simply writing Perl scripts is unlikely to do much damage, CGI Perl scripts *can* make your server vulnerable to attack from outside forces.

Beware! The CGI scripts in this book are not intended to be perfect from a security standpoint, they are intended to teach you specific, individual tasks without distracting you with other concepts, like security. Before publishing (using them for testing and personal study is probably fine) *any* CGI scripts that you have copied from this book, or indeed that you have copied from anywhere or written yourself, you must be sure that they pose no security risk to your system. You may want to consult your ISP about possible security risks and make sure to, at the very least, follow the tips outlined in this chapter. Remember that once you start writing your own scripts, or using scripts written by others (including the ones from this book), it is **your responsibility** to close all security loopholes that exist.

Read the security FAQs

This chapter includes a few very basic strategies you can employ to reduce your risk. I also recommend reading as much about security as you can find out on the Web. Paul Phillips has compiled a useful list of pages with information about CGI security at *http://www.go2net.com/people/paulp/cgi-security/* (**Figure C.1**). Perhaps the most important and most comprehensive of these is Lincoln Stein's World Wide Web Security FAQ, which is at *http://www.w3.org/Security/Faq/www-security-faq.html* (**Figure C.2**).

Monitoring visitor input

The first rule of CGI security is that you should never trust your visitors to input what you think they're going to input. Even with the best of intentions, visitors sometimes don't understand what information you're asking for. And in more serious situations, visitors may be actively trying to trash—or spy on—your server's files.

Your first line of defense begins with vigilantly checking a visitor's input to make sure it is in the form you expected. For example, if you're asking for a person's name, the data should look like one or two words without special symbols like <, !, or *, among others. Or you might want to ensure that e-mail addresses are in the form *name@domain.com*. You can use search patterns to verify incoming data and to filter out strange looking input *(see page 137)*.

Even if a visitor's choices seem limited by a menu or set of check boxes, there is no guarantee that the visitor won't call your CGI script with their own HTML form—if you let them. You can check the HTTP_REFERER environment variable *(see page 63)* to make sure the page that accesses the script is on your server and, indeed, located in a particular directory.

To check the HTTP_REFERER variable:

Use a regular expression to make sure that the filename and/or path contained in the HTTP_REFERER variable conform to what they should be.

✔ Tip

■ Unfortunately, you can't rely on the HTTP_REFERER variable completely since wily crackers can fool your system with a fake HTTP_REFERER value.

```
1   #!/usr/local/bin/perl
2
3   require "subparseform.lib";
4   &Parse_Form;
5
6   $origin = $ENV{'HTTP_REFERER'};
7   print "Content-type:text/html\n\n";
8
9   if ($origin =~ m#^http://
    www.cookwood.com/#) {
10    print "The page that launched the
      script is on my server";
11    print "<P>The name you entered was
      $formdata{'name'}";
12  } else {
13    print "You can't run this script from
      that location. Sorry.";
14  }
```

6:   This line stores the value of HTTP_REFERER in the $origin scalar variable.
9:   The if conditional checks to see if the page that launches the script is on my server.
10: As long as the page that launches the script is on my server, it will run correctly.
13: If the launching page is not on my server, the visitor gets an error message.

Figure C.3 *You can check the HTTP_REFERER variable to make sure the page from which the script is activated is on your server and not someone else's.*

Figure C.4 *Here's a form created by some visitor who's trying to pass their own data to my script. Notice the URL in the Location dialog box.*

Figure C.5 *The error message will appear unless the HTTP_REFERER variable confirms that the script is being run from a page that is physically located on my (cookwood) server.*

```
1   #!/usr/local/bin/perl
2
3   require "subparseform.lib";
4   &Parse_Form;
5   print "Content-type: text/html\n\n";
6
7   $language = $formdata{'language'};
8
9   if ($language=~/English/) {
10    $filename = "gatetseng.html";
11  } elsif ($language =~ /Catalan/) {
12    $filename = "gatetscat.html";
13  } else {
14    print "Sorry, you can only choose
        between English and Catalan.";
15  }
16
17  open (FILE, "/home/user4/lcastro/WWW/
      personal/$filename") || &Error;
18  @page = <FILE>;
19  close FILE;
20
21  foreach $line (@page) {
22      print $line;
23      }
```

9:   The if conditional looks at the input to see
     which file should be opened, but does not
     rely on the input to determine the filename
     itself.

Figure C.6 *Using the filename itself as the value in the form and then appending that to the path in line 17 would be inviting disaster. You never know what input your visitor is going to give you.*

Figure C.7 *Here some bad visitor is trying to use my script to print out my server's password file.*

Figure C.8 *My script is protected in two ways: first, I've checked the incoming data and only accept it if it looks like what I'm expecting. Second, I don't use the visitor's input directly to create the filename that I reference with the system command (open).*

Watching what is sent to the server

Every time you open communications between your script and the server, say, by opening a file, writing to a file, deleting a file, changing permissions, or piping output to an e-mail program, you should be very careful that your commands cannot be corrupted or co-opted by some enterprising cracker.

You should never, for example, let the visitor collaborate on the filenames or paths to files that will be accessed on the server, unless you can verify the filenames and paths in some manner before using the information. Otherwise you may find that your visitors are inserting damaging commands (say, to delete all the server's files) instead of real paths or filenames.

To verify what is sent to the server:

Before you pass visitor input to a system command, use a regular expression to make sure that it looks the way it should. For example, you can check the path of filenames to ensure that the files are actually on your server and in the proper directory.

Another option is to use the input to choose between different *preset* filenames without letting the visitor directly determine what those filenames will be. That's the tack I've taken in the example.

Avoiding tainted data

Perl has a built-in system that restricts your script from using data that comes from outside the script, like visitor input and environment variables, to affect something else outside the script (like writing to a log file)—unless you've cleaned up the tainted data.

To avoid tainted data:

At the end of the shebang line for your Perl script, type **-T**. If you use unverified outside data to modify a file, directory, or process, you'll get an error message.

Of course, if you *want* to use outside input, you can. But first, you have to verify or *untaint* it. The only way to do that is to run it through a search pattern and then assign the matched part to a scalar variable. That scalar variable will no longer be tainted. The idea is that if you've checked it, it must be OK. It's your responsibility to ensure that your regular expression does a good job of ensuring that the data is what it should be.

To untaint data:

1. Type **$outside_data =~ /regex/;**, where some part of the *regex* is enclosed in parentheses to capture the desired portion of the outside data.

2. Type **$clean_data = $1;**. The scalar variable $1 is automatically set to contain the matched expression from step 1 (see page 150).

✔ Tips

- According to Larry Wall's *Perl Programming*, **every** CGI script should be run with the -T switch.

- To test the script's syntax, type **perl -cT script** (*cf. page 40*).

```
1   #!/usr/local/bin/perl -T
2
3    print "Content-type:text/html\n\n";
4    &Parse_Form;
5
6    $file=$formdata{'name'};
7    $comments=$formdata{'comments'};
8
9    if ($file=~/^(\w+)$/) {
10     $file=$1;
11     open (FILE, ">>$file.txt") ||
          &Error("to write");
12     print FILE "$comments\n";
13
14     open (FILE, "$file.txt") || &Error("to
          read");
15     @lines = <FILE>;
16     close FILE;
17
18     foreach $line (@lines) {
19        print "<P>$line";
20     }
21
22  } else {
23     print "error with test $file";
24  }
25
```

1: The -T at the end of the shebang line turns on taint checking to keep you from unwittingly using outside (tainted) data to modify files, directories, or processes.

6: Lines 6 and 7 contain tainted data, since it comes from visitor input.

9: In order to verify the data from line 6, I use a conditional and a regular expression to make sure the data looks the way it should. The part within parentheses will be saved clean.

10: This line saves the cleansed data back into the $file variable.

11: You cannot use tainted data to write to (modify) another file. In other words, line 11 would generate a tainted data error if lines 9 and 10 didn't exist.

12: You can *print* tainted data—even to an external file—without cleaning it.

14: You can also open a file to read using tainted data without getting an error.

22: If the regular expression fails, the visitor gets an error message.

25: The Error and Parse_Form subroutines are not shown due to space restraints. You can find the full script at the Web site (*see page 22*).

Figure C.9 *Setting manual taint checking keeps you from using outside data without first using a regular expression to verify that the data looks the way it should.*

Unix Essentials

It seems crazy, but one of the biggest obstacles to writing and using Perl CGI scripts has nothing at all to do with Perl or CGI. If your Web site is hosted by a Unix server (which this book supposes), you'll have to deal with Unix, an operating system that you may have little experience with. While some of Unix can be figured out, other parts are only ridiculously simple to those folks who have worked with the system for some time.

If you've never worked with Unix, this chapter will serve as a "basic phrase book" for your journey. You'll get enough information to make yourself understood without a barrage of the details and complexities of the entire operating system. If you *have* worked with Unix, you can use this chapter as a quick reference for those commands whose syntax you may have forgotten.

Telnetting to your Unix server

While you may use a Mac or Windows machine to write your scripts (and indeed the rest of your Web site), you will need access to your Unix server in order to complete the configuration of those scripts. Instead of getting in your car and driving to your ISP and using the Unix server in person, you can use Telnet to create a remote connection that works the same as if you were there in the flesh.

To Telnet to your Unix server:

1. Open the Telnet client on your Mac or PC. (I use BetterTelnet on a Mac and Microsoft Telnet on Windows. Both are free. For more details, see page 255.)

2. Choose the Connect command (however it's called in your program).

3. Type your ISP's name or IP address in the Host Name field.

4. Then click Connect **(Figure D.1)**. A window should appear asking your for your login name **(Figure D.2)**.

5. Type your login name and then press Return. (Ask your ISP if you're not sure what to use; usually it's the same as your e-mail before the @ sign.)

6. Type your password and then press return. You should see your home directory on the Unix server. Depending on the Unix server's settings, it might also tell you whether or not you have e-mail waiting.

✔ Tip

■ The techniques in the rest of this chapter assume that you have first opened a Telnet connection with your Unix server.

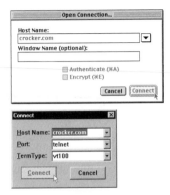

Figure D.1 *Whether you use BetterTelnet for Mac (top) or Microsoft Telnet for Windows, you'll need to type your server name and click Connect to open a Telnet connection to your server.*

Figure D.2 *The connection window shows you just what you'd see if you were at a real Unix terminal. Type your login (mine's lcastro) and your password. Your server (as mine does) may alert you about new mail received, tell you the time, give you your present location (here it's my home directory, indicated by the tilde), your user name, and the prompt. Now you're ready to go. Notice that whether you use a Mac (top) or Windows, the contents of the Telnet window looks pretty much the same.*

Figure D.3 *To close the connection with the server, type* **logout** *or* **exit** *and then press Return or Enter. Shown here again are BetterTelnet for Macintosh (top) and Microsoft Telnet for Windows.*

Logging out ensures that nobody else can get access to your space on the Unix server if you happen to leave your machine for some period of time.

To close a Telnet connection:

1. Type **logout** or **exit** at the Unix prompt and then press Return or Enter.

2. If desired, quit your Telnet program.

✔ Tips

■ If you try to quit your Telnet program before you've officially logged out, it will ask you if you really want to close the connection. Say yes.

■ If your modem disconnects before you've officially logged out, your Telnet program will give you an error. It's not the end of the world, but it's definitely better to logout correctly and then disconnect your modem.

Telnetting to your Unix server

Executing commands in Unix

If you're used to a graphical interface, getting things done in Unix can be a test of your patience and of your typing skills. Instead of double clicking programs and files, you tell Unix what you want it to do by typing commands at the prompt.

The Unix prompt

The Unix prompt, which takes different forms depending on the kind of Unix that is installed on your server and the way that your system administrator has configured it, is Unix's way of telling you it's listening and ready to do your bidding. It might look like a %, $ or, in my case, a >, and it may be accompanied by other data including the date or time, the name of the server, your user name, and the current working directory. Its most important function, however, is to indicate that it's ready for you to type a command.

Typing commands

To get Unix to do something, you have to type out a command at the prompt and then press Return or Enter. All commands (and filenames and paths) are case sensitive. Capital and small letters do matter! Some commands have special options that you can use to customize the command's results. Some commands need an object or *parameter* (like a filename or path to a directory) on which to work. In the rest of this chapter, you'll learn how to use the few basic Unix commands (together with the necessary options and parameters) that are necessary for installing and configuring Perl scripts.

Unix's response

Often when you type a command, Unix's only response is another prompt. You can generally assume that no news is good news.

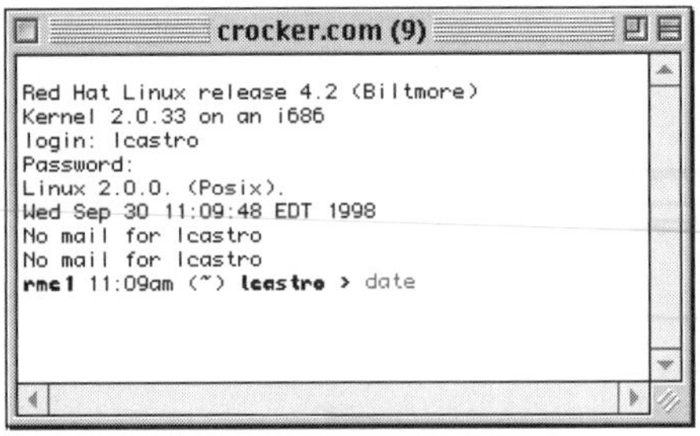

Figure D.4 *On my server, the prompt line shows the server name (rmc1), the time (11:09am), the current working directory (~, which stands for the home directory), and my user name (lcastro), followed by a >, which is the prompt that tells me that Unix is ready for a command. I've typed the command* date *and pressed Return.*

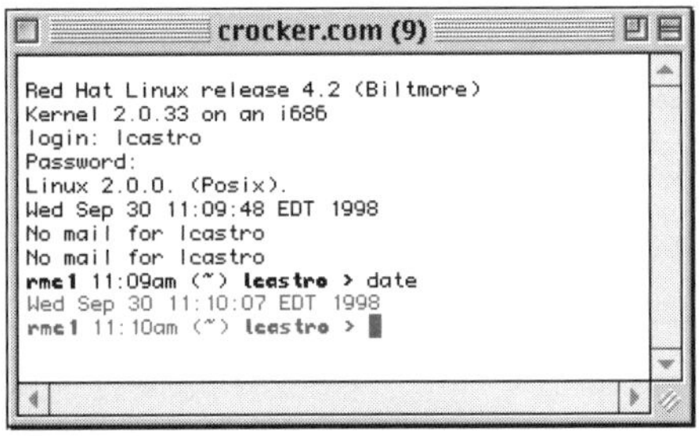

Figure D.5 *Unix displays its response to my command (that is, today's date and time), and then gives me a new prompt line indicating that it is ready for a new command.*

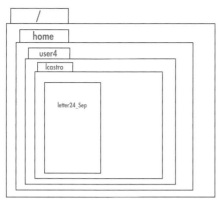

/home/user4/lcastro/letter24_Sep

Figure D.6 *The file* letter24_Sep *is located in the lcastro directory which is in the user 4 directory which is in the home directory which is in the root directory. You represent the root directory with a forward slash (/). You also use a forward slash to separate each successive directory from the next.*

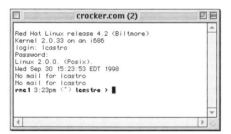

Figure D.7 *On some servers (like mine, shown), when you log in, your home directory is the first directory you see (that is, it's your working directory—see page 246). My server shows the current directory within parentheses before the user name on the prompt line. The tilde is an abbreviation for the home directory.*

Dealing with paths in Unix

On a Mac or Windows machine, when you want to refer to a specific file, you usually just give it a special name—like *letter24_Sep*, or whatever. On Unix, a file is referenced by its complete location on the server, starting from the top or *root* directory. It might look something like this: */home/user4/lcastro/ letter24_Sep*.

So how do you figure out what a file's complete path is? First, you should know that the top directory on all Unix servers is called *root* and is represented by a forward slash (/) to save typing. Then each directory within the root directory is given a name. Directories within other directories are separated by additional slashes. So if a file called *letter24_Sep* is in the *lcastro* directory inside the *user4* directory inside the *home* directory inside the *root* directory, it would have a full path like the one at the end of the last paragraph.

Your home directory

There is one directory on the server that has special significance for you: your *home* directory. (Typically, your home directory is the directory you see when you first connect to the server via Telnet or an FTP program.) This is your little corner of the server where you have full access and in which you can create, upload, edit, and delete files and directories. Nobody else (except maybe your system administrator) has access to your home directory or its contents.

Although most Unix servers recognize the tilde (~) as an abbreviation for your home directory, you generally should not use this abbreviation when specifying full path names for files, directories, or scripts.

Absolute and relative paths

Paths can be either absolute or relative. An absolute path shows every directory from the root to the actual file. An absolute path is analogous to a complete street address, including name, street, and number, city, state, and zip code, and country. No matter where a letter is sent from, the post office will be able to find the recipient. In terms of absolute paths, this means that no matter where the script that contains the path is located on your server, it will be able to find the designated file.

To give you directions to my neighbor's house, instead of giving her complete address, I might just say "it's three doors down on the right". This is a *relative* address—where it points to depends on where the information is given from. With the same information in a different city, you'd never find my neighbor.

In the same way, a *relative path* describes the location of the desired file with reference to the location of the script that contains the reference to that file. Since most scripts are contained in the cgi-bin directory, the original point of reference is often the same.

The relative path for a file that is in the same directory as the script that references it is simply the file name and extension **(Figure D.9)**. The path for a file in a subdirectory of the current directory is the name of the subdirectory followed by a forward slash and then the name and extension of the desired file **(Figure D.10)**.

Dealing with paths in Unix

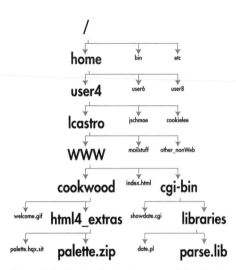

Figure D.8 *Here's a look at just some of the directories and files on my Unix server. It's something like a family tree—each directory may or may not have children (subdirectories) and those children may or may not have children of their own. The trick to creating relative paths is to figure out the relationships between each branch of the family.*

Inside the current directory, there's a file called *showdate.cgi*

"showdate.cgi"

Figure D.9 *Let's assume the script we're writing resides in the cgi-bin directory shown in Figure D.8. To reference another script in the same directory, all you need for a relative path is the name of the script itself.*

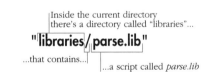

Inside the current directory there's a directory called "libraries"...

"libraries/parse.lib"

...that contains... ...a script called *parse.lib*

Figure D.10 *Again, we're writing a script that will be located in the cgi-bin directory. This time, we want to reference a subroutine that is contained within the libraries directory which is in the cgi-bin directory (see Figure D.8).*

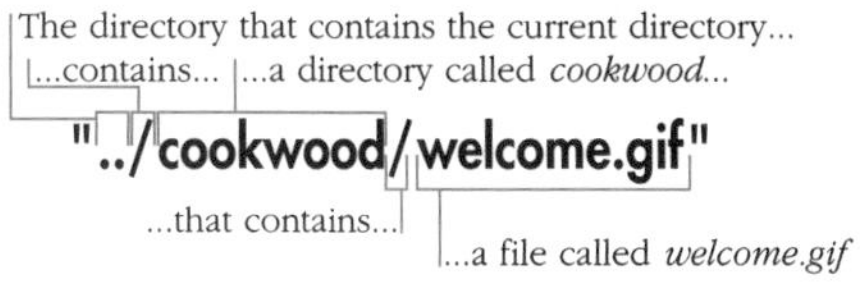

The directory that contains the current directory...
...contains... ...a directory called *cookwood*...

"../cookwood/welcome.gif"

...that contains...
...a file called *welcome.gif*

Figure D.11 *This image, as you can see in Figure D.8 is in a directory (cookwood) that is inside the directory (WWW) that contains the directory (cgi-bin) that contains the script in which this path will appear—whew! In this case, we use two periods and a forward slash to go up a level, and then note the subdirectory, followed by a forward slash, followed by the filename.*

/home/user4/lcastro/WWW/
cookwood/html4_extras/palette.zip

../cookwood/html4_extras/palette.zip

http://www.cookwood.com/
cookwood/html4_extras/palette.zip

Figure D.12 *Always assuming that this path will appear in a script that resides in the cgi-bin directory, at top we have an absolute path to the palette.zip file, in the middle there's a relative path to that same file, and at bottom the corresponding URL for the file is displayed.*

To reference a file in a directory at a *higher* level of the file hierarchy, use two periods and a forward slash **(Figure D.11)**. You can combine and repeat the two periods and forward slash to reference any file on the server that you have access to.

Relative paths can sometimes be useful but they're not nearly as prevalent as relative URLs in an HTML document. One problem is that it's not always clear where the script is located that contains the reference to the file. For example, even though I store CGI scripts in a cgi-bin directory, my server considers those scripts as residing within a virtual lcastro directory *inside* the cgi-bin directory. Obviously, this would affect all my relative paths. Absolute paths are always the same, regardless of the location of the script that contains them.

URLs vs. paths

While URLs often look something like paths, or use paths, they are not identical. A URL starts with a protocol, like *http:* and is then followed by the server name or IP address as it is identified out on the Web. Depending on how your server is set up, the path that comes after the server name starts with your *Web directory* which generally is somewhere within your home directory (but not equal to it).

For example, the URL of my home page is *http://www.cookwood.com/index.html*. My server is set up so that my Web directory is */home/user4/lcastro/WWW/*. Therefore, the path on the server of the index.html file referred to by that URL is */home/user4/lcastro/WWW/index.html*. It would be very unusual for the root directory of the server and the Web directory to be the same.

Changing the working directory

While you can visualize several folders or directories at a time on your Mac or PC, in Unix you look at one directory at a time. The directory you happen to be looking at is called the *working directory*. Any commands that you type without filenames will affect the contents of the working directory and any relative paths or filenames that you reference will be with respect to the working directory.

By default, when you Telnet (or FTP) to the server, the initial working directory is your home directory. You can change the working directory as needed to save time typing complicated relative paths (or long absolute ones).

To change the working directory:

1. Type **cd** (which stands for *change directory*).

2. Type **path**, where *path* is the absolute or relative path that describes the location of the directory that you want to designate as the new working directory.

3. Press Return or Enter.

✔ Tips

■ To make your home directory the current working directory, don't type a path after **cd** (just press Return or Enter).

■ For more information on constructing absolute and relative paths, consult *Absolute and relative paths* on page 244.

Figure D.13 *Type* **cd** *followed by the relative path (with respect to the current working directory) of the directory that you want to designate as the new working directory. Notice how the new location (in parentheses on the prompt line) reflects the change).*

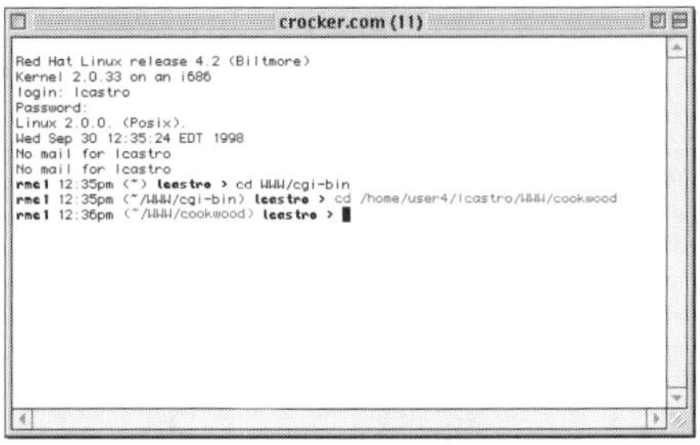

Figure D.14 *You can also use an absolute path name with the cd command. Again, the new working directory is displayed on the prompt line. Your server may not show the current working directory at every prompt line, but it will still change it with cd.*

Figure D.15 *If your server doesn't tell you where you are at all times (like mine), you can type pwd to see the full path of the current working directory.*

Finding out where you are

Depending on how your server is configured, it's not always obvious what the working directory is currently set to. You can use the pwd (*p*rint *w*orking *d*irectory) command to find out.

To find out where you are:

Type **pwd**. The full path of the current working directory is displayed.

Listing directory contents

To see what is in the working directory, you can list its contents.

To list a directory's contents:

1. Navigate to the directory whose contents you wish to see. (In other words, make the desired directory the working directory—see page 246.)

2. Type **ls** (that's a letter *l* and an *s*).

3. If desired, type **-l** (that's a letter *l* too) to view the permissions, modification date, user group, and other data about the directory's contents.

✔ Tip

■ There are other adjustments you can make to the listing command, including sorting the contents by modification date (-t), listing the contents on a single line (-m), and others. For a full listing, type **man ls** *(see page 252)*. When using more than one setting, you can combine them together: **ls -lt** is perfectly legitimate, although you can use **ls -l -t** if you like that better.

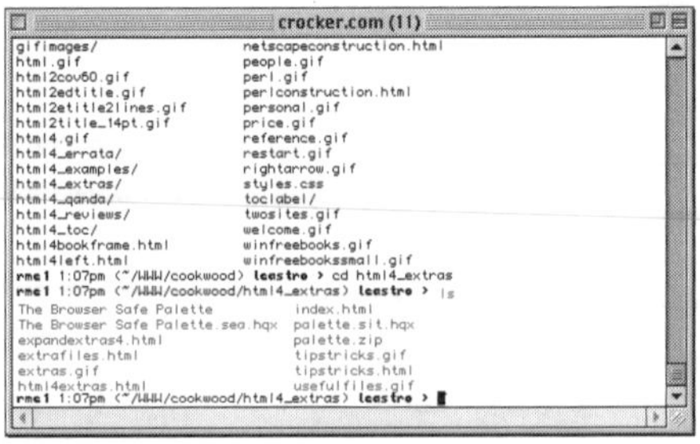

Figure D.16 *Type* **ls** *to list the contents of the current working directory.*

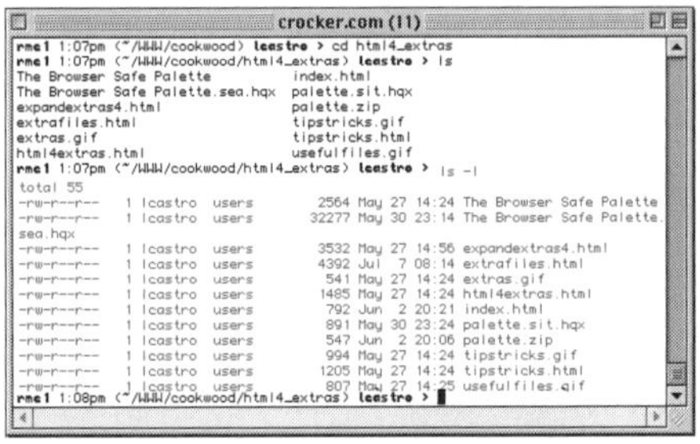

Figure D.17 *Type* **ls -l** *to list the contents of the current working directory together with information about the permissions, modification date, and more.*

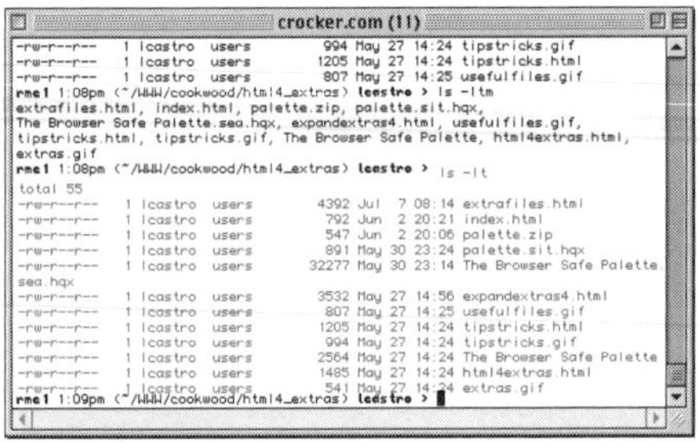

Figure D.18 *Type* **ls -lt** *to list the contents of the current working directory with extra information, and sorted by modification date.*

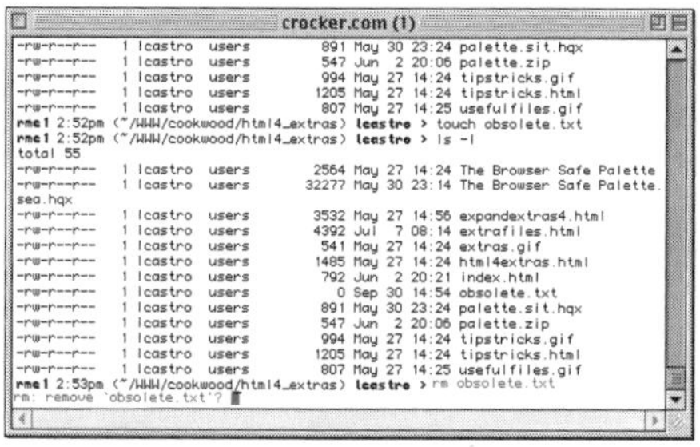

Figure D.19 *Type* **rm filename** *to delete a file. Depending on your server, you might get a warning like the one shown here asking if you really want to delete the file. Type* **y** *if so, or anything else, if not.*

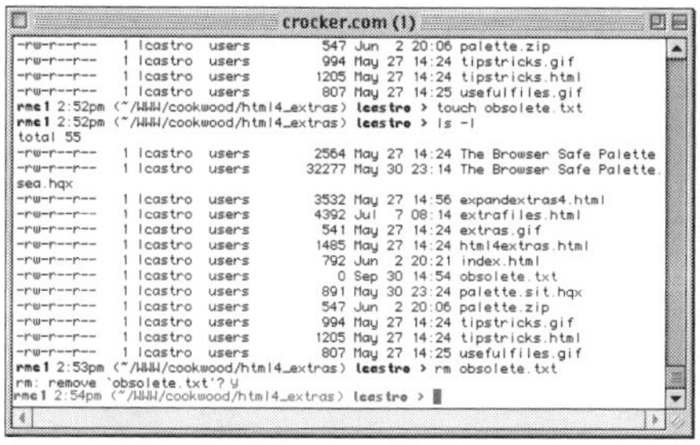

Figure D.20 *Generally, Unix won't confirm that the file has been deleted. It just gives you another prompt.*

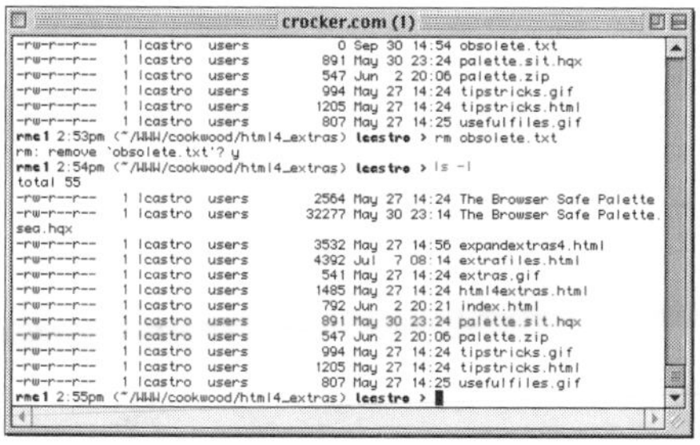

Figure D.21 *If you want to make sure that the file has been eliminated, type* **ls -l** *to check the contents of the directory from which it should have disappeared (see page 248).*

Eliminating files

Getting rid of old and obsolete files is an essential part of keeping your Unix space organized and effective. In addition, since your ISP probably limits the amount of space that you have at your disposal, you'll want to make sure you're not wasting any of that space on files you no longer need.

To eliminate files:

1. If desired, navigate to the directory that contains the file you want to eliminate (that is, change the working directory to the directory that contains the file in question).

2. Type **rm filename**, where *filename* is either the complete filename with the full path starting from the root directory or includes a relative path with respect to the current working directory.

✔ Tips

- Depending on your server's configuration, you may or may not get an alert asking if you really want to remove the file. (Type *y* or *Y* to confirm the deletion, or anything else to cancel it.) At any rate, once you remove it, it's gone forever. There's no getting it back.

- How do you *create* a file—say, for a log? You can create an empty text file with pico, or with your local text editor and then upload it.

Eliminating files

Creating and eliminating directories

You have full control over the contents of your home directory, including any files and directories contained within the home directory. As with your personal computer, it's often helpful to create additional subdirectories within the home directory so that you can organize your files better.

To create a directory:

1. If desired, navigate to the directory in which you want to create a new directory (that is, change the working directory to the directory that should contain the new directory).

2. Type **mkdir path**, where *path* is the absolute or relative (with respect to the working directory) path of the new directory.

To eliminate a directory:

1. If desired, navigate to the directory that contains the directory you want to delete (that is, change the working directory to the directory that contains the obsolete directory).

2. Make sure the directory to be deleted is empty. For more information on removing files, see page 249.

3. Type **rmdir path**, where *path* is the absolute or relative (with respect to the working directory) path of the obsolete directory.

✔ Tips

- There is no "undo". Once you remove a directory, it's gone for good.

- You can often use your FTP program to add and remove directories as well.

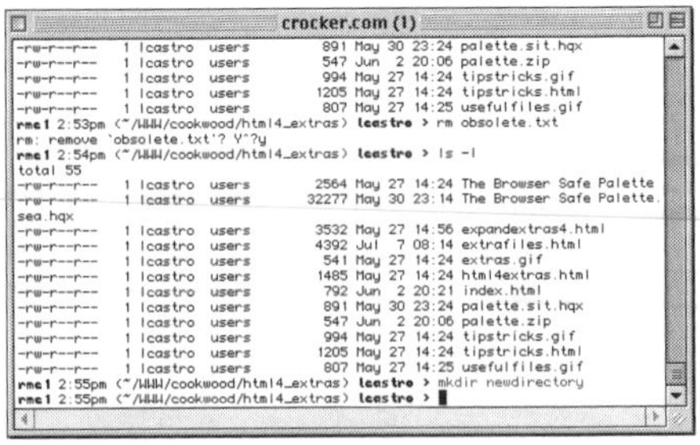

Figure D.22 *Type* **mkdir** *and then the name of the new directory (including its path, if desired) to create the new directory. Again, Unix offers no response except for a new prompt.*

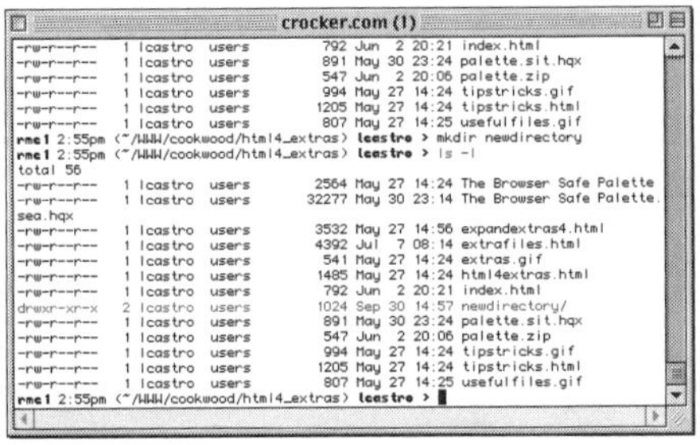

Figure D.23 *The nervous (and skeptical) among you can type* **ls -l** *to make sure that the new directory has been created. (I always do.)*

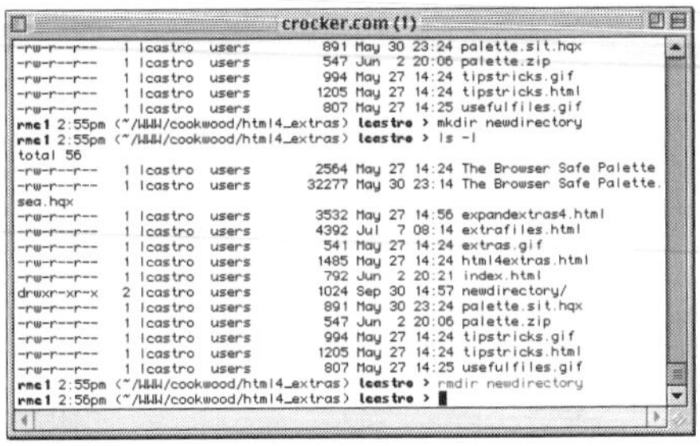

Figure D.24 *You can only remove a directory if it's empty.*

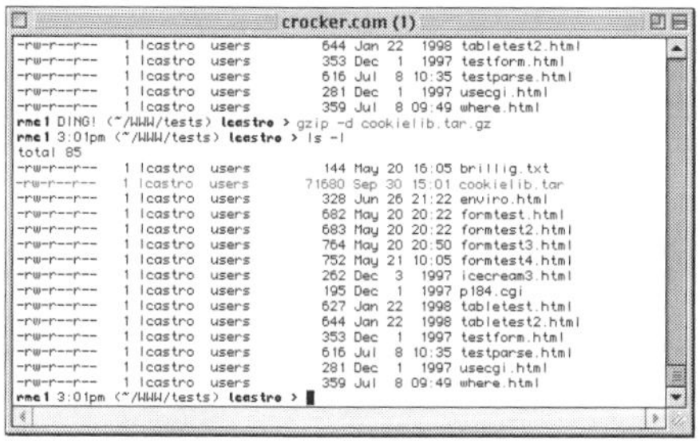

Figure D.25 *Type* **gzip -d** *and then the name of the tarred and zipped file that you want to decompress. The original file disappears and in its place you'll find an uncompressed tarred file.*

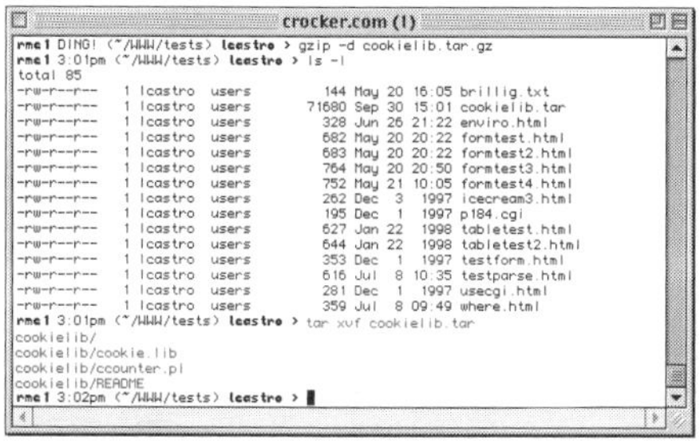

Figure D.26 *Type* **tar xvf** *followed by the name of the uncompressed tar file to extract the files it contains. Unix will display which files and directories it has created.*

Decompressing tar and zipped files

Unix files are often compressed in tar (tape archive) and zip formats. Once you upload the files to your server you can use Unix commands to extract the scripts.

To decompress files on the Unix server:

1. Download the compressed scripts—with extensions like .tar, .tar.gz, .tar.Z, etc.—from the Web site to your hard disk *(see page 219)*.

2. Then upload the compressed scripts from your hard disk to your server *(see page 36)*.

3. Telnet to the Unix server *(see page 240)*.

4. Navigate to the directory that contains the file you want to decompress *(see page 246)*.

5. Type **gzip -d filename.tar.gz**, where *filename.tar.gz* is the name of the file (and its extensions) that contains the compressed script.

6. Press Return or Enter. You should now have a file that ends in .tar in your directory **(Figure D.25)**.

7. Type **tar xvf filename.tar** to extract the script from the tar file created in steps 5–6.

8. Press Return or Enter. Unix displays the extracted files **(Figure D.26)**.

Decompressing tar and zipped files

Getting help with Unix

You can always find a little bit more help about a Unix command by looking at the manual page that is stored on the server itself. While these manual pages tend to be brief and cryptic, usually they'll give you enough clues to get a general idea of what the command does.

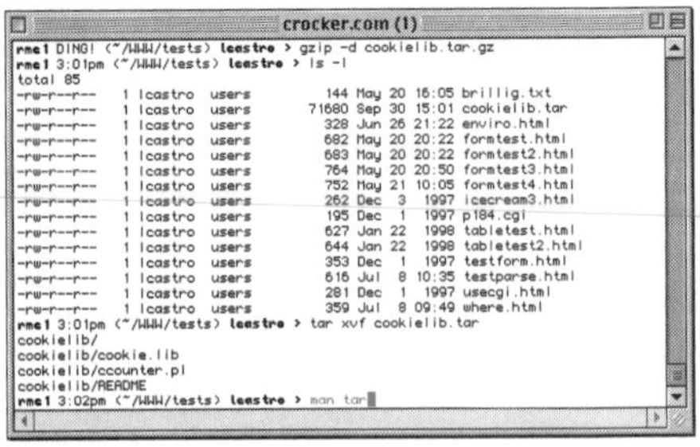

To get help with Unix:

1. Type **man**.

2. Type **command**, where *command* is the Unix function that you want help with **(Figure D.27)**.

3. Press Return or Enter. A screenful of information appears about the desired command **(Figure D.28)**.

4. Press space to see the next screenful of information **(Figure D.29)**.

   Or press **q** to quit out of the online manual and return to the Unix prompt.

✔ Tip

■ You can get information about the online manual itself by typing **man man**.

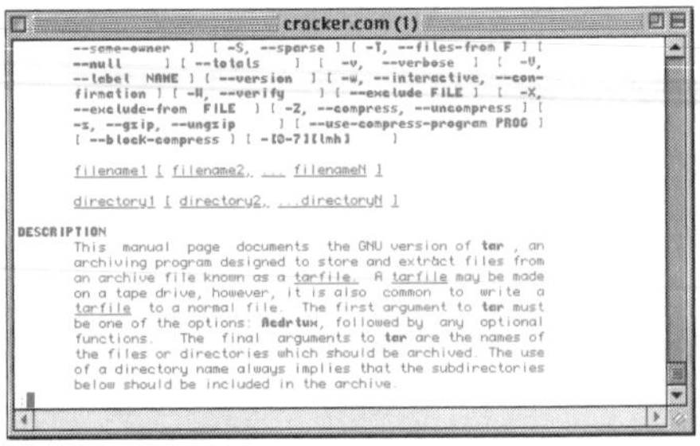

Figure D.27 *Type* **man** *and then the name of the command that you want to learn more about. Then press Return or Enter.*

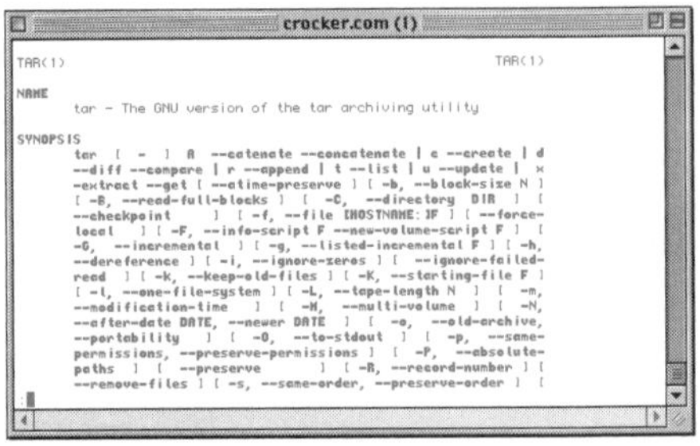

Figure D.28 *The first page of the online manual for the command you have chosen is displayed. Press space to see the following page.*

Figure D.29 *Keep pressing space to pass from page to page or press* **q** *to leave the online manual and return to the Unix prompt.*

Perl and CGI Resources

Besides this book, you don't need much to write a Perl CGI script. Nevertheless, there are a few tools and extra sources of information that can make your job a lot easier.

Two caveats: First, printed material about the Web is often notoriously out of date. Feel free to check the updated lists of links on my Web site *(see page 22)*. Second, the lists on the following pages are by no means exhaustive. The Web is a huge and ever-changing collection of bits and bytes. If you don't find what you're looking for on these pages, jump to any search service on the Web (e.g., *http://altavista.digital.com*) and look for *Perl, CGI, scripts*, or whatever it is you need.

Text editors

Text editors

You can use *any* text editor to write Perl scripts, including SimpleText on the Macintosh, WordPad for Windows, or vi or pico in Unix systems. As long as you save the file as text-only and upload it to the Unix server with ASCII or text (but not Binary), you'll be fine.

Nevertheless, there are several specialized text editors that offer a few extra features specially for Perl (and HTML) programmers.

BBEdit for Macintosh

In my opinion, the best text editor for the Mac is BBEdit, published by Bare Bones Software. It has strong search and replace features, a great HTML editor and validator (if you need it), and can save files with Unix line endings so you don't have to worry if you've uploaded the file in Text or Binary format. You can find more information about both the shareware and commercial versions of the program at *http://web.barebones.com* **(Figure E.1)**.

UltraEdit for Windows

The best text editor for Windows that I've come across is UltraEdit. Again, it lets you create text files with Unix line endings, use regular expressions to search and replace, indent blocks of text in Perl programming style, and much more. You can download an evaluation copy at *http://www.ultraedit.com*.

If you're not convinced by UltraEdit, Elizabeth Knuth has a very useful review site for Windows text editors. It's at *http://www.users.csbsju.edu/~eknuth/obcomp/htmled16.html* **(Figure E.2)**.

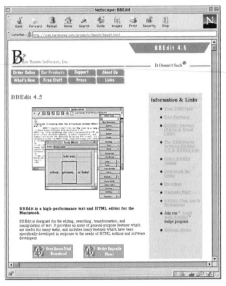

Figure E.1 *BBEdit's home page lists its myriad features and lets you download an evaluation copy or order a full version ($119).*

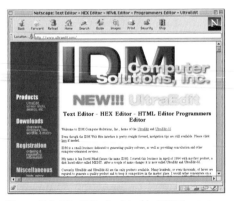

Figure E.2 *UltraEdit, developed by IDM Computer Solutions, has an extensive home page that explains its features and offers a 45-day evaluation period before requesting the $30 shareware fee.*

Figure E.3 *This is BetterTelnet's Web site, where you can get more information and download the program.*

Telnet programs

While text editors *(see page 254)* can get very fancy, Telnet programs are still pretty basic looking. What can you expect from a program that tries to emulate a Unix terminal? While I'm sure there are many more options out there, here are the Telnet programs that I recommend.

BetterTelnet for Macintosh

The standard for Telnet programs for many years in the Macintosh community was NCSA Telnet, developed by the same folks who created Mosaic, an early and now almost obsolete browser. BetterTelnet **(Figure E.3)** is based on NCSA Telnet but has a much cleaner interface and less bugs. It's at *http://www.cstone.net/~rbraun/mac/telnet/.*

Microsoft Telnet for Windows

The easy solution for telnetting on Windows machines is using Microsoft Telnet which comes with the system software. It's nothing special, but it gets the job done.

Telnet programs

Other folks' scripts

There are hundreds of scripts already written that you can download and use on your site. Some of these scripts are free, others require some sort of compensation to the programmer. While you can find scripts all over the Web, there are four particularly good places to look.

The CGI Resource Index

The CGI Resource Index, published by Matt's Script Archive, Inc. (see below), lists hundreds of links to Perl CGI scripts, documentation, books, magazine articles, programmers, and jobs. While the huge quantity of information is sometimes a bit overwhelming, it is a great place to get a sense for what's out there. It's at *http://www.cgi-resources.com* **(Fig. E.4)**.

Matt's Script Archive

Also known as MSA, Matt's Script Archive is one of the most popular script repositories on the Web. Created by teenager Matt Wright, the site offers several solid, useful, free Perl CGI scripts. It's at *http://www.worldwidemart.com /scripts*.

Extropia.com

Another famous source for free Perl CGI scripts is Extropia.com, created by Selena Sol and Gunther Birznieks. Though recently sporting a more commercial look, Extropia offers many useful scripts that its authors have generously released to the public domain. They now offer support for those scripts—for a fee. You can find them at *http://www.extropia.com*.

The WebScripts Archive

While not the biggest nor the most popular, Darryl Burgdorf's site houses what I consider to be the best documented and easiest to implement collection of Perl CGI scripts. You'll find them at: *www.awsd.com/scripts*.

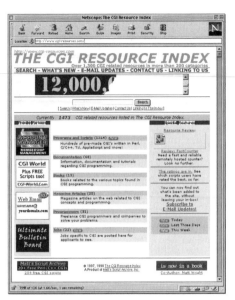

Figure E.4 *The CGI Resource Index is a helpful collection of links to CGI-related information on the Web, including hundreds of Perl scripts that you can download for your own use.*

Figure E.5 *O'Reilly and Associates' www.perl.com site is the place to go for Perl-related resources. You can get an idea of the variety of information available from the category listings down the left side of the site's pages.*

Learning more

While this book has hopefully been a good start, there are many resources that you can tap to further your studies and improve your scripts.

www.perl.com

This huge site is home to a vast collection of Perl-related resources, including news about Perl events, a complete mirror to CPAN where you can find both Perl interpreters and hundreds of Perl scripts and modules, as well as information about books, magazines, security issues, training, and much, much more **(Figure E.5)**.

FAQs

There are several important FAQs about Perl and CGI. While some of these FAQs are annoyingly condescending, they also offer a wealth of information. You should read all of them before posting anything to any of the newsgroups listed below. Otherwise, you'll most likely be flamed. You can find a list of Perl related FAQs at *http://language.perl.com/ faq/index.html* **(Figure E.6)**.

Newsgroups

There are two especially important newsgroups for folks writing Perl CGI scripts, one for Perl questions and one for CGI related questions. Although the folks on both newsgroups are very knowledgeable and more than willing to share their experience, they are not so happy about fielding questions that are answered in the FAQs or that fall outside the scope of each particular newsgroup. With that in mind, post questions specifically about Perl programming to *comp.lang.perl.misc* **(Figure E.7)**. Posts about using Perl to write CGI scripts are more welcome on *comp. infosystems.www.authoring.cgi* **(Figure E.8)**.

Online documentation

Perl's complete documentation can be found online. In fact, it's often identical to what you'll find in *Programming Perl* (see below). You can find the online manual at: *http://language.perl.com/info/documentation.html.*

Other books

In this book, you'll learn about creating Perl CGI scripts—specifically for getting, processing, and returning information through your Web pages. If you are interested in non-Web related applications for Perl scripts, try *Learning Perl* (affectionately known as the *Llama* book), by Randal Schwartz and Tom Christiansen or *Programming Perl* (the *Camel* book), by Larry Wall, Schwartz, and Christiansen. Both are in their second edition and published by O'Reilly & Associates, and both are geared towards experienced programmers interested in learning Perl.

Companion Web sites

This book has two companion Web sites that can both help you with the information contained herein as well as point you to other valuable resources. For more information, consult *The Perl and CGI VQS Guide Web Site* on page 22.

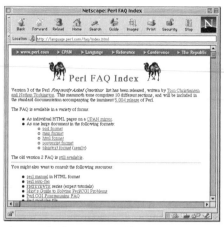

Figure E.6 *There are several helpful FAQ files about Perl. You can find a full list of them at* http://language.perl.com/faq/index.html.

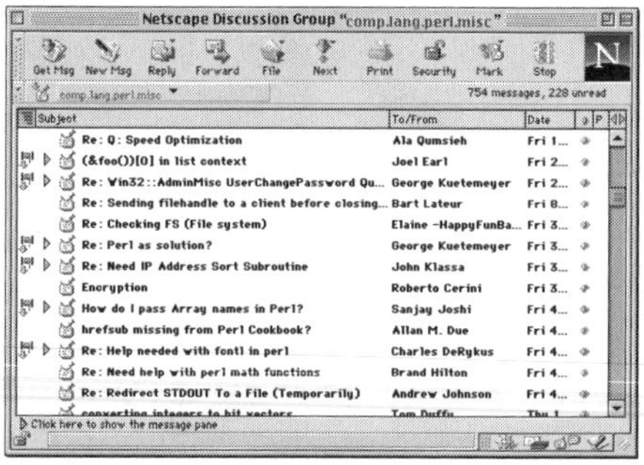

Figure E.7 *Post Perl-specific questions to the Perl programming newsgroup:* comp.lang.perl.misc. *This newsgroup is not very fond of fielding CGI-related questions.*

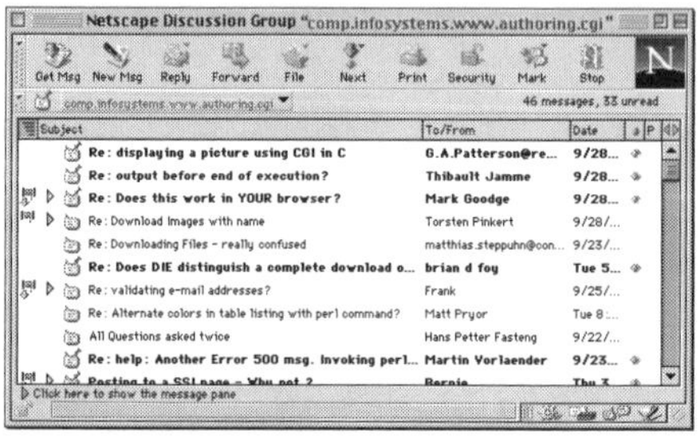

Figure E.8 *Post CGI-related questions (even about Perl) to the* comp.infosystems.www.authoring.cgi *newsgroup.*

Learning more

Index

Symbols

& (ampersand)
  and HTML 178
  and subroutines 119, 121
  default data 58
  inputting data 57
&& (double ampersand), logical and
  operator 105
* (asterisk)
  multiplication operator 75
  quantifier in search patterns 154
** (double asterisk), exponential powers 77
@ (at sign)
  @_ (underscore array), and subroutines
      120
  and hashes 129
  array variables 25
  arrays 83–99
  escaping in e-mail addresses 209
[ ] (brackets)
  and character classes 146, 147
  for individual elements of array 84
^ (caret)
  limiting location of search patterns 149
  negating character classes 147
{ } (curly brackets)
  and hashes 128, 129
  closing 115
  in search patterns 155
/ (division) 75
  See also forward slashes
$ (dollar sign)
  $&, and found data 140
  $n, in search patterns 158
  $`, and found data 140
  $´, and found data 140
  as Unix prompt 242
  for individual elements
      of arrays 84
      of hashes 128
  limiting location of search patterns 149
  scalar variables 25
= (equals sign)
  combined with other operators 81
  inputting arrays 70
  inputting hashes 71
  inputting scalar data 69
  storing result of operation 74

== (double equals signs), equal to
  comparison operator 102
=~ (binding operator) 139
  and finding 138
!= (not equal to), comparison operator 102
> (greater than)
  and writing to files 190
  as Unix prompt 242
  comparison operator 102
>= (greater than or equal to), comparison
  operator 102
>> (double greater than), and appending
  files 190
< (less than)
  and reading files 190
  comparison operator 102
<= (less than or equal to), comparison
  operator 102
- (minus/hyphen)
  and search patterns 146
  subtraction operator 75
-- (double minus), decrement operator 82
  and for block 113
% (percent sign)
  as Unix prompt 242
  hash variables 25
  modulus operator 78
. (period)
  concatenation 79
  wildcard in search patterns 144
+ (plus)
  addition operator 75
  quantifier in search patterns 153
++ (double plus), increment operator 82
  and for block 113
  and while conditionals 110
(pound symbol)
  and debugging 215
  and matching 138
  for comments 35
? (question mark)
  and non-greedy quantifiers 156
  default data 58
  inputting data 57
  quantifier in search patterns 152
~ (tilde), on Unix servers 243
| (vertical bar)
  alternation, in search patterns 157
  piping, and e-mailing output 207

| | (double vertical bar)
  and verifying file/directory operations *192*
  logical or operator *105*
1;, and subroutines *124*

A

A tag (HTML) *56*
absolute paths *244*
access
  exclusive *194*
  to directories *200*
ACTION attribute, in FORM tag (HTML) *46*
active images *55*
adding elements to array *90, 91*
addition *26, 75*
Aladdin Expander for Windows *220*
Aladdin Systems *220*
AltaVista (search engine) *219*
alternation. *See* matching one element or
  another
anchoring, and search patterns *149*
appending files *190*
AppleScript *16*
arguments in subroutines *119, 121*
arrays *83–99*
  adding items
    in particular positions *95*
    to beginning *90*
    to end *91*
  associative. *See* hashes
  combining *92*
  converting to hashes *71*
  creating from scalar *86*
  description *25*
  getting multiple items *89*
  getting particular item *84*
  inputting *70*
  length *85, 88*
  modifying all elements *87*
  number of elements *88*
  numbering elements *83, 84*
  printing as HTML list *185*
  removing first item *93*
  removing last item *94*
  repeating block for each element *114*
  replacing items *95*
  replacing multiple items *96*
  reversing order of items *99*
  sorting *98*
ASCII
  order *98*
  uploading, vs. Binary *254*
  values of characters *103*

assignment *69*
  combined with operation *81*
associative arrays. *See* hashes
associativity *76*
avoiding tainted data *238*

B

\b, in search patterns *149*
\B, in search patterns *149*
backslashes
  and here documents *180*
  escaping @ in e-mail addresses *209*
  escaping special symbols in HTML tags *178*
  in search patterns *144*
bang symbol (!) *32*
Bare Bones Software *254*
BASE tag (HTML), for simplifying paths *181*
BBEdit for Macintosh *254*
BetterTelnet *240, 255*
binary assignment operator *81*
Binary uploading, vs. ASCII *254*
Birznieks, Gunther *256*
blocks
  executing at least once *112*
  in conditional statements *101*
  of text, in forms *49*
  repeating certain number of times *113*
books, other *258*
borrowing scripts *217–222*
browsers
  creating output for *34*
  determining visitor's *62*
  need for output *193*
  running scripts *41*
bullets, and password boxes in forms *48*
Burgdorf, Darryl *256*
  The WebScripts Archive *219*
  WebBBS script *222*
buttons, in forms
  fancy *53*
  radio *50*
  reset *54*
  submit *53*

C

C (language) *16*
Camel book. *See Programming Perl*
carriage returns, deleting *210*
cat (Unix program) *207*
cd, Unix command *246*

CGI
    description *16*
    newsgroup *257*
CGI Resource Index *256*
CGI.pm module *179*
cgi-bin directory *37*
    and URLs *41*
changing
    arrays *87*
    permissions *39*
        from within a script *205*
        security *237*
    working directory *203*
character classes *146–147*
    and parentheses *151*
    shorthands *148*
chdir function *203*
checkboxes *51*
    creating *51*
    splitting values into array *86*
CHECKED attribute, in INPUT tag (HTML)
    for check boxes *51*
    for radio buttons *50*
checking
    files and directories *199*
    syntax *40*
        with tainted data *238*
chmod
    Perl function *205*
    Unix command *39, 233*
chomp function *210*
chop function *210*
Christiansen, Tom *258*
classes, character
    and search patterns *146*
    negated *147*
    shorthands *148*
cleaning data *238*
close function *196*
closedir function *202*
closing
    directories *202*
    files *196*
closing curly brackets, on same line *115*
COLS attribute, in TEXTAREA tag (HTML) *49*
combining arrays *92*
commands, executing in Unix *242*
commas
    and cookies *168*
    for separating operands *26*
comments *35*
    and debugging *215*

common errors *212–213*
    changing permissions *39*
    checking syntax *40*
    MIME content line *34*
Common Gateway Interface. *See* CGI
comparing
    multiple *105*
    numbers *102*
    strings *103*
comparison operators *102, 103*
compressed scripts *220*
computer languages, description *14*
concatenation *79*
    with quotation marks *28*
conditional statements *101–115*
    basic *106*
    comparing numbers *102*
    comparing strings *103*
    constructing *101*
    do *112*
    else *107*
    elsif *108*
    executing at least once *112*
    false conditions *107, 109*
    for *113*
    foreach *114*
    if *106*
    multiple, independent conditions *108*
    nesting *115*
    repeating blocks *110, 111*
    repeating certain number of times *113*
    repeating for each element in array *114*
    testing multiple comparisons *105*
    unless *109*
    until *111*
    while *110*
    without comparisons *104*
conditions
    false *107, 109*
    multiple, independent *108*
configuring scripts *221*
connecting strings *79*
    with quotation marks *28*
constants *24*
contents, listing directory's
    in script *201*
    in Unix *248*
Content-type, line *34*
    for cookies *168*
CONTENT_LENGTH, environment variable
    61, 227
context *26*

cookies
  and security *166, 169, 173, 176*
  deleting your own *167*
  description *166*
  domain *171*
  editing your own *167*
  expiration date *170*
  HTTP Cookie Library *169*
  limiting to part of server *172*
  limiting to secure connections *173*
  limits *169*
  looking at your browser's *167*
  reading and using *174*
  refused *169, 176*
  sending *168*
  sending multiple *169*
copyrights, and borrowed scripts *222*
CPAN *257*
creating
  checkboxes *51*
  data *44*
  default data *58*
  directories *204*
    in Unix *250*
  files *191*
    in Unix *249*
  forms *46*
  links *56*
  menus *52*
  password boxes *48*
  radio buttons *50*
  reset buttons *54*
  scripts *30*
  search patterns *142*
    tips for *143*
  submit buttons *53*
  subroutines *118*
  text areas *49*
  text boxes *47*
curly brackets, closing, on same line *115*
curly quotation marks *28*
current directory. *See* working directory
customizing scripts *222*

D

-d (checking directories) *199*
\d, in search patterns *148*
\D, in search patterns *148*
data
  cleaning tainted *238*
  creating *44*
  default *58*
  getting from visitors *43*

getting into script *65–71*
inputting
  arrays *70*
  from environment variables *68*
  from form *66*
  hashes *71*
  scalars *69*
  with link *57, 66*
  labeling *44*
  monitoring *237*
  remembering *161–176*
  sent with link *60*
  types *23–25*
deactivating code *215*
debugging *211–216*
  and commenting *35, 215*
  and extra printing *216*
  checking syntax *40*
  common errors *212–213*
  creating error subroutine *214*
decompressing
  files, in Unix server *251*
  scripts *220*
decrementing variables *82*
default
  data *58*
  permissions *233*
delete function *134*
deleting
  directories *206*
  extra returns *210*
  files *198*
    in Unix *249*
  security *237*
delimiters, and matching *138*
DHTML *17*
directories *189–210*
  accessing *200*
  and paths *243*
  cgi-bin *37*
    and URLs *41*
  checking status *199*
  closing *202*
  creating *204*
    in Unix *250*
    permissions *233*
  deleting *206*
    in Unix *250*
  home directory *243*
  listing contents *248*
  owner *232*
  permissions *39, 231*
  reading contents *201*
  removing *206*

root *243*
  verifying operations *192*
  vs. files in Unix *199*
  working *203*
    changing in Unix *246*
division *75*
  getting remainder of *78*
do *112*
documentation, online
  for Perl *258*
  for Unix *252*
documenting scripts *35*
dollars and cents, formatting *187*
domain, of cookies *171*
double quotation marks *28*
downloading scripts *219*
  compression *220*

E

-e (checking file status) *199*
each function *132*
editors, text. *See* text editors
elements, of an array *25*
else *107*
elsif *108*
e-mail
  address, for book *20, 22*
  preparing to send output *207*
  security *237*
  sending output via *208*
%ENV hash *59*
  See also environment variables
environment variables *59–64*
  See also hashes *127*
  and parsing forms *60*
  CONTENT_LENGTH *61*
  HTTP_COOKIE *174*
  HTTP_REFERER *63*
  HTTP_USER_AGENT *62*
  inputting data *68*
  QUERY_STRING *61*
  REQUEST_METHOD *60*
  viewing all *64*
eq (equal to), comparison operator *103*
error messages *214*
errors
  common *212–213*
    "Document contains no data" *193*
  subroutine *192, 214*
exclamation point (!) *32, 102*
exclusive access *194*

executing
  commands in Unix *242*
  scripts *41*
    permissions *231*
exists function *135*
exit
  Perl function *192, 214*
  Unix command *241*
expanding
  files, in Unix server *251*
  scripts *220*
expiration date, for cookies *170*
exponential powers *77*
extensions of scripts *31*
  downloaded uncompressed *220*
  for subroutines *124*
external files. *See* files
external subroutines *124*
  using *125*
extra returns *210*
Extropia.com *256*

F

false conditions *107, 109*
FAQs
  Perl *257*
  security *235*
Fetch (for Macintosh) *36*
file extensions of scripts *31*
  downloaded uncompressed *220*
  for subroutines *124*
filehandles
  and exclusive access *194*
  and opening files *190*
  and writing to external files *193*
  definition *189*
filenames
  and security *237*
  See also extensions
files *189–210*
  and security *189*
  appending *190*
  checking status *199*
  closing *196*
  creating *191*
    in Unix *249*
  deleting *198*
    in Unix *249*
  exclusive access *194*
  extensions *31, 220*
  moving *197*
  opening *190*
    security *237*

owner *232*
permissions *39, 231*
reading from *190, 195*
removing *198*
renaming *197*
saving *254*
uploading *254*
verifying operations *192*
vs. directories in Unix *199*
writing to *190, 193*
filtering out bad data *236*
finding *138*
  and replacing *139*
  search patterns *138, 142*
  using found data *140*
  where you are in Unix *247*
first line *32*
fixing errors *211–216*
flock function *194*
flocking files *194*
footer and header subroutines (HTML) *182*
for *113*
foreach *114*
  and modifying arrays *87*
  getting key-value pairs from hash *133*
FORM tag (HTML) *46*
formatting
  dollars and cents *187*
  numbers and strings *186*
  time *188*
  with HTML *178*
%formdata hash, and form-parsing script *67, 229*
form-parsing script *66*
  determining the method *224*
  GET method *226*
  POST method *227*
  storing name-value pairs in hash *228*
  using parsed data *230*
forms *43–58*
  active images *55*
  and labeling data *44*
  bullets *48*
  buttons *53*
  checkboxes *51*
  creating *46*
  default data *58*
  default values *54*
  free-form text *47*
  hidden fields *163*
  inputting data *66*
  menus *52*
  NAME attribute *44*

parsing *223–230*
password boxes *48*
radio buttons *50*
reset button *54*
structure of *46*
submit buttons *53*
submitting with image *55*
text areas *49*
text blocks *49*
text boxes *47*
VALUE attribute *44*
forward slashes *143*
free-form text, in forms *47*
Friedl, Jeffrey, and *Mastering Regular Expressions 142*
FTP programs
  and removing and creating directories *250*
  Fetch (for Macintosh) *36*
  WS_FTP Pro (for Windows) *38*
functions *26*
  result vs. return value *27*
  user-defined. *See* subroutines

G

g (global) operator, for matching and substituting *139*
ge (greater than or equal to), comparison operator *103*
general syntax *33*
GET method *46, 61, 224*
  getting name-value pairs *226*
  vs. POST method *60*
getting
  help *20, 22*
    with Unix *252*
  Perl *18*
  scripts *219*
GIF images, in forms *55*
greediness, in search patterns *156*
grep (Unix program) *207*
gt (greater than), comparison operator *103*
guestbooks *195*
gzip, Unix command *251*

H

hashes *127–135*
  and single quotation marks *128*
  checking if key exists *135*
  converting arrays into *71*
  description *25, 127*

getting
   all keys *131*
   all values *130*
   each key and value *132*
   several values with keys *129*
   value with key *128*
inputting *71*
order *71*
printing as HTML table *184*
removing key-value pairs *134*
header and footer subroutines (HTML) *182*
help, getting *20, 22*
   online documentation *258*
   with Unix *252*
here documents *180*
hexadecimal codes, including in string *24*
hidden fields
   adding to HTML form *163*
   description *162*
   processing *165*
   storing collected data in *164*
   transitory nature *165*
home directory *243*
HREF attribute, in A tag (HTML) *56*
HTML
   and backslashes *178*
   and newlines *178*
   and Perl *17*
   and quotation marks *163*
   CGI.pm module *179*
   editors *254*
   formatting output *178*
   forms *43–58*
   header and footer subroutines *182*
   hidden fields *163*
   labels, and NAME attribute *45*
   learning more *17, 53*
   presentation in book *20*
   printing *177–188*
      arrays *185*
      hash as table *184*
      headers and footers *117, 120*
   tags, and compatibility *62*
HTTP Cookie Library *169*
HTTP_COOKIE, environment variable *174*
HTTP_REFERER, environment variable *63, 236*
   and security *63*
HTTP_USER_AGENT, environment variable *62*

I

i (ignore)
   for matching *138*
   for substituting *139*
if *106*
images
   active (in forms) *55*
   simplifying paths to *181*
   to submit data *55*
incrementing variables *82*
INPUT tag (HTML)
   for active images *55*
   for check boxes *51*
   for password boxes *48*
   for radio buttons *50*
   for reset button *54*
   for submit button *53*
   for text boxes *47*
inputting data
   arrays *70*
   from environment variables *68*
   from form *66*
   hashes *71*
   scalar *69*
   with link *57, 66*
Internet Explorer *34*
Internet service providers. *See* ISPs
interpolating *28*
interpreters, Perl *18*
   checking syntax *40*
   location of *32*
ISPs *19*

J

JavaScript *17, 62*
joining data, with quotation marks *28*
JPEG images, in forms *55*

K

keys
   function *131*
      getting key-value pairs *133*
   getting from hash *131*
Knuth, Elizabeth *254*

L

labeling data *44*
le (less than or equal to), comparison operator *103*
leading zeros *188*
learning more *257*
Learning Perl 258
length of arrays *88*
libraries *125*
   HTTP Cookie Library *169*
limiting cookies *172*
   to secure connections *173*
line numbering *20*
links
   activating scripts with *56*
   and HTTP_REFERER environment variable *63*
   appended data *60*
   inputting data with *57, 66*
   simplifying paths to *181*
listing directory contents *248*
lists. *See* arrays
literal *24*
Llama book. *See Learning Perl*
location
   limiting in search patterns *149*
   of Perl interpreter *32*
   of scripts on server *37*
log files *195*
logical and operator *105*
logical or operator *105*
logout, Unix command *241*
ls, Unix command *232, 248*
lt (less than), comparison operator *103*

M

m (match) operator *138*
   description *137*
Macintosh
   and this book *21*
   getting Perl *18*
   text editors *254*
   uploading from with Fetch *36*
mail. *See* e-mail
making directories
   in Unix *250*
   with Perl *204*
man, Unix command *252*
Mastering Regular Expressions 142
match operator *138*
   description *137*

matching *138*
   character from group *146*
   characters not in group *147*
   how many *151*
   one character *144*
   one element or another *157*
   specifying how many *155*
   string of characters *145*
   using what was matched *158*
mathematical operators *75*
Matt's Script Archive *256*
MAXLENGTH attribute, in INPUT tag (HTML)
   for password boxes *48*
   for text boxes *47*
menus
   creating *52*
   splitting values into array *86*
method
   determining *224*
   POST vs. GET *60*
METHOD attribute, in FORM tag (HTML) *46*
Microsoft Telnet *240, 255*
MIME content line
   creating *34*
   for cookies *168*
mkdir
   Perl function *204*
   Unix command *250*
modifying arrays *87*
modulus *78*
monitoring
   data sent to server *237*
   visitor input *236*
moving files *197*
Mozilla, and determining browser *62*
MULTIPLE attribute, in SELECT tag (HTML) *52*
multiple items from array *89*
multiple operators *76*
multiple optional elements, in search patterns *154*
multiplication *26, 75*

N

\n
   in search patterns *158*
   See also newlines
NAME attribute (HTML)
   and HTML labels *45*
   for active images *55*
   for checkboxes *51*
   for hidden fields *163*
   for menus *52*

for radio buttons *50*
for text areas *49*
for text boxes *47, 48*
in form-parsing script *127*
in forms *44*
omitting for reset button *54*
omitting for submit button *53*
and %formdata hash *67*
name-value pairs *66, 67*
navigating in Unix *203*
ne (not equal to), comparison operator *103*
negated character class *147*
nesting conditional statements *115*
Netscape Communicator *34*
newlines
    and HTML *178*
    and writing to external files *193*
newsgroups about Perl and CGI *257*
number of elements, in arrays *88*
numbering lines of code *20*
numbers *23*
    comparing *102*
    formatting *186*
        as dollars and cents *187*
    leading zeros *188*
    padding *188*
    raising to exponential power *77*
    vs. strings *102, 103*

O

1;, and subroutines *124*
online manual
    for Perl *258*
    for Unix *252*
open function *190*
    and e-mailing output *207*
opendir function *200*
opening
    directories *200*
    files *190*
        security *237*
operating and assigning *81*
operations, storing result *74*
operators *26*
    comparison operators for numbers *102*
    comparison operators for strings *103*
    logical and *105*
    logical or *105*
    mathematical *75*
    multiple *76*
    result vs. return value *27*
    shortcuts *81*
OPTION tag (HTML) *52*

order
    and hashes *71*
    of characters in class *146*
output
    creating *34*
    formatting *178*
    sending via e-mail *208*
owner, of file/directory *232*
O'Reilly & Associates *258*

P

padding numbers and strings *188*
pairs of elements. *See* hashes
parentheses
    and character classes *151*
    and functions *26*
    and quantifiers, in search patterns *151*
    and subroutines *119*
    to assign elements of array to one or more
        variables *85*
    using what was matched in search patterns
        158
parsing forms *60, 66, 117, 223–230*
    and environment variables *60*
    definition *66*
    script *66, 223–230*
        creating a subroutine for *223*
password boxes *48*
paths
    absolute vs. relative *244*
    adjusting in borrowed scripts *221*
    and directories *243*
    and opening files *191*
    and security *237*
    for cookies *172*
    in Unix *243*
    simplifying *181*
    vs. URLs *245*
PCs. *See* Windows
Peachpit's Web site, for this book *22*
Perl
    and HTML *17*
    building blocks *23–28*
    data *23–25*
    FAQs *257*
    getting *18*
    history *15*
    home page *257*
    interpreters *18*
        location of *32*
    newsgroups *257*
    numbering lines *20*
    online documentation *258*

other books *258*
presentation in book *20*
suitability for Web applications *15*
version *18*
writing *23*
See also scripts
permissions *39, 205, 231–234*
and creating files *191*
and external subroutines *124*
and new directories *204*
changing *39*
from within a script *205*
deciding on code *234*
default *233*
recommended *39*
security *237*
types of *231*
viewing *231*
Phillips, Paul, and security FAQs *235*
pico (text editor) *23, 254*
creating scripts with *31*
piping output *207*
placeholders *24*
platforms
and this book *21*
determining visitor's *62*
pop function *94*
POST method *46, 224*
and environment variables *61*
getting name-value pairs *227*
vs GET method *60*
powers, exponential *77*
PRE tag, and here documents *180*
precedence, of operators *76*
print function *34*
and debugging *216*
and quotation marks *28*
writing to external files *193*
See also printing, printf function, and
sprintf function
printf function *186, 187, 188*
printing *177–188*
and quotation marks *34*
arrays as HTML list *185*
hashes *184*
HTML code *180*
HTML documents *178*
HTML headers and footers *117, 120*
several lines at a time *180*
problems, fixing *211–216*
program, definition of *14*
Programming Perl 258
prompt, Unix *242*
push function *91*
pwd, Unix command *247*

Q

quantifiers
* (asterisk) *154*
+ (plus) *153*
? (question mark) *152*
and greediness *156*
description *151*
m and n *155*
non-greedy *156*
QUERY_STRING, environment variable *61,
224, 226*
question-and-answer board, for this book *22*
quotation marks *23, 28*
and here documents *180*
and HTML *163, 178*
and printing *34*
and qw *70*
qw (quote word)
and arrays *70*
and hashes *71*

R

-r (checking read permissions) *199*
radio buttons *50*
ranges, in search patterns *146*
read function *227*
read permissions *231*
readdir function *201*
reading
cookies *174*
directory contents *201*
external files *190, 195*
refused cookies *176*
regex *142*
See also search patterns
regular expressions *142*
See also search patterns, finding, finding
and replacing
relative paths *244*
remainder, of division *78*
remembering data *161–176*
removing
directories *206*
in Unix *250*
extra returns *210*
files *198*
in Unix *249*
first item from array *93*
last item in array *94*
rename function *197*
renaming files *197*

repeating
    blocks 110
        certain number of times 113
        for each element in array 114
        if condition is false 111
    strings 80
REQUEST_METHOD, environment variable
    60, 224
require function 125
reset button 54
resetting forms 54
resources 253–258
    learning more 257
    online documentation 258
    other folks' scripts 256
    Telnet programs 255
    text editors 254
result, vs. return value 27
return function 123
return values
    and subroutines 122
    setting in subroutine 123
    vs. result 27
returns, carriage
    and writing to external files 193
    eliminating extra 210
    including in string 24
reversing contents of array 99
rm, Unix command 249
rmdir
    Perl function 206
    Unix command 250
root directory 243
ROWS attribute, in TEXTAREA tag (HTML) 49
running scripts 41

S

s (substitute) operator 139
    description 137
\s, in search patterns 148
\S, in search patterns 148
scalar function 88
scalars 73–82
    adding 75
    concatenation 79
    decrementing 82
    description 25
    dividing 75
    exponential power 77
    incrementing 82
    inputting data 69
    modulus operator 78
    multiplying 75

operating and assigning 81
precedence of operators 76
repeat operator 80
shortcuts 81
splitting into array 86, 141
storing result of operation 74
subtracting 75
Schwartz, Randal 258
scripts
    activating with links 56
    and URLs 41
    borrowing 256
    changing permissions 39
    checking syntax 40
    comments 35
    common errors 212–213
    configuring 221
    copyright 222
    creating 30
        and uploading 31
    customizing 222
    debugging 211–216
    definition 14
    documenting 35
    downloading 219
        compression 220
    executing 41
    expanding 220
    extensions 31
    general syntax 33
    getting 219
    getting data 65–71
    inputting data 43
        with link 57
    location on server 31
    other folks' 256
    owner 232
    parsing data 66
    permissions 231–234
    running 41
    saving 254
    shebang line 32
    starting 32
    syntax 40
    uploading 31, 254
        Macintosh 36
        Windows 38
    using other folks' 217–222, 256
search patterns
    * (asterisk) quantifier 154
    \n 158
    $n 158
    + (plus) quantifier 153
    ? (question mark) quantifier 152

anchoring *149*
and security *236*
character classes *146*
character from group *146*
characters not in group *147*
constructing *142*
finding *138*
finding and replacing *139*
how many *151*
hyphens *146*
limiting location *149*
parentheses *151, 158*
quantifiers
    description *151*
    greediness *156*
ranges *146*
repeating elements *158*
shorthands for character classes *148*
single characters *144*
strings *145*
tips *143*
using what was matched *158*
wildcards *144*
security *235–238*
    ability to run CGI scripts *19*
    and cookies *166, 169, 173, 176*
    and files *189*
    FAQs *235*
    HTTP_REFERER environment variable *63*
    monitoring
        data sent to server *237*
        visitor input *236*
    tainted data *238*
SELECT tag (HTML) *52*
SELECTED attribute, in OPTION tag (HTML) *52*
semicolons (;) *33*
    and cookies *168*
    and HTML *178*
sending
    cookies *168*
    output via e-mail *208*
sendmail (Unix program) *207, 208*
servers
    and environment variables *59, 68*
    assumed in this book *21*
    changing permissions *39*
    location of scripts *31, 37*
    See also Unix servers
shebang line *32*
    and external subroutines *124*
    avoiding tainted data *238*
    in borrowed scripts *221*
shift function *93*

SimpleText *23, 254*
    creating scripts *30*
simplifying paths to images/links *181*
single quotation marks *28*
    and hashes *128*
SIZE attribute (HTML)
    for password boxes *48*
    for text boxes *47*
    in SELECT tag *52*
slashes. *See* backslashes, forward slashes
slices
    of array *89*
    of hash *129*
Sol, Selena *256*
sort function *98*
    for hashes *131*
sorting arrays *98*
spaces
    and cookies *168*
    and ranges in search patterns *146*
    and search patterns *143*
split function *86, 141*
    and cookies *174*
    description *137*
splitting scalars into arrays *86, 141*
sprintf function *186, 187, 188*
SRC attribute, in INPUT tag (HTML) *55*
Standard Input *61*
    See also STDIN
STDIN *227*
    See also Standard Input
Stein, Lincoln
    CGI.pm module *179*
    World Wide Web Security FAQ *235*
storing data in hidden fields *164*
straight quotation marks *28*
strings *23*
    and mathematical operators *75*
    comparing *103*
    connecting *79*
    formatting *186*
    repeating *80*
    vs. numbers *102, 103*
StuffIt Expander *220*
sub function *118*
submit buttons *53*
    and HTTP_REFERER variable *63*
    creating *53*
    multiple *53*
    vs. active images *55*
subroutines *117–125*
    1; *124*
    and arguments *121*
    creating *223*

creating simple *118*
description *117*
errors *214*
external *124*
  and permissions *124*
  and shebang line *124*
  using *125*
HTML headers and footers *182*
legal names *118*
location of *118*
parsing forms *223–230*
return values *122*
  setting *123*
storing in separate file *124*
using *121*
using simple *119*
with arguments (input) *120*
with no arguments *119*
substitute operator *139*
  description *137*
substituting *139*
subtraction *75*
symbols
  and search patterns *143*
  backslashes *178*
syntax
  checking *40*
    with tainted data *238*
  general *33*

T

-T, avoiding tainted data *238*
tables, creating from hash *184*
tabs, including in string *24*
tainted data, avoiding *238*
Tan, Christian (Dimmy) *181*
tar files *251*
tar, Unix command *251*
tcl (language) *16*
Telnet, Microsoft *240, 255*
Telnet programs *255*
  BetterTelnet (for Macintosh) *240, 255*
  closing connection *241*
  Microsoft Telnet (for Windows) *240, 255*
  opening connection *240*
templates *195*
testing
  checking syntax *40*
  on local computer *18*
text areas creating *49*
text blocks, in forms *49*
text boxes *47*

text editors *23, 30, 254*
  BBEdit for Macintosh *254*
  for Windows, review site *254*
  UltraEdit for Windows *254*
TEXTAREA tag (HTML) *49*
tilde (Unix servers) *243*
time, formatting *188*
TYPE attribute, in INPUT tag (HTML)
  for active images *55*
  for check boxes *51*
  for password boxes *48*
  for radio buttons *50*
  for reset button *54*
  for submit button *53*
  for text boxes *47*
types of data *23–25*

U

UltraEdit for Windows *254*
umask *233*
Unix prompt *242*
Unix servers *239–252*
  ~ (tilde) *243*
  and other folks' scripts *219*
  basics *239–252*
  changing working directory *246*
  creating files *249*
  creating scripts on *31*
  decompressing files *251*
  deleting files *249*
  directories, creating and removing *250*
  documentation *252*
  executing commands *242*
  files vs. directories *199*
  finding where you are *247*
  getting help *252*
  getting Perl *18*
  groups *231*
  home directory *243*
  in this book *21*
  listing directory contents *248*
  navigating *203*
  online documentation *252*
  paths *243, 244*
  permissions *231*
  pico *31, 254*
  prompt *242*
  telnetting to *240*
  text editors *31*
  vi *254*
  writing scripts *31*
unless *109*
unlink function *198*

unshift function *90*
untainting data *238*
until *112*
updating variables *74*
uploading scripts *31*
  and changing permissions *39*
  from Macintosh *36*
  from Windows *38*
URLs
  for scripts *41*
  in links *56*
  vs. paths *245*
using
  cookies *174*
  what was matched *158*

V

VALUE attribute (HTML)
  and active images *55*
  and %formdata hash *67*
  and TEXTAREA tag *49*
  for check boxes *51*
  for hidden fields *163*
  for menus (in OPTION tag) *52*
  for radio buttons *50*
  for reset button *54*
  for submit button *53*
  for text boxes *47*
  in forms *44*
values function *130*
values, in hashes *128, 130*
variables *24*
  environment *59–64*
    and parsing forms *60*
    CONTENT_LENGTH *61*
    HTTP_REFERER *63*
    HTTP_USER_AGENT *62*
    inputting data *68*
    QUERY_STRING *61*
    REQUEST_METHOD *60*
    viewing all *64*
  joining with quotation marks *28*
  updating value *74*
verifying
  data sent to server *237*
  file and directory operations *192*
version of Perl *18*
vi (Unix program) *254*
visitors
  determining browser and platform *62*
  getting data from *43*
  monitoring input *236*
  where from *63*
Visual Basic *16*

W

-w (checking write permissions) *199*
\w, in search patterns *148*
\W, in search patterns *148*
Wall, Larry *15, 258*
Web site, for this book *22*
WebScripts Archive *256*
where you are, in Unix servers *247*
whereis, Unix command *207*
which, Unix command *32*
while *112*
  and reading external files *195*
Windows
  and this book *21*
  getting Perl *18*
  text editors *254*
  uploading scripts *38*
  Windows NT *21*
word processors *23, 30, 254*
WordPad *23, 254*
  creating scripts *30*
working directory, changing *203*
  in Unix *246*
World Wide Web Security FAQ *235*
WRAP attribute, in TEXTAREA tag (HTML) *49*
Wright, Matt
  CGI Resource Index *256*
  cookie library *169*
  Matt's Script Archive *256*
write permissions *231*
writing
  Perl code *33*
  Perl scripts *23*
  scripts *30, 254*
    See also text editors
  to files *190, 193*
    security *237*
WS_FTP, uploading scripts with *38*
www.perl.com *257*

X

-x (checking execute permissions) *199*
x (repeat operator) *80*

Y

Yahoo (search engine) *219*

Z

zeros, leading *188*
zipped files *251*